EDUCATION IN A COMPETITIVE AND GLOBALIZING WORLD

U.S. SCIENCE, TECHNOLOGY, ENGINEERING AND MATHEMATICS (STEM) EDUCATION

EDUCATION IN A COMPETITIVE AND GLOBALIZING WORLD

Additional books in this series can be found on Nova's website under the Series tab.

Additional E-books in this series can be found on Nova's website under the E-books tab.

MATHEMATICS RESEARCH DEVELOPMENTS

Additional books in this series can be found on Nova's website under the Series tab.

Additional E-books in this series can be found on Nova's website under the E-books tab.

EDUCATION IN A COMPETITIVE AND GLOBALIZING WORLD

U.S. SCIENCE, TECHNOLOGY, ENGINEERING AND MATHEMATICS (STEM) EDUCATION

CATHERINE L. GROVER
EDITOR

Nova Science Publishers, Inc.
New York

Copyright © 2011 by Nova Science Publishers, Inc.

All rights reserved. No part of this book may be reproduced, stored in a retrieval system or transmitted in any form or by any means: electronic, electrostatic, magnetic, tape, mechanical photocopying, recording or otherwise without the written permission of the Publisher.

For permission to use material from this book please contact us:
Telephone 631-231-7269; Fax 631-231-8175
Web Site: http://www.novapublishers.com

NOTICE TO THE READER

The Publisher has taken reasonable care in the preparation of this book, but makes no expressed or implied warranty of any kind and assumes no responsibility for any errors or omissions. No liability is assumed for incidental or consequential damages in connection with or arising out of information contained in this book. The Publisher shall not be liable for any special, consequential, or exemplary damages resulting, in whole or in part, from the readers' use of, or reliance upon, this material. Any parts of this book based on government reports are so indicated and copyright is claimed for those parts to the extent applicable to compilations of such works.

Independent verification should be sought for any data, advice or recommendations contained in this book. In addition, no responsibility is assumed by the publisher for any injury and/or damage to persons or property arising from any methods, products, instructions, ideas or otherwise contained in this publication.

This publication is designed to provide accurate and authoritative information with regard to the subject matter covered herein. It is sold with the clear understanding that the Publisher is not engaged in rendering legal or any other professional services. If legal or any other expert assistance is required, the services of a competent person should be sought. FROM A DECLARATION OF PARTICIPANTS JOINTLY ADOPTED BY A COMMITTEE OF THE AMERICAN BAR ASSOCIATION AND A COMMITTEE OF PUBLISHERS.

Additional color graphics may be available in the e-book version of this book.

LIBRARY OF CONGRESS CATALOGING-IN-PUBLICATION DATA

U.S. science, technology, engineering, and mathematics (STEM) education /
[edited by] Catherine L. Grover.
p. cm.
Includes index.
ISBN 978-1-61122-549-5 (hardcover)
1. Science--Study and teaching (Higher)--United States. 2. Science--Study
and teaching (Graduate)--United States. 3. Science and state--United
States. I. Grover, Catherine L.
Q183.3.A1U16 2010
507.1'173--dc22
2010042636

Published by Nova Science Publishers, Inc. † New York

CONTENTS

Preface		vii
Chapter 1	Students Who Study Science, Technology, Engineering, and Mathematics (STEM) in Postsecondary Education *National Center for Education Statistics*	1
Chapter 2	Science, Technology, Engineering, and Mathematics (STEM) Education: Background, Federal Policy, and Legislative Action *Jeffrey J. Kuenzi*	29
Chapter 3	Moving Forward to Improve Engineering Education *National Science Board, National Science Foundation*	57
Chapter 4	National Action Plan for Addressing the Critical Needs of the U.S. Science, Technology, Engineering and Mathematics Education System *National Science Board, National Science Foundation*	101
Chapter Sources		195
Index		197

PREFACE

A large majority of secondary school students fail to reach proficiency in math and science, and many are taught by teachers lacking adequate subject matter knowledge. When compared to other nations, the math and science achievement of U.S. pupils and the rate of STEM degree attainment appear inconsistent with a nationa considered the world leader in scientific innovation. In a recent international assessment of 15-year old students, the U.S. ranked 28th in math literacy and 24th in science literacy. Moreover, the U.S. ranks 20th among all nations in the proportion of 24-year olds who earn degrees in natural science or engineering. This book provides background and context to understand the legislative developments in STEM and examines the federal role in promoting STEM education and policy

Chapter 1- Rising concern about America's ability to maintain its competitive position in the global economy has renewed interest in STEM education. In 2005, for example, three preeminent U.S. scientific groups—the National Academy of Science, the National Academy of Engineering, and the Institute of Medicine—jointly issued a report, *Rising Above the Gathering Storm: Energizing and Employing America for a Brighter Economic Future*, that called for strengthening the STEM pipeline from primary through postsecondary education (National Academy of Science 2005). This chapter recommended increasing investment in STEM programs, enhancing the STEM teaching force, and enlarging the pool of students pursuing degrees and careers in STEM fields. Similar policy recommendations have come from other organizations and government agencies (Government Accountability Office 2006; National Science Board 2007; U.S. Department of Education 2006).

Chapter 2- There is growing concern that the United States is not preparing a sufficient number of students, teachers, and practitioners in the areas of science, technology, engineering, and mathematics (STEM). A large majority of secondary school students fail to reach proficiency in math and science, and many are taught by teachers lacking adequate subject matter knowledge.

When compared to other nations, the math and science achievement of U.S. pupils and the rate of STEM degree attainment appear inconsistent with a nation considered the world leader in scientific innovation. In a recent international assessment of 15-year-old students, the U.S. ranked 28th in math literacy and 24th in science literacy. Moreover, the U.S. ranks 20th among all nations in the proportion of 24-year-olds who earn degrees in natural science or engineering.

Chapter 3- This chapter of the National Science Board (Board) lays out our findings and recommendations for the National Science Foundation (NSF) to support innovations in engineering education programs. The Board, established by Congress in 1950, provides oversight for, and establishes the policies of, NSF. It also serves as an independent body of advisors to the President and Congress on national policy issues related to science and engineering research and education.

Chapter 4- The National Science Board (Board) is pleased to present a national action plan to address pressing issues in U.S. science, technology, engineering, and mathematics (STEM) education. In this action plan the Board identifies priority actions that should be taken by all stakeholders, working together cooperatively, to achieve measurable improvements in the Nation's STEM education system.

In: U.S. Science, Technology, Engineering and Mathematics... ISBN: 978-1-61122-549-5
Editor: Catherine L. Grover © 2011 Nova Science Publishers, Inc.

Chapter 1

STUDENTS WHO STUDY SCIENCE, TECHNOLOGY, ENGINEERING, AND MATHEMATICS (STEM) IN POSTSECONDARY EDUCATION

National Center for Education Statistics

INTRODUCTION

Rising concern about America's ability to maintain its competitive position in the global economy has renewed interest in STEM education. In 2005, for example, three preeminent U.S. scientific groups—the National Academy of Science, the National Academy of Engineering, and the Institute of Medicine—jointly issued a report, *Rising Above the Gathering Storm: Energizing and Employing America for a Brighter Economic Future*, that called for strengthening the STEM pipeline from primary through postsecondary education (National Academy of Science 2005). This chapter recommended increasing investment in STEM programs, enhancing the STEM teaching force, and enlarging the pool of students pursuing degrees and careers in STEM fields. Similar policy recommendations have come from other organizations and government agencies (Government Accountability Office 2006; National Science Board 2007; U.S. Department of Education 2006).

Although information about the number of students completing degrees in STEM fields is available (Goan and Cunningham 2006; U.S. Department of Education 2008), less is known about students' undergraduate progress through the STEM pipeline (Anderson and Kim 2006). This Statistics in Brief focuses on undergraduate students, examining students' entrance into and persistence toward degree completion in STEM fields. It is designed to provide a profile of undergraduates who pursue and complete STEM degrees. It addresses three questions: (1) Who enters STEM fields? (2) What are their educational outcomes (i.e., persis-tence and degree completion) several years after beginning postsecondary education? (3) Who persisted in and completed a STEM degree after entrance into a STEM field of study?

Definition of STEM Fields and Entrance

What Are STEM Fields? STEM fields can include a wide range of disciplines. For example, the National Science Foundation (NSF) defines STEM fields broadly, including not only the common categories of mathematics, natural sciences, engineering, and computer and information sciences, but also such social/behavioral sciences as psychology, economics, sociology, and political science (Green 2007). Many recent federal and state legislative efforts, however, are aimed at improving STEM education mainly in mathematics, natural sciences, engineering, and technologies (Kuenzi, Matthews, and Mangan 2006; National Governors Association 2007). For this reason, this Statistics in Brief excludes social/behavioral sciences from the definition of STEM fields. STEM fields, as defined here, include mathematics; natural sciences (including physical sciences and biological/agricultural sciences); engineering/engineering technologies; and computer/information sciences. For more details about classifications of STEM fields, see the crosswalk in the Technical Notes section.

How Is Entrance into a STEM Field Defined? To identify students entering STEM fields, this Statistics in Brief uses their reported major field of study and considers anyone a STEM entrant if that student has reported a major (first or second major if that information is available) in a STEM field at any time during his or her postsecondary enrollment (to the extent that the data allow). This definition attempts to capture all students who enter STEM fields, including early entrants, later entrants, those who changed majors, and those with a second major in a STEM field. For example, in the 1996/01 Beginning Postsecondary Students Longitudinal Study (BPS:96/01) (the major data source for this study), STEM entrance is identified by students' major field as reported in the base-year survey of 1995–96 and in the 1998 and 2001 follow-up surveys. Students reporting a STEM major field of study at one or more of these three times are considered STEM entrants between 1995–96 and 2001.[1] In the 20 03–04 National Postsecondary Student Aid Study (NPSAS:04) and the Education Longitudinal Study of 20 02/06 (ELS:02/06) (two additional data sources for this study), STEM entrance is identified by students' major and secondary major field reported at the time of interview. For brevity, this study refers to students who entered STEM fields as *STEM entrants* and those who never entered (including those with only non-STEM majors and those with an undeclared major[2]) as *non-STEM entrants*.

Data Sources and Analysis Samples

This study primarily uses longitudinal data from the 1995-96 Beginning Postsecondary Students Longitudinal Study (BPS:96/01). This survey began in 1995–96 with a nationally representative sample of approximately 12,000 first-time students who enrolled in postsecondary education in 1995–96. These students were interviewed again in 1998 and, for the last time, in 2001, about 6 years after their initial college entry. The longitudinal design of BPS permits examination of student entrance, persistence, and attainment in STEM fields over the period of time in which most students complete a bachelor's degree. To examine students' paths to STEM degrees, this study used a sample of about 9,000 BPS students who participated in the initial survey in 1996 and the two follow-up surveys in 1998 and 2001 and who reported a major (including "undeclared major") in at least one of three data collections.

This study also draws data from two other surveys to provide information about STEM participation among different undergraduate populations. The first is the 2003–04 National Postsecondary Student Aid Study (NPSAS:04), a cross-sectional survey of undergraduate and graduate/first-professional students enrolled in U.S. postsecondary institutions in 2003–04. Focusing on all undergraduates (a sample of about 80,000), NPSAS:04 provides information about the prevalence of STEM majors among U.S. undergraduates in 2003–04. The second data source is the Education Longitudinal Study of 2002/06 (ELS:02/06). Unlike BPS and NPSAS, which include postsecondary students of all ages, ELS represents a more homogeneous group: high school graduates from the senior class of 2004. Using a subsample of these graduates who were enrolled in postsecondary education in 2006 (about 8,500), this study examines STEM entrance among a more traditional college-age population. For details on the BPS:96/01, NPSAS:04, and ELS:02/06 data, see the Technical Notes below.

All findings reported below are descriptive and do not imply any causal relationship. All comparisons in this study were tested for statistical significance using Student's t statistic to ensure that differences were larger than might be expected due to sampling variation. All differences cited are statistically significant at the .05 level. Adjustments were not made for multiple comparisons. Consequently, some differences noted here might not be significant if a multiple comparison procedure was used. Standard errors for all estimates are available at http://nces.ed.gov/das/library/reports.asp.

Organization of the Statistics in Brief

This Statistics in Brief is organized into four major sections. The first section provides an overview of STEM entrance among various undergraduate populations. The next section looks at the demographic and academic characteristics of students who entered STEM fields in postsecondary education. The third section examines rates of overall persistence and degree completion for both students who entered STEM fields and those who did not. The last section focuses on only STEM entrants and examines their rates of persistence and degree completion in STEM fields.

ENTRANCE INTO STEM FIELDS: AN OVERALL PICTURE

How many postsecondary students entered STEM fields? Answers to this question depend on the undergraduate population and period of enrollment examined. Based on a nationally representative undergraduate sample from NPSAS:04, some 14 percent of all undergraduates enrolled in U.S. postsecondary institutions in 2003–04 were enrolled in a STEM field, including 5 percent in computer/information sciences, 4 percent in engineering/engineering technologies, 3 percent in biological/agricultural sciences, and less than 1 percent each in physical sciences and mathematics (table 1).

Although NPSAS:04 covers undergraduates of all ages, ELS:02/06 looked at students who were of traditional college age: some 15 percent of 20 03–04 high school graduates enrolled in postsecondary education in 2006 reported a STEM major. Compared to students in NPSAS:04, the traditional college-age students of ELS:02/06 enrolled in mathematics and natural sciences (including physical sciences and biological/agricultural sciences) at higher rates and enrolled in computer/ information sciences at a lower rate.

Unlike the one-time snapshots provided by NPSAS:04 and ELS:02/06, BPS:96/01 follows the enrollment of beginning postsecondary students over 6 years, thereby offering a fuller picture of STEM entrance. Based on BPS:96/0 1, a total of 23 percent of beginning postsecondary students entered a STEM field at some time during their postsecondary enrollment from 1995–96 to 2001 (figure 1 and table 1). Overall, 77 percent of 1995–96 beginning postsecondary students never entered a STEM field during their enrollment through 2001, including 72 percent who entered only non- STEM fields and 5 percent who never declared a major. In STEM fields, a higher percentage of students entered biological/ agricultural sciences, engineering/engineering technologies, and computer/information sciences (7–8 percent) than mathematics and physical sciences (less than 2 percent for each).

Table 1. Percentage of undergraduates who entered STEM fields, by undergraduate population

Undergraduate population	Total	Mathematics	Natural sciences Total	Physical sciences	Biological/ag ricultural sciences	Engineering/ engineering technologies	Computer/ Information sciences	Non-STEM field	Major undeclared
2003–04 undergraduates	13.7	0.5	4.2	0.7	3.1	4.2	4.9	65.0	21.3
2003–04 high school graduates who were enrolled in postsecondary education in 2006	14.7	0.9	7.1	1.3	5.4	4.7	2.3	60.8	24.5
1995–96 beginning postsecondary students	22.8	1.2	8.3	1.5	7.1	8.3	6.6	72.5	4.7

[1] A student entered a STEM field if his or her major or secondary major field of study was in a STEM field. STEM fields include mathematics, natural sciences (including physical sciences and biological/agricultural sciences), engineering/engineering technologies, and computer/information sciences. In NPSAS:2004, STEM entrance is identified by undergraduates' major and secondary major field as reported in 2003–04. In ELS:02/06, STEM entrance is identified by the major and secondary major field as reported by 2003–04 high school graduates who were enrolled in postsecondary education in 2006. In BPS:96/01, STEM entrance is identified by students' major field as reported in 1995–96, 1998, and 2001, and students who reported a STEM major at one or more of these interview times are considered to have entered a STEM field between 1995–96 and 2001. Estimates for entering specific STEM fields do not sum to the total because some students had a major and a secondary major in different STEM fields or entered more than one STEM field during their postsecondary education.

NOTE: Standard error tables are available at http://nces.ed.gov/das/library/reports.asp.

SOURCE: U.S. Department of Education, National Center for Education Statistics, 2003–04 National Postsecondary Student Aid Study (NPSAS:04); Education Longitudinal Study of 2002 (ELS:2002), Second Follow-up, 2006; and 1996/01 Beginning Postsecondary Students Longitudinal Study (BPS:96/01).

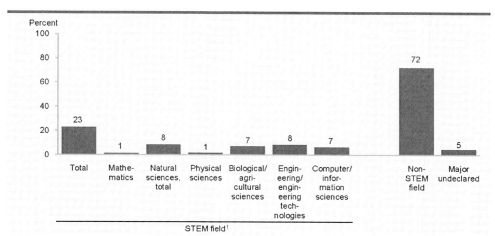

[1] STEM entrance is identified by students' major field as reported in 1995–96, 1998, and 2001. Students who reported a STEM major at one or more of these interview times are considered to have entered a STEM field between 1995–96 and 2001. STEM fields include mathematics, natural sciences (including physical sciences and biological/agricultural sciences), engineering/ engineering technologies, and computer/information sciences. Estimates for entering specific STEM fields do not sum to total because some students entered more than one STEM field between 1995–96 and 2001.

Source: U.S. Department of Education, National Center for Education Statistics, 1996/01 Beginning Postsecondary Students Longitudinal Study (BPS:96/01).

Figure 1. Percentage of 1995–96 beginning postsecondary students who entered STEM fields between 1995–96 and 2001

Students entering STEM fields had enrollment patterns different from those who did not enter STEM fields. Based on BPS:96/01,[3] 52 percent of STEM entrants started their postsecondary education at a 4-year institution, compared to 38 percent of their non-STEM counterparts (table 2). Further, about one-third of STEM entrants who started in a 4-year institution (33 percent) began in a very selective institution, compared to 21 percent among their non-STEM counterparts. A higher percentage of STEM entrants started in a bachelor's degree program (48 percent vs. 35 percent) and a lower percentage attended classes exclusively part time (8 percent vs. 13 percent) when compared to their non-STEM counterparts.

Students entering specific STEM fields generally differed from non-STEM entrants in terms of type of institution attended, degree program, and attendance, but those entering computer/information sciences were an exception. No measurable differences were found between students entering computer/information sciences and their non-STEM counterparts in terms of the type of institution and level of degree program in which they first enrolled. Compared to their non-STEM counterparts, a lower percentage of students entering computer/information sciences attended classes exclusively full time and a higher percentage had mixed full- and part- time enrollment. Further, compared to students who entered natural sciences (more specifically, the physical sciences and biological/agricultural sciences), a higher percentage of students entering computer/information sciences started postsecondary education at public 2-year colleges and less selective institutions, enrolled in sub-baccalaureate programs such as certificate or associate's degree programs, and attended school exclusively part time. In addition, compared to students entering mathematics and engineering/engineering technologies, those entering computer/information sciences attended 4-year institutions and enrolled in bachelor's degree programs at lower rates.

Table 2. Percentage distributions of 1995–96 beginning postsecondary students' first institution type and selectivity, first degree program level, and enrollment intensity through 2001, by STEM entrance between 1995–96 and 2001

STEM entrance between 1995–96 and 2001[2]	First institution type			First institution selectivity[1]		
	4-year Public	2-year Public	Other	Less selective	Selective	Very selective
All students	41.2	45.5	13.3	57.9	17.7	24.4
Students who entered STEM field, total	51.7	39.8	8.5	48.1	19.3	32.6
Mathematics	53.0	46.4	0.6 !	44.8	25.1	30.1
Natural sciences, total	70.9	26.7	2.4 !	42.6	21.1	36.3
Physical sciences	75.9	23.4	0.7 !	43.8	19.7	36.4
Biological/agricultural sciences	70.2	27.1	2.6 !	42.2	21.3	36.4
Engineering/engineering technologies	47.8	42.0	10.2 !	43.5	19.5	37.0
Computer/information sciences	33.2	51.2	15.6	68.5	12.2	19.3
Students who did not enter STEM field, total	38.1	47.2	14.7	61.9	17.0	21.1
Students who entered only non-STEM fields	39.4	45.2	15.4	61.3	17.2	21.5
Students who did not declare a major	18.4	77.5	4.1 !	79.9	10.6 !	9.5 !

STEM entrance between 1995–96 and 2001[2]	First degree program level			Enrollment intensity through 2001		
	Certificate	Associate's degree	Bachelor's degree	Always full-time	Always part-time	Mixed
All students	18.3	43.5	38.2	46.9	12.2	40.9
Students who entered STEM field, total	11.2	40.6	48.2	47.9	8.3	43.8
Mathematics	0.9 !	47.3	51.8	50.7	11.0 !	38.3
Natural sciences, total	3.5	29.5	67.0	57.1	3.1	39.8
Physical sciences	0.9 !	24.8	74.3	46.8	#	53.2
Biological/agricultural sciences	4.0	30.1	65.9	59.0	3.7	37.3
Engineering/engineering technologies	13.7	42.5	43.7	46.4	9.3	44.3
Computer/information sciences	18.8	50.7	30.5	38.0	11.2	50.8
Students who did not enter STEM field, total	20.4	44.4	35.3	46.7	13.3	40.1
Students who entered only non-STEM fields	20.2	43.1	36.7	48.5	10.3	41.2
Students who did not declare a major	22.9	62.9	14.3	19.2	58.5	22.3

[1] This variable only applies to 4-year institutions. The "very selective" institutions are those in which the 25th percentile of SAT/ACT scores of incoming freshman exceeded 1000. The "selective" institutions are research universities I and II, baccalaureate I institutions, and private not-for-profit doctoral universities I and II that do not meet the "very selective" criteria. The "least selective" institutions are all other 4-year institutions.

[2] STEM entrance is identified by students' major field as reported in 1995–96, 1998, and 2001. Students who reported a STEM major at one or more of these interview times are considered to have entered a STEM field between 1995–96 and 2001. STEM fields include mathematics, natural sciences (including physical sciences and biological/agricultural sciences), engineering/ engineering technologies, and computer/information sciences.

Note: Detail may not sum to totals because of rounding. Standard error tables are available at http://nces.ed.gov/das/library/reports.asp.

Source: U.S. Department of Education, National Center for Education Statistics, 1996/01 Beginning Postsecondary Students Longitudinal Study (BPS:96/01).

WHO ENTERS STEM FIELDS?

To address the question of who enters STEM fields, this section looks at various characteristics of beginning postsecondary students who entered STEM fields between 1995 and 2001. The percentage of men entering STEM fields was higher than that of women (33 percent vs. 14 percent) (table 3), especially in the fields of mathematics, engineering/engineering technologies, and computer/ information sciences. Nearly half of Asian/Pacific Islander students (47 percent) entered STEM fields, compared to 19–23 percent of students in each of the other racial/ethnic groups. No measurable differences were found among White, Black, and Hispanic students.[4]

Percentages of students entering STEM fields were higher for younger (age 19 or younger) and dependent students than for older (age 24 or older) and independent students. Compared to their U.S.-born counterparts, a higher percentage of foreign students entered STEM fields overall (34 percent vs. 22 percent), and computer/information sciences in particular (16 percent vs. 6 percent). Compared to students whose family income fell in the bottom 25 percent or whose parents had a high school education or less, a higher percentage of stu-dents from families with income in the top 25 percent or whose parents had at least some college education entered natural sciences, including the biological/ agricultural sciences and physical sciences.

Various academic indicators are associated with STEM entrance as well. For example, the percentage of students entering STEM fields was higher among students who took trigonometry, precalculus, or calculus in high school; earned a grade point average (GPA) of B or higher; had college entrance exam scores in the highest quarter; and expected to attain a graduate degree in the future than among students without these characteristics.

Students entering most STEM fields had similar demographic and academic characteristics, but those entering computer/information sciences were somewhat different. For example, a higher percentage of students age 30 or older, from families with income in the bottom 25 percent, and with an average high school GPA of below B entered the computer/information science fields than did students age 19 or younger, from families with income in the top 25 percent, and with an average high school GPA of B or higher.

POSTSECONDARY OUTCOMES AFTER 6 YEARS

Students take many different paths through postsecondary education. Some attend college full time continuously until they obtain a degree or other credential; others take longer to complete their studies, taking breaks or attending part time. Still others choose to leave college without obtaining a degree or credential. This section compares the overall outcomes of STEM and non-STEM entrants 6 years after their initial college enrollment.[5] In general, STEM entrants had better outcomes than their non-STEM counterparts (table 4). For example, compared to students who never entered STEM fields or who entered only non-STEM fields, those entering STEM fields had a higher rate of completing a bachelor's degree program (35 percent vs. 27–29 percent) and a lower rate of leaving college without earning any degree (27 percent vs. 33–36 percent).

Table 3. Percentage of 1995–96 beginning postsecondary students who entered STEM fields between 1995–96 and 2001, by selected student characteristics.

Selected student characteristic	STEM entrance[1] Total	Mathematics	Natural sciences Total	Physical sciences	Biological/ agricultural sciences	Engineering/ engineering technologies	Computer/ information sciences
All students	22.8	1.2	8.3	1.5	7.1	8.3	6.6
Sex							
Male	32.9	1.7	9.5	1.7	8.0	15.1	9.3
Female	14.5	0.7	7.3	1.3	6.3	2.7	4.3
Race/ethnicity[2]							
White	21.5	1.1	7.8	1.6	6.5	8.4	5.7
Black	20.8	1.8!	6.5	0.5!	6.1	6.4	7.6
Hispanic	22.8	1.3!	9.2	0.7!	8.7	6.8	6.7
Asian/Pacific Islander	47.4	1.1!	19.1	4.3	15.9	15.0	14.9
American Indian/Alaska Native	19.1!	#	4.3!	3.4	0.9	7.1!	8.5!
Age when first enrolled							
19 or younger	24.7	1.5	10.4	1.9	8.9	8.7	5.8
20–23	23.5	0.6!	5.5!	0.7!	5.0!	10.5	7.1
24–29	14.3	0.6!	3.4!	0.6!	2.8!	4.3!	7.2
30 or older	17.1	0.3!	1.4!	0.2!	1.2!	6.3	10.2
Dependency status when first enrolled							
Dependent	25.6	1.5	10.6	1.9	9.1	9.4	6.0
Independent	15.8	0.4!	2.7	0.4!	2.3	5.7	7.9
Immigrant status when first enrolled							
Foreign students/resident aliens	34.2	1.8	8.1	1.5!	7.3	10.6	16.1
Naturalized citizen	30.3	2.1!	10.8	2.8!	8.3!	13.0 !	7.4!
U.S. native	21.6	1.2	8.3	1.5	7.0	7.8	5.9
Language spoken as a child							
Non-English	33.9	3.1!	9.3	1.6	8.0	11.1	13.5
English	21.5	1.0	8.2	1.6	7.0	7.9	5.7
Parents' highest education							
High school diploma or less	20.3	0.9!	5.6	0.9	4.8	7.7	7.3
Some college	24.2	1.6!	9.9	1.9	8.6	7.5	6.6
Bachelor's degree or higher	25.2	1.4	11.1	2.1	9.3	9.4	5.6
Family income (of dependent students)							
Lowest quarter	25.6	2.1!	9.0	1.1	8.1	8.7	7.9
Middle two quarters	24.4	0.8	10.3	2.3	8.4	8.9	6.0
Highest quarter	27.6	2.2	12.6	2.0	11.2	10.8	3.7
Highest level of mathematics completed in high school[3]							
None of the following	16.8	#	5.7	0.3!	5.4	6.8!	5.1
Algebra 2	18.1	0.6!	8.3	0.6!	7.8	4.7	5.0
Trigonometry or precalculus	25.5	1.2	11.4	2.1	9.8	9.0	5.1
Calculus	45.0	3.3	23.1	5.4	18.3	17.0	5.2

Table 3. (Continued)

Selected student characteristic	STEM entrance[1] Total	Mathematics	Natural sciences Total	Physical sciences	Biological/ agricultural sciences	Engineering/ engineering technologies	Computer/ information sciences
High school GPA[3]							
Below B	18.3	0.5!	5.6	0.4	5.3	5.8	7.3
At least B	31.1	1.7	15.9	3.2	13.3	11.3	4.0
Type of high school diploma							
Regular diploma	23.3	1.3	8.9	1.5	7.7	8.4	6.3
No regular diploma	17.9	#	2.5!	1.1!	1.4!	7.3!	8.9
College entrance exam scores							
Not taken or scores unknown	18.7	1.1!	3.3	0.6	2.8	7.5	8.4
Lowest quarter	20.8	0.7!	6.7	0.4!	6.5	6.6	6.9
Middle two quarters	25.0	1.0	11.9	2.3	10.1	8.8	4.8
Highest quarter	51.0	5.2!	28.5	6.0	23.9	16.4	4.8!
Highest degree expected when first enrolled							
No degree or below bachelor's degree	14.7	0.4!	3.1	#	3.1!	4.3	7.8
Bachelor's degree	18.9	0.9!	4.0	0.3!	3.7	8.7	6.7
Graduate/professional degree	28.4	2.0	13.3	2.9	11.0	9.7	5.6

Rounds to zero.

! Interpret data with caution (estimates are unstable).

[1] STEM entrance is identified by students' major field as reported in 1995–96, 1998, and 2001. Students who reported a STEM major at one or more of these interview times are considered to have entered a STEM field between 1995–96 and 2001. STEM fields include mathematics, natural sciences (including physical sciences and biological/agricultural sciences), engineering/ engineering technologies, and computer/information sciences. Estimates for entering specific STEM fields do not sum to the total because some students entered more than one STEM field between 1995–96 and 2001.

[2] The racial/ethnic category of "other" is included in the total but not presented as an individual group due to small sample sizes. Black includes African American, Hispanic includes Latino, and Asian/Pacific Islander includes Native Hawaiian.

[3] This variable only applies to students who took college entrance exams such as the Scholastic Achievement Test (SAT) or the American College Test (ACT). NOTE: Standard error tables are available at http://nces.ed.gov/das/library/reports.asp.

SOURCE: U.S. Department of Education, National Center for Education Statistics, 1996/01 Beginning Postsecondary Students Longitudinal Study (BPS:96/01).

Students who entered computer/information sciences and engineering/engineering technologies did not do as well as students in other STEM fields with respect to attaining a bachelor's degree. On the other hand, the percentage of students earning an associate's degree was higher among these two groups than among those who entered biological/agricultural sciences. The percentage of students earning a certificate was higher among stu-dents who entered computer/information sciences than among those who entered mathematics, biological/ agricultural sciences, and physical sciences. A higher percentage of students who entered computer/information sciences and engineering/engineering technologies left college without earning any credential, compared to students entering physical sciences and biological/ agricultural sciences.

PERSISTENCE IN STEM FIELDS

While a majority of STEM entrants either completed a degree or remained enrolled over 6 years (73 percent, table 4), not all remained in the STEM field they had entered. This section examines students' persistence in STEM fields from several perspectives. Table 5 shows changes among majors; table 6 shows persistence and degree attainment in STEM fields; table 7 focuses on bachelor's degree completion in STEM fields; and table 8 shows the characteristics of students who persisted in STEM fields.

Table 4. Percentage distribution of 1995–96 beginning postsecondary students' degree attainment and persistence as of 2001, by STEM entrance between 1995–96 and 2001

STEM entrance between 1995–96 and 2001[1]	Attained a degree/certificate as of 2001					Did not attain a degree/certificate as of 2001	
	Total	Bachelor's	Associate's	Certificate	No degree, still enrolled	No degree, not enrolled
All students	51.6	28.9	10.3	12.3	14.4	34.0
Students who entered STEM field, total	54.9	34.8	11.1	8.9	18.6	26.6
Mathematics	61.4	49.7	11.0 !	0.6 !	15.2	23.4 !
Natural sciences, total	63.5	52.7	6.5	4.3 !	18.1	18.4
Physical sciences	68.4	55.2	10.6 !	2.6 !	18.6	13.0
Biological/agricultural sciences	62.3	52.2	5.5 !	4.5 !	18.4	19.4
Engineering/engineering technologies	53.0	29.7	15.0	8.4 !	19.3	27.6
Computer/information sciences	46.4	14.8	15.3	16.4	18.4	35.2
Students who did not enter STEM field, total	50.6	27.2	10.1	13.4	13.2	36.2
Students who entered only non-STEM fields	53.3	28.9	10.8	13.6	13.9	32.8
Students who did not declare a major	10.0 !	0.2 !	0.3 !	9.5 !	2.2 !	87.8

! Interpret data with caution (estimates are unstable).

[1] STEM entrance is identified by students' major field as reported in 1995–96, 1998, and 2001. Students who reported a STEM major at one or more of these interview times are considered to have entered a STEM field between 1995–96 and 2001. STEM fields include mathematics, natural sciences (including physical sciences and biological/agricultural sciences), engineering /engineering technologies, and computer/information sciences.

Note: Detail may not sum to totals because of rounding. Standard error tables are available at http://nces.ed.gov/das/library/reports.asp.

Source: U.S. Department of Education, National Center for Education Statistics, 1996/01 Beginning Postsecondary Students Longitudinal Study (BPS:96/01)

Change in Majors

Are college students who start out in STEM fields likely to change to a major outside of STEM? Table 5, which compares students' majors when they first enrolled in 1995–96 with their majors when they were last enrolled through 2001, indicates that 36 percent were no longer in STEM fields when last enrolled through 2001.[6] On the other hand, about 7 percent of students who began with a non-STEM major switched to a STEM field, and 16 percent of those with undeclared majors initially later declared a STEM major.

Table 5. Percentage distribution of 1995–96 beginning postsecondary students' major field when last enrolled through 2001, by major field in 1995–96

	\multicolumn{7}{c	}{Major field when last enrolled through 2001[1]}		
	\multicolumn{6}{c	}{STEM field[2]}		
			\multicolumn{4}{c	}{Natural sciences}			
Major field in 1995–96	Total	Mathematics	Physical Total sciences	Biological/ agricultural sciences	Engineering/ engineering technologies	Computer/ information	Non-STEM field	Major undeclared
All students	17.1	0.7	5.8	1.0	4.8	5.3	5.4	78.1	4.8
STEM field, total	64.1	2.5	19.9!	3.2!	16.6!	28.5!	13.2!	35.9	#
Mathematics	67.7	43.7!	3.1	2.6	0.5	16.7!	4.2	32.3	#
Natural sciences, total	56.8	1.0!	52.2	7.5	44.7	1.8!	1.8!	43.2	#
Physical sciences	72.1	3.3!	59.7	44.1	15.6	5.2!	4.0!	27.9	#
Biological/agricultural sciences	54.5	0.7!	51.1	2.0	49.1	1.3!	1.5	45.5	#
Engineering/engineering technologies	69.2	1.4!	2.3	1.1	1.3	59.7	5.7	30.8	#
Computer/information sciences	65.1	#	0.8!	#	0.8!	3.0!	61.3	34.9	#
Non-STEM field	7.1	0.4!	2.4	0.3!	2.1	1.2	3.1	92.9	#
No major declared	15.8	0.4	6.3	1.5	4.8	3.1	6.0	65.9	18.4

\# Rounds to zero.
! Interpret data with caution (estimates are unstable).
[1] Student's major field of study for the undergraduate program last enrolled through 2001.
[2] STEM fields include mathematics, natural sciences (including physical sciences and biological/agricultural sciences), engineering/engineering technologies, and computer/information sciences.
Note: Detail may not sum to totals because of rounding. Standard error tables are available at http://nces.ed.gov/das/library/reports.asp.
Source: U.S. Department of Education, National Center for Education Statistics, 1996/01 Beginning Postsecondary Students Longitudinal Study (BPS:96/01).

Table 6. Among 1995–96 beginning postsecondary students who entered STEM fields between 1995–96 and 2001, percentage distribution of degree attainment and persistence in STEM fields as of 2001

	Degree attainment and persistence in STEM field as of 2001			
	STEM completers	STEM persisters	STEM leavers	
STEM entrance	Attained a degree or certificate in a STEM field	No STEM degree or certificate but were still enrolled in a STEM field	No STEM degree or certificate and changed to a non-STEM field[1]	Left post-secondary education without a degree or certificate
Students who entered STEM field in 1995–96,2 total	37.1	7.5	27.1	28.3
Mathematics	27.0	1.5 !	32.3	39.1 !
Natural sciences, total	35.4	6.4	34.9	23.3
Physical sciences	41.7	15.3 !	21.0	22.0 !
Biological/agricultural sciences	34.4	5.0	37.0	23.5
Engineering/engineering technologies	40.8	8.6	23.1	27.5
Computer/information sciences	32.6	7.9 !	20.0	39.5
Students who entered STEM field between 1995–96 and 2001,3 total	40.7	12.0	20.6	26.7
Mathematics	46.9	7.2 !	22.5 !	23.3 !
Natural sciences, total	47.3	9.7	24.5	18.5
Physical sciences	58.9	10.3 !	17.8	13.0
Biological/agricultural sciences	45.3	9.5	25.9	19.4
Engineering/engineering technologies	39.9	11.5	20.8	27.8
Computer/information sciences	36.2	17.1	11.4	35.2

[1] This group includes students who had attained one or more degrees only in non-STEM fields and were last enrolled in a non-STEM field as of 2001, or those who had not attained a degree yet and were enrolled in a non-STEM field in 2001.

[2] STEM entrance is identified by students' major field as reported in 1995–96, the first year they were enrolled in postsecondary education. STEM fields include mathematics, natural sciences (including physical sciences and biological/agricultural sciences), engineering/engineering technologies, and computer/ information sciences.

[3] STEM entrance is identified by students' major field as reported in 1995–96, 1998, and 2001. Students who reported a STEM major at one or more of these interview times are considered to have entered a STEM field between 1995–96 and 2001.

Note: Detail may not sum to totals because of rounding. Standard error tables are available at http://nces.ed.gov/das/library/reports.asp.

Source: U.S. Department of Education, National Center for Education Statistics, 1996/01 Beginning Postsecondary Students Longitudinal Study (BPS:96/01).

Students who first majored in various STEM fields shifted their majors out of STEM fields at various rates, ranging from 28 percent for physical sciences to 46 percent for biological/agricultural sciences. Students changed majors within STEM fields as well. For example, 24 percent of initial mathematics majors switched to another STEM field later (with about 17 percent switching to engineering/engineering technologies, for example). Similarly, 28 percent of initial physical sciences majors switched to another STEM field later (notably to biological/agricultural sciences—16 percent). Between 4 and 9 percent of those initially entering computer/information sciences, biological/agricultural sciences, and engineering/engineering technologies later changed to another STEM field.

Degree Attainment and Persistence in STEM Fields

Among students entering a STEM field during their first year of enrollment (table 6), 37 percent completed a degree or certificate in a STEM field (*STEM completers*) over the next 6 years; some 7 percent maintained enrollment in a STEM field, but had not yet completed a degree in a STEM field (*STEM persisters*); and 55 percent left STEM fields (*STEM leavers*) by either switching to a non-STEM field (27 percent)[7] or leaving postsecondary education without earning any credential (28 percent).[8]

Of all STEM entrants between 1995–96 and 2001, some 41 percent had earned a STEM degree or certificate by 2001, and 12 percent remained enrolled in a STEM field as of 2001. About 47 percent had either switched to a non-STEM field (21 percent) or left postsecondary education without a degree or certificate by 2001 (27 percent).

Attainment and persistence rates varied among STEM fields.[9] Taking all STEM entrants between 1995–96 and 2001 as an example, compared to the total percentage for all STEM entrants, a higher percentage of students entering the physical sciences completed a degree in a STEM field (59 percent vs. 41 percent), and a lower per-centage left college without earning a degree or certificate (13 percent vs. 27 percent). Students entering computer/information sciences and engineering/engineering technologies, on the other hand, completed a STEM degree at lower rates than those who entered physical sciences, and they left postsecondary education without a degree at a higher rate than students who entered natural sciences, including physical sciences and biological/agricultural sciences.

Bachelor's Degree Attainment in STEM Fields

A total of 35 percent of all STEM entrants had attained a bachelor's degree by 2001 (table 7). Among these bachelor's degree recipients, 27 percent earned a degree in a STEM field and 8 percent did so in a non-STEM field (figure 2). The bachelor's degree attainment rate in a STEM field was highest for students who entered physical sciences (47 percent) and lowest for those who entered computer/information sciences (12 percent).

A majority of students earned their bachelor's degree in the STEM field they entered. For example, among students who entered the physical sciences between 1995–96 and 2001 and had earned a bachelor's degree by 2001, some 68 percent earned their bachelor's degree in the physical sciences. The percentage of students earning a bachelor's degree in the STEM field they entered ranged from 65 percent for mathematics to 77 percent for computer/information sciences.

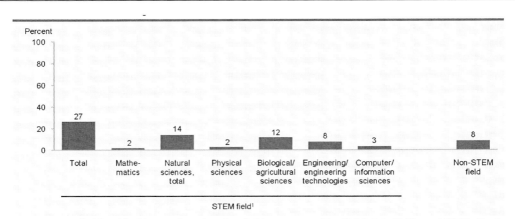

[1] STEM entrance is identified by students' major field as reported in 1995–96, 1998, and 2001. Students who reported a STEM major at one or more of these interview times are considered to have entered a STEM field between 1995–96 and 2001. STEM fields include mathematics, natural sciences (including physical sciences and biological/agricultural sciences), engineering/engineering technologies, and computer/information sciences. Estimates for specific STEM fields may not sum to total because of rounding.

SOURCE: U.S. Department of Education, National Center for Education Statistics, 1996/01 Beginning Postsecondary Students Longitudinal Study (BPS:96/01).

Figure 2. Among 1995–96 beginning postsecondary students who entered a STEM field between 1995–96 and 2001, percentage who attained a bachelor's degree in a STEM or non-STEM field: 2001

Who Is Likely to Complete a Degree or Remain Enrolled in STEM Fields?

The data in table 8 show the associations among various student characteristics and degree completion and persistence in STEM fields. The table focuses only on STEM entrants (non-STEM entrants are excluded). No gender difference was evident in persistence and attainment rates in STEM fields between 1995–96 and 2001. Some racial/ethnic differences were observed, however. Although there were no measurable differences in STEM entrance among White, Black, and Hispanic students (table 3), White students had a higher STEM bachelor's degree completion rate than did Black and Hispanic students. Asian students also had a higher STEM bachelor's degree completion rate than did Black and Hispanic students.

Students' age and dependency status were not only related to STEM entrance (table 3) but also to STEM degree completion. For example, a higher percentage of students who first enrolled in postsecondary education at age 19 or younger completed a bachelor's degree in a STEM field than did those who entered at age 20 or older. Similarly, a higher percentage of dependent students than of independent students completed a STEM bachelor's degree. Differences were also observed in how students left STEM fields. In general, a higher percentage of younger (age 19 or younger) and dependent students left by changing to a non-STEM field, while a higher percentage of their older (age 20–30 or 30 years and older when first enrolled) and independent peers left postsecondary education without earning any credential.

Table 7. Among 1995–96 beginning postsecondary students who entered STEM fields between 1995–96 and 2001, percentage who attained a bachelor's degree in various fields, by STEM entrance between 1995–96 and 2001

STEM entrance between 1995–96 and 2001[1]	Bachelor's degree in any field	Bachelor's degree in STEM field								Bachelor's degree in the same STEM field entered[2]	Bachelor's degree in non-STEM field
		Total	Mathematics	Natural sciences			Engineering/ engineering technologies	Computer/ information sciences			
				Total	Physical sciences	Biological/ agricultural sciences					
Students who entered STEM field, total	34.8	26.5	1.7	14.0	2.5	11.6	7.5	3.3	—	8.3
Mathematics	49.7	36.0	32.5	1.4 !	1.4 !	#	0.5 !	1.6 !	65.4	13.7 !
Natural sciences, total	52.7	40.3	0.7 !	38.5	6.8	31.7	0.7 !	0.3 !	73.1	12.4
Physical sciences	55.2	47.2	2.2 !	43.3	37.6	5.8	1.2 !	0.4 !	68.1	8.0
Biological/agricultural sciences	52.2	39.3	0.4 !	37.9	0.8 !	37.1	0.7 !	0.3 !	71.1	12.9
Engineering/engineering technologies	29.7	23.2	0.9 !	1.0 !	0.4 !	0.6 !	20.8 !	0.6 !	70.0	6.5
Computer/information sciences	14.8	11.8	#	0.1 !	#	0.1 !	0.3 !	11.4	77.4	3.0 !

— Not applicable. # Rounds to zero. ! Interpret data with caution (estimates are unstable).
[1] STEM entrance is identified by students' major field as reported in 1995–96, 1998, and 2001. Students who reported a STEM major at one or more of these interview times are considered to have entered a STEM field between 1995–96 and 2001. STEM fields include mathematics, natural sciences (including physical sciences and biological/agricultural sciences), engineering/engineering technologies, and computer/information sciences.
[2] Among students who earned a bachelor's degree, the percentage who earned the degree in the same STEM field as they entered.
Note: Detail may not sum to totals because of rounding. Standard error tables are available at http://nces.ed.gov/das/library/reports.asp.
Source: U.S. Department of Education, National Center for Education Statistics, 1996/01 Beginning Postsecondary Students Longitudinal Study (BPS:96/01).

Table 8. Among 1995–96 beginning postsecondary students who entered STEM fields between 1995–96 and 2001, percentage who earned STEM degrees, persisted in STEM fields, or left STEM fields as of 2001, by selected student characteristics

Selected student characteristic	STEM completers: Attained a degree or certificate in a STEM field	STEM completers: Attained a bachelor's degree in a STEM field	STEM persisters: No STEM degree or certificate but were still enrolled in a STEM field	STEM leavers: No STEM degree or certificate and changed to a non-STEM field[1]	STEM leavers: Left post-secondary education without a degree or certificate
Total		26.5	12.0	20.6	26.7
Gender					
Male		25.5	12.3	20.3	26.6
Female	40.6	28.4	11.4	21.2	26.8
Race/ethnicity[2]					
White	43.9	29.5	12.1	19.4	24.6
Black	31.7	15.5	9.4	23.8	35.2
Hispanic	33.1	16.3	15.7	19.7	31.6
Asian/Pacific Islander	39.9	31.2	9.4 !	27.0	23.8
Age when first enrolled					
19 or younger	43.0	33.2 r	11.5	23.4	22.1
20–23	37.8	8.9 !	13.0 !	12.2	37.0
24–29	37.1	3.4 !	13.2 !	18.5	31.3
30 or older	26.6	3.5 !	14.6 !	7.8	51.0
Dependency status when first enrolled					
Dependent	42.3	31.7	11.2	22.5	24.0
Independent	35.5	5.5 !	15.6	13.0	35.9
Immigrant status when first enrolled					
Foreign students/resident aliens	40.2	23.8	15.1	15.3	29.5
Naturalized citizen	43.6	30.3	7.5 !	28.9 !	20.0 !
U.S. native	41.1	27.3	12.5	20.7	25.7
Language spoken as a child					
Non-English	39.8	22.3	11.7	21.7	26.9
English	41.5	28.1	12.4	20.6	25.6

Table 8. (Continued)

Degree attainment and persistence in STEM field as of 2001

Selected student characteristic	STEM completers — Attained a degree or certificate in a STEM field	STEM completers — Attained a bachelor's degree in a STEM field	STEM persisters — No STEM degree or certificate but were still enrolled in a STEM field	STEM leavers — No STEM degree or certificate and changed to a non-STEM field1	STEM leavers — Left post-secondary education without a degree or certificate
Parents' highest education					
High school diploma or less	36.1	15.5	10.9	17.2	35.8
Some college	32.9	19.4	13.9	25.3	27.9
Bachelor's degree or higher	50.8	42.0	11.4	22.2	15.5
Type of high school diploma					
High school regular diploma	41.3	28.5	11.9	21.0	25.7
No high school regular diploma	33.6	2.1	13.1 !	15.5 !	37.7
College entrance exam scores					
Lowest quarter	26.3	15.0 !	13.2	22.8	37.8
Middle two quarters	40.5	30.2	12.7	25.7	21.1
Highest quarter	59.1	57.7	9.0	21.0	10.9
Highest level of mathematics completed in high school³					
None of the following	28.1	20.3 !	5.5 !	35.1	31.3
Algebra 2	23.5	12.8	15.3	19.8	41.4
Trigonometry or precalculus	47.4	37.5	10.8	23.4	18.4
Calculus	61.0	58.6	9.1	20.2	9.7
High school GPA3 Below B	27.9	13.1	12.9	14.8	44.4
At least B	52.1	47.3	9.7	24.7	13.4
Highest degree expected when first enrolled					
No degree or degree below bachelor's	36.1	4.2 !	4.7 !	10.8 !	48.4
Bachelor's degree	31.1	15.6	12.8	25.2	30.9
Graduate/professional degree	45.8	36.2	13.6	21.5	19.2
First institution type					
4-year	48.9	45.4	11.4	21.5	18.2
Public 2-year	29.2	7.3	14.0	19.8	37.1
Other	44.9	1.8 !	6.9 !	18.6	29.7

Table 8. (Continued)

Degree attainment and persistence in STEM field as of 2001

Selected student characteristic	STEM completers: Attained a degree or certificate in a STEM field	STEM completers: Attained a bachelor's degree in a STEM field	STEM persisters: No STEM degree or certificate but were still enrolled in a STEM field	STEM persisters: No STEM degree or certificate and changed to a non-STEM field[1]	STEM leavers: Left post-secondary education without a degree or certificate
First institution selectivity[4]					
Less selective	36.1	30.0	16.4	22.1	25.5
Selective	51.8	49.1	8.1	24.4	15.6
Very selective	66.2	65.6	5.8	19.2	8.8
First degree program type					
Certificate	39.3	5.4!	5.4!	15.7	39.7
Associate's	30.0	7.5	14.2	21.0	34.8
Bachelor's	50.1	47.5	11.7	21.4	16.8
Enrollment intensity between 1995–96 and 2001					
Always full-time	51.0	41.4	6.7	21.3	20.9
Always part-time	17.8!	#	14.8!	10.7!	56.8
Mixed	34.0	15.3	17.3	21.7	27.0

Rounds to zero.
! Interpret data with caution (estimates are unstable).
[1] This group includes students who had attained one or more degrees only in non-STEM fields and were last enrolled in a non-STEM field as of 2001, or those who had not attained a degree yet and were enrolled in a non-STEM field in 2001.
[2] American Indian/Alaska Native and "other" students are included in the total but not presented as an individual group due to small sample sizes. Black includes African American, Hispanic includes Latino, and Asian/Pacific Islander includes Native Hawaiian.
[3] This variable only applies to students who took college entrance exams such as the Scholastic Achievement Test (SAT) or the American College Test (ACT).
[4] This variable only applies to 4-year institutions. The "very selective" institutions are those in which the 25th percentile of SAT/ACT scores of incoming freshman exceeded 1000. The "selective" institutions are research universities I and II, baccalaureate I institutions, and private not-for-profit doctoral universities I and II that do not meet the "very selective" criteria. The "least selective" institutions are all other 4-year institutions.

NOTE: STEM entrance is identified by students' major field as reported in 1995–96, 1998, and 2001. Students who reported a STEM major at one or more of these interview times are considered to have entered a STEM field between 1995–96 and 2001. STEM fields include mathematics, natural sciences (including physical sciences and biological/agricultural sciences), engineering/engineering technologies, and computer/information sciences. Standard error tables are available at http://nces.ed.gov/das/library/reports.asp.

SOURCE: U.S. Department of Education, National Center for Education Statistics, 1996/01 Beginning Postsecondary Students Longitudinal Study (BPS:96/01).

Although a higher percentage of foreign students and students who spoke a language other than English as a child entered STEM fields than did their U.S.-born and English-speaking counterparts (table 3), no measurable differences were found in rates of completion of STEM degrees or persistence in STEM fields.

Parents' education levels were related to STEM degree attainment. The overall STEM degree completion rates as well as STEM bachelor's degree completion rates were higher among students whose parents had at least a 4- year college degree than among those whose parents did not attain that level of education. In addition, a lower percentage of students whose parents had a bachelor's or higher degree left postsecondary education without earning a credential than did their counterparts whose parents did not have a bachelor's degree.

Strong academic preparation in high school was associated with a higher STEM degree completion rate. For example, students who took trigonometry, precalculus, or calculus in high school; earned a high school GPA of B or higher; obtained college entrance exam scores in the highest quarter; and expected to attain a graduate degree in the future all had higher rates of STEM degree completion (including STEM bachelor's degrees) and lower rates of leaving college without earning any credential than did their peers without these characteristics.

Student outcomes in STEM fields also were related to the type of institution in which they first enrolled, their degree program, and full- or part-time attendance. STEM entrants who started their postsecondary education in a 4-year or selective institution, who nitially enrolled in a bachelor's degree program, and who attended school either exclusively full time or mixed full- and part-time attendance generally had higher STEM degree completion rates (including completing bachelor's degrees in STEM fields) than did their counterparts without these characteristics.

SUMMARY

To understand who enters into and completes undergraduate programs in STEM fields, this Statistics in Brief examined data from three major national studies: the 1995–96 Beginning Postsecondary Students Longitudinal Study (BPS:96/0 1); the 2003–04 National Postsecondary Student Aid Study (NPSAS:04); and the Education Longitudinal Study of 20 02/06 (ELS:02/06). STEM fields, as defined in this study, include mathematics, natural sciences (including physical sciences and biological/agricultural sciences), engineering/ engineering technologies, and computer/information sciences. This study used students' reported major field of study to identify STEM entrants and considered a STEM entrant anyone who reported a major in a STEM field at any time during his or her postsecondary enrollment.

Looking only at single points in time, STEM majors accounted for 14 percent of all undergraduates enrolled in U.S. postsecondary education in 2003–04 and 15 percent of 2003–04 high school graduates who were enrolled in postsecondary education in 2006. The STEM entrance rate increased, however, when estimated over students' postsecondary careers with longitudinal data. For example, 23 percent of 1995–96 first-time be-ginning postsecondary students majored in a STEM field at some point between 1995–96 and 2001. In general, the percentage of students entering STEM fields was higher among male students, younger and dependent students, Asian/Pacific Islander students, foreign students or those who spoke a language other than English as a child, and students with more advantaged family background characteristics and strong academic preparation than among their counterparts who did not have these characteristics.

After 6 years of initial college enrollment, STEM entrants generally did better than non-STEM entrants in terms of bachelor's degree attainment and overall persistence. However, not all STEM entrants stayed in their fields. Roughly one-third of students who entered a STEM field during the first year switched to a non- STEM field over the next 6 years. Among all STEM entrants between 1995–96 and 2001, 53 percent persisted in a STEM field by either completing a degree in a STEM field or staying enrolled in a STEM field, and a total of 47 percent left STEM fields by either switching to a non-STEM field or leaving postsecondary education without earning any credential.

STEM entrants with different characteristics had different STEM completion rates. For example, STEM bachelor's degree completion rates were higher among younger students (age 19 or younger when first enrolled in postsecondary education), White or Asian/Pacific Islander students, students with at least one parent who had a 4- year college degree, and those who demonstrated a high level of academic preparation for postsecondary education, chose a 4-year or a selective institution, enrolled in a bachelor's degree program when they began college, and attended school either full time or mixed full-time with part-time attendance.

Although students in various STEM fields were generally alike in terms of their demographic, academic, and enrollment characteristics and their outcomes, those entering computer/information sciences differed in many respects. According to the BPS data, older students, students from low-income families, and those less academically prepared enrolled in computer/information sciences more often than did their peers who were younger, from high-income families, or more academically prepared. Moreover, compared to other STEM students, a larger percentage of computer/information sciences majors attended public 2-year institutions, enrolled in subbaccalaureate programs, and attended classes exclusively part time. These findings are consistent with trends reported in the *Digest of Education Statistics* (U.S. Department of Education 2008) indicating that the number of associate's degrees awarded in computer/information sciences has increased 155 percent from 1994–95 to 2005–06, accounting for about one-third of all degrees awarded in the field of computer/information sciences in 2005–06. In the fields of biological/agricultural sciences, physical sciences, mathematics, and engineering, the number of associate's degrees accounted for 2–9 percent of all degrees awarded. In other words, more students seem to be seeking subbaccalaureate opportunities in computer/information sciences than in other STEM fields.

REFERENCES

[1] Anderson, E. & Kim, D. (2006). *Increasing the Success of Minority Students in Science and Technology*. Washington, DC: American Council on Education.

[2] Berkner, L., He, S. & Cataldi, E. F. (2002). Descriptive Summary of 1995–96 Beginning Postsecondary Students: Six Years Later (NCES 2003-151). *National Center for Education Statistics*, U.S. Department of Education. Washington, DC.

[3] Cominole, M., Siegel, P., Dudley, K., Roe, D. & Gilligan, T. (2006). 2004 National Postsecondary Student Aid Study (NPSAS:04) Full-Scale Methodology Report (NCES 2006- 180). National Center for Education Statistics, *Institute of Education Sciences*, U.S. Department of Education. Washington, DC.

[4] Goan, S. & Cunningham, A. (2006). Degree Completions in Areas of National Need, 1996−97 and 2001−02 (NCES 2006-154). National Center for Education Statistics, *Institute of Education Sciences*, U.S. Department of Education. Washington, DC.

[5] Government Accountability Office (GAO). (2006). Science, *Technology, Engineering, and Mathematics Trends and the Role of Federal Programs* (GAO-06-702T). Washington, DC: Author.

[6] Green, M. (2007). *Science and Engineering Degrees*: 1966−2004 (NSF 07-307). Arlington, VA: National Science Foundation.

[7] Ingels, S. J., Pratt, D. J., Wilson, D., Burns, L. J., Currivan, D., Rogers, J. E. & Hubbard-Bednasz, S. (2007). *Education Longitudinal Study of 2002 (ELS:02) Base-Year to Second Follow-up Public Use Data File Documentation* (NCES 2008-347). National Center for Education Statistics, Institute of Education Sciences, U.S. Department of Education. Washington, DC.

[8] Kuenzi, J., Matthews, C. & Mangan, B. (2006). Science, *Technology, Engineering, and Mathematics (STEM) Education Issues and Legislative Options*. Congressional Research Report. Washington, DC: Congressional Research Service.

[9] National Academy of Science, Committee on Science, Engi-neering, and Public Policy (COSEPUP). (2005). *Rising Above the Gathering Storm: Energizing and Employing America for a Brighter Economic Future*. Washington, DC: National Academies Press.

[10] National Governors Association (NGA). (2007). *Building a Science, Technology, Engineering and Math Agenda*. Washington, DC: Author.

[11] National Science Board (NSB). (2007). *A National Action Plan for Addressing the Critical Needs of the U.S. Science, Technology, Engineering, and Mathematics Education System*. Arlington, VA: National Science Foundation.

[12] U.S. Department of Education. (2006). A Test of Leadership: *Charting the Future of U.S. Higher Education*. Washington, DC.

[13] U.S. Department of Education, Institute of Education Sciences, National Center for Education Statistics. (2008). *Digest of Education Statistics*, 2007 (NCES 200 8- 022). Washington, DC.

[14] Wine, J. S., Heuer, R. E., Wheeless, S. C., Francis, T. L., Franklin, J. W. & Dudley, K. M. (2002). Beginning Postsecondary Students Longitudinal Study 1996–2001 (BPS:96/01) Methodology Report (NCES 2002-171). *National Center for Education Statistics*, U.S. Department of Education. Washington, DC.

TECHNICAL NOTES

This section describes data sources, study samples, weights, and derived variables used for this Statistics in Brief. It also includes a crosswalk for the specific contents of the STEM categorization for various major fields of study.

Data Sources

The 1995–96 Beginning Postsecondary Students Longitudinal Study. The 1995–96 Beginning Postsecondary Students Longitudinal Study (BPS:96) is composed of a subset of the students who participated in the 1995–96 National Postsecondary Student Aid Study (NPSAS:96). NPSAS:96 consisted of a nationally representative sample of students enrolled in all levels of postsecondary education during the 1995–96 academic year. The BPS:96 initial sample (approximately 12,400 students) was derived from that sample and is a nationally representative sample of students who began postsecondary education for the first time in 1995–96. The first follow- up of the BPS cohort (BPS:96/98) was conducted in 1998, approximately 3 years after these students first enrolled. About 10,300 of the students who first began in 1995–96 were located and interviewed in the 1998 follow-up, for an overall weighted response rate of 80 percent. The second BPS follow-up (BPS:96/0 1) was conducted in 2001, approximately 6 years after initial college entry. All respondents to the first follow-up and a sample of nonrespondents in 1998 were eligible to be interviewed. More than 9,100 students were located and interviewed in the 2001 follow-up, for an overall weighted response rate of 76 percent. Information about beginning students in BPS:96/0 1 was obtained from student interviews conducted in the base year and follow-ups and from various sources used for NPSAS data collection. For further details on the BPS:96/0 1 data, refer to the report *Beginning Postsecondary Students Longitudinal Study: 1996–2001 (BPS:96/01) Methodology Report* (Wine et al. 2002).

The 2003–04 National Postsecondary Student Aid Study. The 2003–04 National Postsecondary Student Aid Study (NPSAS:04) provides comprehensive data for the undergraduate and graduate/first-professional student populations in the academic year 2003–04 and determines how students and their families pay for postsecondary education. The target population consists of all eligible students enrolled at any time between July 1, 2003, and June 30, 2004, in Title IV postsecondary institutions in the United States or Puerto Rico. A two-stage sampling design was used to collect the data for NPSAS:04. The first stage involved selecting eligible institutions, and the second stage involved selecting eligible respondents within each eligible institution. More than 90,000 undergraduate, graduate, and first- professional students participated in the survey. Upon the completion of data collection, the weighted institutional response rate was 80 percent, and the weighted student response rate was 91 percent, resulting in an overall response rate of 72 percent. For further details on the NPSAS:04 data, refer to the report *2004 National Postsecondary Study Aid Study (NPSAS:04) Full-Scale Methodology Report* (Cominole et al. 2006).

The Education Longitudinal Study of **2002/06.** The Education Longitudinal Study of 2002/06 (ELS:02/06) provides data about the critical transitions experienced by high school students as they proceed through high school and into postsecondary education or their early careers. Currently, this survey has four major data components: the base-year interview, the first follow-up interview, the high school transcript data collection, and the second follow-up interview. The base-year interview was carried out in a nationally representative probability sample of about 750 participating public, Catholic, and other private schools in the spring term of the 200 1–02 academic year. Of about 17,600 eligible selected sophomores, about 15,400 completed a base-year questionnaire, for a weighted response rate of 87 percent. The first follow-up interview took place in the spring of 2004, when most sample members were seniors in high school. Seniors in 2004 who were not in the base-year sampling frame were eligible for selection into the sample. Of about 16,500 eligible sample members, about 15,000 participated in an interview, for a weighted response rate of 89 percent. The second follow-up interview took place in 2006, when most sample members were 2 years past high school graduation and had entered the labor force or postsecondary education. Of about 15,900 eligible sample members, about 14,200 completed an interview, for a weighted response rate of 88 percent. For further details on the design and structure of ELS:02/06, refer to the report *Education Longitudinal Study of 2002 (ELS:02) Base-Year to Second Follow-up Public Use Data File Documentation* (Ingels et al. 2007).

Analysis Samples and Weights

Three analysis samples were used for this Statistics in Brief. For analyses of the BPS:96/01 data, the sample consisted of all 1995–96 beginning postsecondary students who participated in the two follow-up surveys in 1998 and 2001 and who reported a major, including "undeclared major," in at least one of three data collections (about 9,000 students selected). Less than 1 percent of students had missing information about their undergraduate major. For analyses of the NPSAS:04 data, the sample consisted of all undergraduates enrolled in all types of postsecondary institutions during the 2003–04 academic year (about 80,000 selected). For analyses of the ELS:02/06 data, the sample consisted of all 2003–04 high school graduates who were enrolled in postsecondary education and who also reported a major (including "undeclared major") in the 2006 interview (about 8,400 selected). Less than 1 percent of high school graduates did not report their major field of study. High school graduates are students who completed high school with a regular or honors diploma.

All estimates in this Statistics in Brief were weighted to compensate for unequal probability of selection into the survey sample and to adjust for nonresponse. The weight variable used for analysis of the BPS data is WTC00, a longitudinal weight designed for 1995–96 beginning postsecondary students who also participated in the two follow-up surveys. The weight variable used for analysis of the NPSAS data is WTA00, a cross-sectional weight applied to all undergraduates in NPSAS:04. The weight variable used for analysis of the ELS data is WTF000, which was designed for an analysis involving all second follow-up respondents in 2006.

Variables Used in the Analyses

All variables used in this Statistics in Brief were from the BPS:96/01, NPSAS:04, and ELS:02/06 Data Analysis System (DAS), a software application developed by NCES to generate tables from the survey data. The DAS can be accessed electronically at http://nces.ed.gov/das. This section provides detailed information on the STEM-related variables constructed specifically for this study. All other variables used in this study were taken directly from the surveys. Interested readers can obtain detailed descriptions of these variables from previous reports online.

STEM Related Variables

Major field of study with a focus on STEM fields (STEMMAJ): This variable was constructed in all three datasets. In NPSAS:04, it indicates undergraduates' major field of study (including secondary major) during the 2003−04 academic year with a focus on STEM fields and was constructed from students' major field of study (MAJORS) and secondary major field of study (N4MAJ2B). In ELS:02/06, this variable indicates the postsecondary enrollee's major field of study (including secondary major) in 2006 with a focus on STEM fields and was constructed from students' responses regarding their declared major (F2B22), major field of study (F2MAJOR2), and secondary major field of study (F2B24). In BPS:96/01, this variable indicates whether 1995–96 beginning postsecondary students ever majored in a STEM field through 2001 and was constructed from students' major field of study as reported in 1995– 96 (SEMAJ1Y1), 1998 (SEMAJ1B1), and 2001 (SEMAJ2B).

The individual STEM fields described below are dichotomous variables (yes/no) constructed from one or more variables in each of the three datasets. In NPSAS:04, the variables indicate STEM majors in 2003–04; in ELS:02/06, variables indicate STEM majors in 2006; and in BPS:96/0 1, variables indicate STEM majors at any time during enrollment up to 6 years after first enrolling in 1995–06.

Major in mathematics (MAJMATH): In NPSAS:04, this variable indicates whether a student's major field of study (including secondary major) in 2003–04 was in mathematics and was constructed from students' major field of study (MAJORS) and secondary major field of study (N4MAJ2B). In ELS:02/06, it indicates whether a postsecondary enrollee's major field (including secondary major field) in 2006 was in mathematics and was constructed from students' responses regarding their declared major (F2B22), major field of study (F2MAJOR2), and secondary major field of study (F2B24). In BPS:96/01, it indicates whether 1995−96 beginning postsecondary students ever majored in mathematics through 2001 and was constructed from students' major field of study as reported in 1995−96 (SEMAJ1Y1), 1998 (SEMAJ1B1), and 2001 (SEMAJ2B).

Major in science (MAJSCI): In NPSAS:04, this variable indicates whether a student's major field of study (including secondary major) in 2003–04 was in science and was constructed from students' major field of study (MAJORS) and secondary major field of study (N4MAJ2B). In ELS:02/06, it indicates whether a postsecondary enrollee's major field (including secondary major field) in 2006 was in science and was constructed from students' responses regarding their declared major (F2B22), major field of study (F2MAJOR2), and secondary major field of study (F2B24). In BPS:96/01, it indicates whether 1995–96 beginning postsecondary students ever majored in science through 2001 and was constructed from students' major field of study as reported in 1995–96 (SEMAJ1Y1), 1998 (SEMAJ1B1), and 2001 (SEMAJ2B).

Major in physical sciences (MAJPHY): In NPSAS:04, this variable indicates whether a student's major field of study (including secondary major) in 2003–04 was in physical sciences and was constructed from students' major field of study (MAJORS) and secondary major field of study (N4MAJ2B). In ELS:02/06, it indicates whether a postsecondary enrollee's major field (including secondary major field) in 2006 was in physical sciences and was constructed from students' responses regarding their declared major (F2B22), major field of study (F2MAJOR2), and secondary major field of study (F2B24). In BPS:96/01, it indicates whether 1995–96 beginning postsecondary students ever majored in physical sciences through 2001 and was constructed from students' major field of study as reported in 1995–96 (SEMAJ1Y1), 1998 (SEMAJ1B1), and 2001 (SEMAJ2B).

Major in biological/agricultural sciences (MAJBIO): In NPSAS:04, this variable indicates whether a student's major field of study (including secondary major) in 2003–04 was in biological/agricultural sciences and was constructed from students' major field of study (MAJORS) and secondary major field of study (N4MAJ2B). In ELS:02/06, it indicates whether a postsecondary enrollee's major field (including secondary major field) in 2006 was in biological/agricultural sciences and was constructed from students' responses regarding their declared major (F2B22), major field of study (F2MAJOR2), and secondary major field of study (F2B24). In BPS:96/01, it indicates whether 1995–96 beginning postsecondary students ever majored in biological/agricultural sciences through 2001 and was constructed from students' major field of study as reported in 1995–96 (SEMAJ1Y1), 1998 (SEMAJ1B1), and 2001 (SEMAJ2B).

Major in Engineering/Engineering Technologies (MAJENG): In NPSAS:04, this variable indicates whether a student's major field of study (including secondary major) in 2003–04 was in engineering/ engineering technologies and was constructed from students' major field of study (MAJORS) and secondary major field of study (N4MAJ2B). In ELS:02/06, it indicates whether a postsecondary enrollee's major field (including secondary major field) in 2006 was in engineering/engineering technologies and was constructed from students' responses regarding their declared major (F2B22), major field of study

(F2MAJOR2), and secondary major field of study (F2B24). In BPS:96/01, it indicates whether 1995–96 beginning postsecondary students ever majored in engineering/engineering technologies through 2001 and was constructed from students' major field of study as reported in 1995–96 (SEMAJ1Y1), 1998 (SEMAJ1B1), and 2001 (SEMAJ2B).

Major in computer/information sciences (MAJCOMP): In NPSAS:04, this variable indicates whether a student's major field of study (including secondary major) in 20 03–04 was in computer/information sciences and was constructed from students' major field of study (MAJORS) and secondary major field of study (N4MAJ2B). In ELS:02/06, it indicates whether a postsecondary enrollee's major field (including secondary major field) in 2006 was in computer/information sciences and was constructed from students' responses regarding their declared major (F2B22), major field of study (F2MAJOR2), and secondary major field of study (F2B24). In BPS:96/01, it indicates whether 1995–96 beginning postsecondary students ever majored in computer/information sciences through 2001 and was constructed from students' major field of study as reported in 1995–96 (SEMAJ1Y1), 1998 (SEMAJ1B1), and 2001 (SEMAJ2B).

Degree attainment in STEM field as of 2001 (STEMDEG): This variable was constructed from BPS:96/01. It indicates whether a 1995–96 beginning postsecondary student had attained a degree/credential in a STEM field by 2001. The variable was constructed from students' major field of study as reported in 1995–96 (SEMAJ1Y1), 1998 (SEMAJ1B1), and

2001 (SEMAJ2B), and the dates of completing a certification (DGDTCT2B), associate's degree (DGDTAA2B), and bachelor's degree (DGDTBA2B).

Bachelor's degree attainment in STEM field as of 2001 (BAMAJ): This variable was constructed from BPS:96/01. It indicates whether a 1995–96 beginning postsecondary student had attained a bachelor's degree in a STEM field by 2001. The variable was constructed from students' major field of study as reported in 1995–96 (SEMAJ1Y1), 1998 (SEMAJ1B1), and 2001 (SEMAJ2B), and the date of completing a bachelor's degree (DGDTBA2B).

Persistence in STEM field as of 2001 (STEMPER1): This variable was constructed from BPS:96/0 1. It indicates 1995–96 beginning postsecondary students' persistence in STEM fields as of 2001, including whether or not they had attained a degree/credential in a STEM field and whether or not they were enrolled in a STEM field as of 2001. The variable was constructed from students' attainment and enrollment as of 2001 (PRENLV2B), major field of study as reported in 1995–96 (SEMAJ1Y1), 1998 (SEMAJ1B1), and 2001 (SEMAJ2B), and the dates of completing a certification (DGDTCT2B), associate's degree (DGDTAA2B), and bachelor's degree (DGDTBA2B).

Other Variables

Variables from BPS:96/01
    Type of first institution enrolled (ITNPSAS)
    Selectivity of first institution (INSTSEL)
    Degree program when first enrolled (DGPGMY1)
    Enrollment intensity through 2001 (ENIPTT2B)
    Gender (SBGENDER)
    Race/ethnicity (SBRACECI)
    Dependency status when first enrolled (SBDEP1Y1)
    Age when first enrolled (SBAGFM)
    Immigrant status when first enrolled (ORIGIN)
    Language spoken as a child (SBLANG)
    Parents' highest level of education (PBEDHI3)
    Family income (of dependent students) (PCTDEP)
    Highest level-math in high school (HCMATHHI)
    High school GPA (HCGPAREP)
    Type of high school diploma (HSDIPLOM)
    College entrance exam score (TESATDER)
    Highest degree expected when first enrolled (EPHDEGY1)
    Persistence and degree attainment as of 2001 (PRENRL2B)
    Major field when first enrolled (SEMAJ1Y1)
    Major field when last enrolled 2001 (SEMAJ2B)

    Information on these variables can be accessed from previous reports online at
    http://nces.ed.gov/pubsearch/pubsinfo.asp?pubid=2003151

http://nces.ed.gov/pubsearch/pubsinfo.asp?pubid=2001163
http://nces.ed.gov/pubsearch/pubsinfo.asp?pubid=2003157

Crosswalk of STEM Categorization and Major Fields of Study in BPS:96/01, NSPAS:04, and ELS:02/06

STEM Categorization	Major Field of Study		
	BPS:96/01	NPSAS:04	ELS:02/06
Mathematics	Mathematics and statistics	Mathematics and statistics	Mathematics and statistics
Natural sciences	Agriculture	Agricultural/related sciences	Agricultural/natural resources/related
	Agricultural sciences	Natural resources/conservation	Biological/biomedical sciences
	Natural resources	Biological/biomedical sciences	Physical sciences
	Forestry	Physical sciences	Science technologies/technicians
	Biological sciences	Other natural sciences	
	Physical sciences	Science technologies/technicians	
Physical sciences	Physical sciences	Physical sciences	Physical sciences
Biological/ agricultural sciences	Agriculture	Agricultural/related sciences	Agricultural/natural resources/related
	Agricultural sciences	Natural resources/conservation	Biological/biomedical sciences
	Natural resources	Biological/biomedical sciences	
	Forestry		
	Biological sciences		
Engineering/ engineering technologies	Electrical engineering	Engineering	Engineering technologies/technicians
	Chemical engineering	Engineering technologies/ technicians	
	Civil engineering		
			Mechanical engineering
			Other engineering
			Engineering technology
Computer/ information sciences	Computer programming	Computer/information sciences	Computer/information sciences/ support technicians
	Data processing		
	Computer/information sciences		

In: U.S. Science, Technology, Engineering and Mathematics... ISBN: 978-1-61122-549-5
Editor: Catherine L. Grover © 2011 Nova Science Publishers, Inc.

Chapter 2

SCIENCE, TECHNOLOGY, ENGINEERING, AND MATHEMATICS (STEM) EDUCATION: BACKGROUND, FEDERAL POLICY, AND LEGISLATIVE ACTION

Jeffrey J. Kuenzi

SUMMARY

There is growing concern that the United States is not preparing a sufficient number of students, teachers, and practitioners in the areas of science, technology, engineering, and mathematics (STEM). A large majority of secondary school students fail to reach proficiency in math and science, and many are taught by teachers lacking adequate subject matter knowledge.

When compared to other nations, the math and science achievement of U.S. pupils and the rate of STEM degree attainment appear inconsistent with a nation considered the world leader in scientific innovation. In a recent international assessment of 15-year-old students, the U.S. ranked 28th in math literacy and 24th in science literacy. Moreover, the U.S. ranks 20th among all nations in the proportion of 24-year-olds who earn degrees in natural science or engineering.

A 2005 study by the Government Accountability Office found that 207 distinct federal STEM education programs were appropriated nearly $3 billion in FY2004. Nearly three-quarters of those funds and nearly half of the STEM programs were in two agencies: the National Institutes of Health and the National Science Foundation. Still, the study concluded that these programs are highly decentralized and require better coordination. Though uncovering many fewer individual programs, a 2007 inventory compiled by the American Competitiveness Council also put the federal STEM effort at $3 billion and concurred with many of the GAO findings regarding decentralization and coordination.

STEM education (and competitiveness) issues have received a lot of attention in recent years. Several high-profile proposals were forwarded by the academic and business communities. In February of 2006, the President released the American Competitiveness Initiative. During the 109th Congress, three somewhat modest STEM education programs were passed and signed into law. Finally, in the spring and summer of 2007, some of the major STEM education legislative proposals were combined into the America Competes Act of 2007, passed by the 110th Congress and signed by the President on August 9, 2007.

This chapter provides the background and context to understand these legislative developments. The report first presents data on the state of STEM education in the United States. It then examines the federal role in promoting STEM education. The report concludes with a discussion of the legislative actions recently taken to address federal STEM education policy.

INTRODUCTION

There is growing concern that the United States is not preparing a sufficient number of students, teachers, and professionals in the areas of science, technology, engineering, and mathematics (STEM).[1] Although the most recent National Assessment of Educational Progress (NAEP) results show improvement in U.S. pupils' knowledge of math and science, the large majority of students still fail to reach adequate levels of proficiency. When compared to other nations, the achievement of U.S. pupils appears inconsistent with the nation's role as a world leader in scientific innovation. For example, among the 40 countries participating in the 2003 Program for International Student Assessment (PISA), the U.S. ranked 28th in math literacy and 24th in science literacy.

Some attribute poor student performance to an inadequate supply of qualified teachers. This appears to be the case with respect to subject-matter knowledge: many U.S. math and science teachers lack an undergraduate major or minor in those fields — as many as half of those teaching in middle school math. Indeed, postsecondary degrees in math and physical science have steadily decreased in recent decades as a proportion of all STEM degrees awarded. Although degrees in some STEM fields (particularly biology and computer science) have increased in recent decades, the overall proportion of STEM degrees awarded in the United States has historically remained at about 17% of all postsecondary degrees awarded. Meanwhile, many other nations have seen rapid growth in postsecondary educational attainment — with particularly high growth in the number of STEM degrees awarded. According to the National Science Foundation, the United States currently ranks 20th among all nations in the proportion of 24-year-olds who earn degrees in natural science or engineering. Once a leader in STEM education, the United States is now far behind many countries on several measures.

What has been the federal role in promoting STEM education? A study by the Government Accountability Office (GAO) found 207 distinct federal STEM education programs that were appropriated nearly $3 billion in FY2004.[2] A more recent study by the newly established Academic Competitiveness Council (ACC) found 105 STEM education programs that were appropriated just over $3 billion in FY2006.[3] The ACC report attributed the difference between the number of programs found by the two inventories to (1) programmatic changes, (2) differing definitions of what constitutes a "program," and (3) GAO's reliance on unverified, agency- reported data.[4] Apart from these differences, both reports came to similar conclusions. Both found that federal STEM education programs had multiple goals, provided multiple types of assistance, and were targeted at multiple groups, but that the bulk of this effort supports graduate and post-doctoral study in the form of fellowships to improve the nation's research capacity. Both studies concluded that the federal effort is highly decentralized and could benefit from stronger coordination, while noting that the creation of the National Science and Technology Council in 1993 was a step in the right direction.[5] The ACC study also contained an evaluative portion and concluded that "there is a general dearth of evidence of effective practices and activities in STEM education."[6]

Several pieces of legislation have been introduced in the 110th Congress that would support STEM education in the United States. Many of the proposals in these bills have been influenced by the recommendations of several reports recently issued by the scientific, business, and policy-making communities. Of particular influence has been a report issued by the National Academy of Sciences (NAS), *Rising Above the Gathering Storm: Energizing and Employing America for a Brighter Economic Future* — also known as the "Augustine" report. Many of the recommendations appearing in the NAS report are also contained in the Administration's *American Competitiveness Initiative*.[7] Among the report's many recommendations, five are targeted at improving STEM education. These five recommendations seek to increase the supply of new STEM teachers, improve the skills of current STEM teachers, enlarge the pre-collegiate pipeline, increase postsecondary degree attainment, and enhance support for graduate and early-career research.

The purpose of this chapter is to put these legislative proposals into a useful context. The first section analyzes data from various sources to build a more thorough understanding of the status of STEM education in the United States. The second section looks at the federal role in promoting STEM education, providing a broad overview of nearly all of the programs in federal agencies and a detailed look at a few selected programs. Finally, the third section discusses legislative options currently being considered to improve STEM education. This discussion focuses primarily on the proposals that have seen congressional action to date.

STEM EDUCATION IN THE UNITED STATES

Elementary and Secondary Education

Assessments of Math and Science Knowledge. National-level assessment of U.S. students' knowledge of math and science is a relatively recent phenomenon, and assessments in other countries that provide for international comparisons are even more recent. Yet the limited information available thus far is beginning to reveal results that concern many individuals interested in the U.S. educational system and the economy's future competitiveness. The most recent assessments show improvement in U.S. pupils' knowledge of math and science; however, the large majority still fail to reach adequate levels of proficiency. Moreover, when compared to other nations, the achievement of U.S. students is seen by many as inconsistent with the nation's role as a world leader in scientific innovation.

The National Assessment of Educational Progress (NAEP) is the only nationally representative, continuing assessment of elementary and secondary students' math and science knowledge. Since 1969, NAEP has assessed students from both public and nonpublic schools at grades 4, 8, and 12. Students' performance on the assessment is measured on a 0-500 scale, and beginning in 1990 has been reported in terms of the percentages of students attaining three achievement levels: *basic*, *proficient*, and *advanced*.[8]

Proficient is the level identified by the National Assessment Governing Board as the degree of academic achievement that all students should reach, and "represents solid academic performance. Students reaching this level have demonstrated competency over challenging subject matter." In contrast, the board states that "Basic denotes partial mastery of the knowledge and skills that are fundamental for proficient work at a given grade."[9]

The most recent NAEP administration occurred in 2005. Figure 1 displays the available results from the NAEP math tests administered between 1990 and 2005. Although the proportion of 4th and 8th grade students achieving the proficient level or above has been increasing each year, overall math performance in these grades has been quite low. The percentage performing at the basic level has not improved in 15 years. About two in five students continue to achieve only partial mastery of math. In 2005, only about one-third of 4th and 8th grade students performed at the proficient level in math — 36% and 30%, respectively.[10] The remainder of students — approximately 20% of 4th graders and just over 30% of 8th graders — scored below the basic level.

The results among 12th grade students are mixed. Although the percent scoring at the basic level is higher among these students than among 4th and 8th grade students, the percent scoring proficient or above is smaller. Moreover, the results from recent years indicate that these percentages are in decline. [Note: changes in the testing instrument may account for much if not all of this drop.[11]]

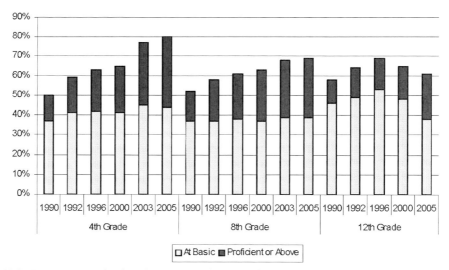

Source: U.S. Department of Education, National Center for Education Statistics, The Nation's Report Card, various years.

Figure 1. NAEP Math Scores, Selected Years: 1990-2005

Similarly low levels of achievement have been found with regard to knowledge of science. Less than one-third of 4th and 8th grade students and less than one-fifth of 12th grade students score at or above proficient in science. In 2005, the percentage of 4th, 8th, and 12th grade students scoring proficient or above was 29%, 29%, and 18%, respectively; compared to 27%, 30%, and 18% in 2000 and 28%, 29%, and 21% in 1996.[12]

U.S. Students Compared to Students in Other Nations. Another relatively recent development in the area of academic assessment has been the effort by a number of nations to produce reliable cross-national comparison data.[13] The Trends in International Mathematics and Science Study (TIMSS) assesses achievement in these subjects at grades 4 and 8 among students in several countries around the world. TIMSS has been administered to 4th grade students on two occasions (1995 and 2003) and to 8th grade students on three occasions (1995, 1999, and 2003). In the latest administration, 25 countries participated in assessments of their 4th grade students, and 45 countries participated in assessments of their 8th grade students. Unlike NAEP, TIMSS results are reported only in terms of numerical scores, not achievement levels.

U.S. 4th grade pupils outscored the international average on the most recent TIMSS assessment.[14] The international average score for all countries participating in the 2003 4th grade TIMSS was 495 in math and 489 in science.[15] The average score for U.S. students was 518 in math and 536 in science. U.S. 4th grade students outscored students in 13 of the 24 countries participating in the math assessment in 2003. In science, U.S. students outperformed students in 16 of the 24 countries. Among the 10 Organization for Economic Co-operation and Development (OECD) member states participating in the 2003 TIMSS, U.S. 4th grade students ranked fourth in math and tied for second in science.

U.S. 8th grade pupils also outscored the international average. Among 8th grade students, the international average on the 2003 TIMSS was 466 in math and 473 in science. The average score for U.S. students was 504 in math and 527 in science. Among the 44 countries participating in the 8th grade assessments in 2003, U.S. students outscored students in 25 countries in math and 32 countries in science. Twelve OECD countries participated in the 8th grade TIMSS in 2003 — five outscored the United States in math and three outscored the United States in science.

TIMSS previously assessed students at grade 4 in 1995 and grade 8 in 1995 and 1999. Although there was no measurable difference between U.S. 4th graders' average scores in 1995 and 2003, the standing of the United States declined relative to that of the 14 other countries participating in both math and science assessments. In math, U. S. 4th graders outperformed students in nine of these countries in 1995, on average, compared to six countries in 2003. In science, U.S. 4th graders outperformed students in 13 of these countries in 1995, on average, compared to eight countries in 2003.

Among 8th graders, U.S. scores increased on both the math and science assessments between 1995 and 2003. The increase in scores translated into a higher ranking of the United States relative to other countries. In math, 12 of the 21 participating countries outscored U. S. 8th graders in 1995, while seven did so in 2003. In science, 15 of the 21 participating countries outscored U. S. 8th graders in 1995, while 10 did so in 2003. Table 1 displays the 2003 TIMSS math and science scores of 4th and 8th grade students by country (scores in **bold** are higher than the U.S. score).

Table 1. TIMSS Scores by Grade and Country/Jurisdiction, 2003

	4th Grade Math	4th Grade Science	8th Grade Math	8th Grade Science
International Average	495	489	466	473
United States	518	536	504	527
United Kingdom	**531**	**540**	—	—
Tunisia	339	314	410	404
Sweden	—	—	499	524
South Africa	—	—	264	244
Slovenia	479	490	493	520
Slovak Republic	—	—	**508**	517
Singapore	**594**	**565**	**605**	**578**
Serbia	—	—	477	468
Scotland	490	502	498	512
Saudi Arabia	—	—	332	398
Russian Federation	**532**	526	**508**	514
Romania	—	—	475	470
Philippines	358	332	378	377
Palestinian National Authority	—	—	390	435
Norway	451	466	461	494
New Zealand	493	520	494	520
Netherlands	**540**	525	**536**	**536**
Morocco	347	304	387	396
Moldova, Republic of	504	496	460	472
Malaysia	—	—	**508**	510
Macedonia, Republic of	—	—	435	449
Lithuania	**534**	512	502	519
Lebanon	—	—	433	393
Latvia	**536**	532	**508**	512
Korea, Republic of	—	—	**589**	**558**
Jordan	—	—	424	475
Japan	**565**	**543**	**570**	**552**
Italy	503	516	484	491
Israel	—	—	496	488
Iran, Islamic Republic of	389	414	411	453
Indonesia	—	—	411	420
Hungary	**529**	530	**529**	**543**
Hong Kong SAR	**575**	**542**	**586**	**556**
Ghana	—	—	276	255
Estonia	—	—	531	552
Egypt	—	—	406	421
Cyprus	510	480	459	441
Chinese Taipei	**564**	**551**	**585**	**571**

Table 1. (Continued)

	4th Grade		8th Grade	
	Math	Science		Math
Chile	—	—	387	413
Bulgaria	—	—	476	479
Botswana	—	—	366	365
Belgium-Flemish	**551**	518	**537**	516
Bahrain	—	—	401	438
Australia	499	521	505	527
Armenia	456	437	478	461

Source: U.S. Department of Education, National Center for Education Statistics, *Highlights From the Trends in International Mathematics and Science Study (TIMSS) 2003*, NCES 2005-005, Dec. 2004.

The Program for International Student Assessment (PISA) is an OECD- developed effort to measure, among other things, mathematical and scientific literacy among students 15 years of age, that is, roughly at the end of their compulsory education.[16] In 2003, U.S. students scored an average of 483 on math literacy — behind 23 of the 29 OECD member states that participated and behind four of the 11 non-OECD countries. The average U.S. student scored 491 on science literacy — behind 19 of the 29 OECD countries and behind three of the 11 non-OECD countries. **Table 2** displays the 2003 PISA scores on math and science literacy by country (scores in **bold** are higher than the U.S. score).

Table 2. PISA Math and Science Scores, 2003

	2003	
	Math	Science
OECD Average	**500**	**500**
United States	483	491
Turkey	423	434
Switzerland	**527**	**513**
Sweden	**509**	**506**
Spain	**485**	487
Slovak Republic	**498**	**495**
Portugal	466	468
Poland	**490**	**498**
Norway	**495**	484
New Zealand	**524**	**521**
Netherlands	**538**	**524**
Mexico	385	405
Luxembourg	**493**	483
Korea, Republic of	**542**	**538**
Japan	**534**	**548**
Italy	466	487

Table 2. (Continued)

	2003 Math	2003 Science
OECD Average	**500**	**500**
Ireland	503	505
Iceland	515	495
Hungary	490	503
Greece	445	481
Germany	503	502
France	511	511
Finland	544	548
Denmark	514	475
Czech Republic	517	523
Canada	533	519
Belgium	529	509
Austria	506	491
Australia	524	525
Non-OECD Countries		
Uruguay	422	438
United Kingdom	508	518
Tunisia	359	385
Thailand	417	429
Serbia and Montenegro	437	436
Russian Federation	468	489
Macao SAR	527	525
Liechtenstein	536	525
Latvia	483	489
Indonesia	360	395
Hong Kong SAR	550	540

Source: U.S. Department of Education, National Center for Education Statistics, *International Outcomes of Learning in Mathematics Literacy and Problem Solving*, NCES 2005-003, Dec. 2004.

Table 3. Teachers Lacking a Major or Minor in Subject Taught, 1999-2000

	Middle School	High School
English	44.8%	13.3%
Foreign language	27.2%	28.3%
Mathematics	51.5%	14.5%
Science	40.0%	11.2%
Social science	29.6%	10.5%
ESL/bilingual education	57.6%	59.4%
Arts and music	6.8%	6.1%
Physical/health education	12.6%	9.5%

Source: U.S. Department of Education, National Center for Education Statistics, *Qualifications of the Public School Teacher Workforce: Prevalence of Out-of-Field Teaching 1987-88 to 1999-2000*, NCES 2002-603, May 2002.

Math and Science Teacher Quality

Many observers look to the nation's teaching force as a source of national shortcomings in student math and science achievement. A recent review of the research on teacher quality conducted over the last 20 years revealed that, among those who teach math and science, having a major in the subject taught has a significant positive impact on student achievement.[17] Unfortunately, many U.S. math and science teachers lack this credential. The Schools and Staffing Survey (SASS) is the only nationally representative survey that collects detailed data on teachers' preparation and subject assignments.[18] The most recent administration of the survey for which public data are available took place during the 1999-2000 school year. That year, there were just under 3 million teachers in U.S. schools, about evenly split between the elementary and secondary levels. Among the nation's 1.4 million public secondary school teachers, 13.7% reported math as their main teaching assignment and 11.4% reported science as their main teaching assignment.[19]

Nearly all public secondary school math and science teachers held at least a baccalaureate degree (99.7%), and most had some form of state teaching certification (86.2%) at the time of the survey.[20] However, many of those who taught middle school (classified as grades 5-8) math and science lacked an undergraduate or graduate major or minor in the subject they taught. Among middle-school teachers, 51.5% of those who taught math and 40.0% of those who taught science did not have a major or minor in these subjects. By contrast, few of those who taught high school (classified as grades 9-12) math or science lacked an undergraduate or graduate major or minor in that subject. Among high school teachers, 14.5% of those who taught math and 11.2% of those who taught science did not have a major or minor in these subjects.[21] **Table 3** displays these statistics for teachers in eight subject areas.

Given the link between teachers' undergraduate majors and student achievement in math and science, these data appear to comport with some of the NAEP findings discussed earlier. Recall that those assessments revealed that only about one-third of 4th and 8th grade students performed at the proficient or higher level in math and science. On the other hand, at the high school level, the data seem to diverge. While four-fifths of math and science teachers at this level have a major in the subject, only two-fifths of high school students scored proficient or above on the NAEP in those subjects.

Postsecondary Education

STEM Degrees Awarded in the United States. The number of students attaining STEM postsecondary degrees in the U.S. more than doubled between 1960 and 2000; however, as a proportion of degrees in all fields, STEM degree awards have stagnated during this period.[22] In the 2002-2003 academic year, more than 2.5 million degrees were awarded by postsecondary institutions in the United States.[23] That year, just under 16% (399,465) of all degrees were conferred in STEM fields; all STEM degrees comprised 14.6% of associate degrees, 16.7% of baccalaureate degrees, 12.9% of master's degrees, and 34.8% of doctoral degrees.[24] **Table 4** displays the distribution of degrees granted by academic level and field of study.

Table 4. Degrees Conferred by Level and Field of Study, 2002-2003

	Associate	Baccalaureate	Master's	Doctoral	Total
All fields	632,912	1,348,503	512,645	46,024	2,540,084
STEM fields, total	92,640	224,911	65,897	16,017	399,465
STEM, percentage of all fields	14.6%	16.7%	12.9%	34.8%	15.7%
Biological and biomedical sciences	1,496	60,072	6,990	5,003	73,561
Computer and information sciences	46,089	57,439	19,503	816	123,847
Engineering and engineering technologies	42,133	76,967	30,669	5,333	155,102
Mathematics and statistics	732	12,493	3,626	1,007	17,858
Physical sciences and science technologies	2,190	17,940	5,109	3,858	29,097
Non-STEM fields, total	540,272	1,123,592	446,748	30,007	2,140,619
Business	102,157	293,545	127,545	1,251	524,498
Education	11,199	105,790	147,448	6,835	271,272
English language and literature/letters	896	53,670	7,413	1,246	63,225
Foreign languages and area studies	1,176	23,530	4,558	1,228	30,492
Liberal arts and sciences, general studies, and humanities	216,814	40,221	3,312	78	260,425
Philosophy, theology, and religious studies/vocations	804	18,270	6,677	1,983	27,734
Psychology	1,784	78,613	17,123	4,831	102,351
Social sciences	5,422	115,488	12,109	2,989	136,008
History	316	27,730	2,525	861	31,432
Other	199,704	366,735	118,038	8,705	693,182

Source: U.S. Department of Education, National Center for Education Statistics, *Digest of Education Statistics, 2004*, NCES 2005-025, Oct. 2005, Table 249-252..

At the associate and baccalaureate levels, the number of STEM degrees awarded was roughly equivalent to the number awarded in business. In 2002-2003, 92,640 associate degrees and 224,911 baccalaureate degrees were awarded in STEM fields, compared to 102,157 and 293,545, respectively, in business. However, nearly twice as many master's degrees were granted in business (127,545) as in STEM (65,897), and an even larger number of master's degrees were awarded in education (147,448). At the doctoral level, STEM plays a larger role. Doctoral degrees awarded in STEM fields account for more than one-third of all degrees awarded at this level. Education is the only field in which more doctoral degrees (6,835) were awarded than in the largest three STEM fields — biology, engineering, and the physical sciences (5,003, 5,333, and 3,858, respectively).

Specialization within STEM fields also varies by academic level. Engineering was among the most common STEM specialties at all levels of study in 2002-2003. Biology was a common specialization at the baccalaureate and doctoral levels, but not at the master's level. Computer science was common at all but the doctoral level. Physical sciences was a common specialization *only* at the doctoral level.

Figure 2 displays the trends in STEM degrees awarded over the last three decades (excluding associate degrees). The solid line represents the number of STEM degrees awarded as a proportion of the total number of degrees awarded in all fields of study. The flat line indicates that the ratio of STEM degrees to all degrees awarded has historically hovered at around 17%. The bars represent the number of degrees awarded in each STEM sub-field as a proportion of all STEM degrees awarded. The top two segments of each bar reveal a consistent decline, since 1970, in the number of degrees awarded in math and the physical sciences. The bottom segment of each bar shows a history of fluctuation in the number of degrees awarded in biology over the last 30 years. The middle two segments in the figure represent the proportion of degrees awarded in engineering and computer science. The figure reveals a steady decline in the proportion of STEM degrees awarded in engineering since 1980, and a steady increase in computer science degrees (except for a contraction that occurred in the late 1980s following a rapid expansion in the early 1980s).

U.S. Degrees Awarded to Foreign Students. The increased presence of foreign students in graduate science and engineering programs and in the scientific workforce has been and continues to be of concern to some in the scientific community. Enrollment of U.S. citizens in graduate science and engineering programs has not kept pace with that of foreign students in these programs. According to the National Science Foundation (NSF) Survey of Earned Doctorates, foreign students earned one-third of all doctoral degrees awarded in 2003.

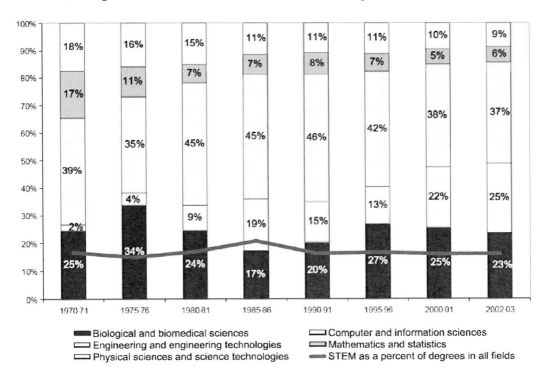

Figure 2. STEM Degrees Awarded, 1970-2003

Doctoral degrees awarded to foreign students were concentrated in STEM fields. The NSF reports that foreign students earned "more than half of those [awarded] in engineering, 44% of those in mathematics and computer science, and 35% of those in the physical sciences."[25] Many of these degree recipients remain in the United States to work. The same NSF report indicates that 53% of those who earned a doctorate in 1993 remained in the U.S. as of 1997, and 61% of the 1998 cohort were still working in the United States in 2003. In addition to the number of foreign students in graduate science and engineering programs, a significant number of university faculty in the scientific disciplines are foreign, and foreign doctorates are employed in large numbers by industry.[26]

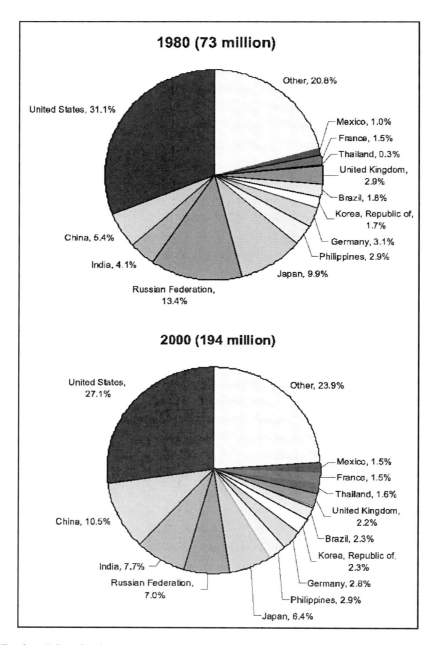

Figure 3. Tertiary Education by Country, 1980 and 2000

Table 5. Field of Study, by Selected Region and Country, 2002 (or the Most Recent Year Available)

Region/Country	All Fields	STEM Fields	Percent STEM
All Regions	9,057,193	2,395,238	26.4%
Asia	3,224,593	1,073,369	33.3%
China	929,598	484,704	52.1%
India	750,000	176,036	23.5%
Japan	548,897	351,299	64.0%
South Korea	239,793	97,307	40.6%
Middle East	445,488	104,974	23.6%
Europe	2,682,448	713,274	26.6%
France	309,009	83,984	27.2%
Spain	211,979	55,418	26.1%
United Kingdom	282,380	72,810	25.8%
Central/Eastern Europe	1,176,898	319,188	27.1%
Russia	554,814	183,729	33.1%
North/Central America	1,827,226	341,526	18.7%
Mexico	321,799	80,315	25.0%
United States	1,305,730	219,175	16.8%
South America	543,805	96,724	17.8%
Brazil	395,988	61,281	15.5%

Source: National Science Foundation, *Science and Engineering Indicators, 2006, Volume 1*, Arlington, VA, NSB 06-01, January 2006, Table 2-37.

International Postsecondary Educational Attainment. The United States has one of the highest rates of postsecondary educational attainment in the world. In 2003, the most recent academic year for which international data are available, 38% of the U.S. population aged 25-64 held a postsecondary degree — 9% at the *tertiary-type B* (vocational level) and 29% at the *tertiary-type A* (university level) or above. The OECD compiled comparison data from 30 OECD member states and 13 other nations. Three countries (Canada, Israel, and the Russian Federation) had larger shares at the two tertiary levels combined; however, all three had lower rates at the tertiary-type A level. At the tertiary-type A level, only one country (Norway) had a rate as high as the United States. The average for OECD member states was 16% at tertiary-type A and 8% at tertiary-type B.[27]

China and India were not included in the OECD data. Reliable information on postsecondary educational attainment is very difficult to obtain for these countries.

The World Bank estimates that, in 1998, tertiary enrollment of the population between 18 and 24 years old was 6% in China and 8% in India, up from 1.7% and 5.2%, respectively, in 1980.[28] Based on measures constructed by faculty at the Center for International Development (CID), the National Science Foundation (NSF) has generated an estimate of the distribution of the world's population that possesses a tertiary education.[29] The NSF estimates that the number of people in the world who had a tertiary education more than doubled from 73 million in 1980 to 194 million in 2000. Moreover, the two fastest-growing countries were China and India. China housed 5.4% of the world's tertiary degree holders in 1980, and India had 4.1%; by 2000, the share in these countries was 10.5% and 7.7%, respectively. Indeed, as

Figure 3 indicates, China and India were the only countries to substantially increase their share of the world's tertiary degree-holders during that period.

International Comparisons in STEM Education. The NSF has compiled data for many countries on the share of *first university* degrees awarded in STEM fields.[30] According to these data, the United States has one of the lowest rates of STEM to non-STEM degree production in the world. In 2002, STEM degrees accounted for 16.8% of all first university degrees awarded in the United States (the same NCES figure reported at the outset of this section). The international average for the ratio of STEM to non-STEM degrees was 26.4% in 2002. Table 5 displays the field of first university degrees for regions and countries that award more than 200,000 university degrees annually. Among these nations, only Brazil awards a smaller share (15.5%) of STEM degrees than the United States. By contrast, the world leaders in the proportion of STEM degrees awarded are Japan (64.0%) and China (52.1%). Although the U.S. ranks near the bottom in the proportion of STEM degrees, it ranks third (behind Japan and China) in the absolute number of STEM degrees awarded.

FEDERAL PROGRAMS THAT PROMOTE STEM EDUCATION

Government Accountability Office Study

According to a 2005 Government Accountability Office (GAO) survey of 13 federal civilian agencies, in FY2004 there were 207 federal education programs designed to increase the number of students studying in STEM fields and/or improve the quality of STEM education.[31] About $2.8 billion was appropriated for these programs that year, and about 71% ($2 billion) of those funds supported 99 programs in two agencies. In 2004, the National Institutes of Health (NIH) received $998 million that funded 51 programs, and the National Science Foundation (NSF) received $997 million that funded 48 programs. Seven of the 13 agencies had more than five STEM-related education programs. In addition to the NIH and NSF, only three other agencies received more than $100 million for STEM-related education programs. In FY2004, the National Aeronautics and Space Administration (NASA) received $231 million that funded five programs, the Department of Education (ED) received $221 million that funded four programs, and the Environmental Protection Agency (EPA) received $121 million that funded 21 programs.

The GAO study found that most of the 207 programs had multiple goals, provided multiple types of assistance, and were targeted at multiple groups. The analysis identified six major program goals, four main types of assistance, and 11 target groups. The findings revealed that federal STEM education programs are heavily geared toward attracting college graduates into pursuing careers in STEM fields by providing financial assistance at the graduate and postdoctoral levels. Moreover, improving K-12 teacher education in STEM areas was the least frequent of the major goals, improving infrastructure was the least frequent of the main types of assistance, and elementary and secondary students were the least frequent group targeted by federal STEM education programs.[32]

The major goals of these programs were found by GAO to be the following (the number of programs with this goal is shown in parentheses):

- attract and prepare students at all educational levels to pursue coursework in STEM areas (114),
- attract students to pursue STEM postsecondary degrees (two-year through Ph.D.) and postdoctoral appointments (137),
- provide growth and research opportunities for college and graduate students in STEM fields (103),
- attract graduates to pursue careers in STEM fields (131),
- improve teacher education in STEM areas (73), and
- improve or expand the capacity of institutions to promote STEM fields (90).

The four main types of assistance provided by these programs were as follows (the number of programs providing this service is shown in parentheses):

- financial support for students or scholars (131),
- institutional support to improve educational quality (76),
- support for teacher and faculty development (84), and
- institutional physical infrastructure support (27).

The 11 target groups served by these programs were the following (the number of programs targeting them is shown in parentheses):

- elementary school students (28),
- middle school students (34),
- high school students (53),
- two-year college students (58),
- four-year college students (96),
- graduate students (100),
- postdoctoral scholars (70),
- elementary school teachers (39),
- secondary school teachers (50),
- college faculty or instructional staff (79), and
- institutions (82).

Academic Competitiveness Council Study

The Academic Competitiveness Council (ACC) was created by the Deficit Reduction Act of 2005 (P.L. 109-171). Section 401 A(a)(2)(B) of the act charged the ACC with conducting a year-long study to

(i) identify all federal programs with a mathematics or science focus;
(ii) identify the target populations being served by such programs;
(iii) determine the effectiveness of such programs;
(iv) identify areas of overlap or duplication in such programs; and
(v) recommend ways to efficiently integrate and coordinate such programs.

The ACC found 105 STEM education programs that were appropriated just over $3 billion in FY2006.[33] The authors of the ACC report attributed the difference between the number of programs found by the GAO and ACC inventories to have occurred for three reasons:

> First, programmatic changes occurred between the time of the GAO study and the time of the ACC effort. Second, the ACC program inventory and GAO report used different definitions and guidelines for program inclusion. Specifically, the ACC effort included all federal agencies that supported STEM education programs while the GAO report did not. Lastly, differences in the program inventories arose because the GAO report was based solely on agency-reported data, whereas the ACC program inventory was also verified by the Office of Management and Budget.[34]

According to the ACC inventory, three agencies account for nearly 80% of all federal STEM education spending in FY2006. Figure 4 displays total federal spending for that year by agency. According to the ACC, 29% ($924 million) of total federal STEM funds went to NSF, 27% ($855 million) went to NIH (through the Department of Health and Human Services (HHS)), and 23% ($706 million) went to ED.

Apart from these differences, both the GAO and ACC studies came to similar findings and conclusions about the state of the federal effort to promote STEM education. Both found that federal STEM education programs had multiple goals, provided multiple types of assistance, and were targeted at multiple groups. Both concluded that the federal effort is highly decentralized and could benefit from stronger coordination, while noting that the creation of the National Science and Technology Council in 1993 was a step in the right direction.[35] The ACC report states that these programs

> support activities in a wide variety of areas, including STEM curriculum development; teacher professional development, recruitment, and retention; institutional support (including programs to strengthen the educational capabilities of minority-serving or similar institutions); mentoring; student financial assistance; outreach and recognition to motivate interest in or continued work in STEM fields; and research aimed at improving STEM education.[36]

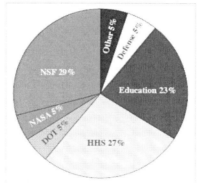

Source: U.S. Department of Education, *Report of the Academic Competitiveness Council*, Washington, D.C., 2007

Figure 4. Federal STEM Education Funding FY2006, by Agency

Like the GAO results, the ACC study found that much of the federal effort in this area comes through NSF and NIH support for graduate and post-doctoral study in the form of fellowships to improve the nation's research capacity. The ACC identified 27 federally funded STEM graduate and post-doctoral fellowship and traineeship programs with a total funding of $1.46 billion in FY2006, which is 47% of the total FY2006 federal funding in STEM education. The ACC found an additional 43 STEM programs in nine agencies primarily focused on improving undergraduate education that received 30% ($943 million) of the total FY2006 funds. The remaining 23% of federal STEM education funds went to 24 K-12 programs ($574 million) and 11 STEM "informal education and outreach" programs ($137 million).[37]

Program Effectiveness. The ACC study went beyond the scope of the GAO study in one key area: the ACC was asked to evaluative the effectiveness of federal STEM education programs. Due to the short time frame allotted to the study, the ACC could not conduct its own evaluations and, instead, had to solicit examples of evaluations from the agencies administering the programs. After a review of the examples submitted, the ACC concluded that "there is a general dearth of evidence of effective practices and activities in STEM education."[38]

In particular, the report states that, "Of the 115 examples submitted: 10 evaluations were scientifically rigorous evaluations that produced preliminary findings about a program or project's impact on education outcomes."[39] Of the ten evaluations that were considered to be "scientifically rigorous," only three had been completed, were found to have a "meaningful positive impact," and had published results in academic journals. The report's critique continued by stating that, "even these well-designed studies with seemingly positive impacts would require additional replication and validation before they could be useful" in determining what policies and programs to promote.[40]

Description of Selected Federal STEM Programs

The GAO and ACC reports did not provide much detail on specific federal STEM programs.[41] This section describes the major federal STEM education programs including the kinds of activities they support and how they operate at the federal, state, and/or local levels. These are the largest STEM education programs administered by the agencies with the largest STEM education budgets, including NIH, NSF, and ED.

NIH Ruth L. Kirschstein National Research Service Awards. First funded in 1975, the Kirschstein National Research Service Awards (KNRSA) constitute the large majority of HHS/NIH's spending on STEM education.[42] Most of these funds are used to support the Kirschstein Training Grants that provide graduate and postdoctoral fellowships in health-related fields. About 15-20% of the funds support the Kirschstein Postdoctoral Fellowships and Kirschstein Predoctoral Fellowships. The Training Grants are awarded to institutions to develop or enhance research training opportunities for individuals, selected by the institution, who are training for careers in specified areas of interest to the institution or principal investigator. The Fellowship Grants are awarded directly to individuals from various organizations within the NIH (e.g., the National Institute on Aging) to support the particular research interests of the individual receiving the award.

Kirschstein Award applicants must be U.S. citizens or nationals, or permanent resident aliens of the United States — individuals on temporary or student visas are not eligible. Predoctoral trainees must have received a baccalaureate degree by the starting date of their appointment, and must be training at the postbaccalaureate level and be enrolled in a program leading to a Ph.D. in science or in an equivalent research doctoral degree program. Health-profession students who wish to interrupt their studies for a year or more to engage in full-time research training before completing their professional degrees are also eligible. Postdoctoral trainees must have received, as of the beginning date of their appointment, a Ph.D., M.D., or comparable doctoral degree from an accredited domestic or foreign institution.

Institutional grants are made for a five-year period. Trainee appointments are normally made in 12-month increments, although short-term (two- to three-month) awards are available. No individual trainee may receive more than five years of aggregate Kirschstein support at the predoctoral level or three years of support at the postdoctoral level, including any combination of support from institutional training grants and individual fellowship awards. The annual stipend for predoctoral trainees in 2005 was about $12,000, and the postdoctoral stipend was between $20,000 and $32,000 (depending on years of experience).

In FY2004, Training Grants were awarded to 293 institutions in all but six states. A total of 2,356 grants were awarded, which funded nearly 9,000 predoctoral fellowships and nearly 5,500 postdoctoral fellowships. The Fellowship Grant programs supported around 2,500 pre- and postdoctoral students in 2004. The large majority of the Training Grants were awarded through the National Institute of General Medical Sciences.

NSF Graduate Research Fellowships. The NSF Graduate Research Fellowships is the largest of that agency's STEM education programs. These fellowships also represent one of the longest-running federal STEM programs (enacted in 1952). The purpose of this program is to increase the size and diversity of the U.S. workforce in science and engineering. The program provides three years of support to approximately 1,000 graduate students annually in STEM disciplines who are pursuing research-based master's and doctoral degrees, with additional focus on women in engineering and computer and information sciences. In 2006, 907 awards were given to graduate students studying in nine major fields at 150 instituions.

Applicants must be U.S. citizens or nationals, or permanent resident aliens of the United States; must have completed no more than twelve months of full-time graduate study at the time of their application; and must be pursuing an advanced degree in a STEM field supported by the National Science Foundation.[43] The fellows' affiliated institution receives a $40,500 award — $30,000 for a 12-month stipend and $10,500 for an annual cost-of-education allowance. These awards are for a maximum of three years and usable over a five-year period, and provide a one-time $1,000 International Research Travel Allowance. All discipline-based review panels, made up of professors, researchers, and others respected in their fields, convene for three days each year to read and evaluate applications in their areas of expertise. In 2005, there were 29 such panels made up of more than 500 experts.

NSF Mathematics and Science Partnerships. The Mathematics and Science Partnerships program is among the NSF's largest STEM education programs. Since its inception in 2002,

this program has awarded grants that support four types of projects (the number of awards is shown in parentheses):
- Comprehensive Partnership projects (12) to implement change inmathematics and science education across the K-12 continuum;
- Targeted Partnership projects (28) to improve K-12 student achievement in a narrower grade range or disciplinary focus in mathematics and/or science;
- Institute Partnership projects (8) to focus on improving middle and high school mathematics and science through the development of school-based intellectual leaders and master teachers; and
- Research, Evaluation & Technical Assistance projects (22) to build research, evaluation, and infrastructure capacity for the MSP.

One of the Comprehensive Partnership projects is between the Baltimore County Public Schools (BCPS) and the University of Maryland, Baltimore County (UMBC). The two main goals of the UMBC-BCPS STEM Partnership are to (1) facilitate the implementation, testing, refinement, and dissemination of promising practices for improving STEM student achievement, and (2) improve teacher quality and retention in selected high-need elementary, middle, and high schools in Baltimore County Public Schools. Centered on creating and evaluating performance-based pre-service (internship) teacher education programs and sustainable professional development programs for teachers and administrators, the project is designed to increase K-12 student achievement in STEM areas by increasing teacher and administrator knowledge. Ongoing assessments of student work and the differentiation of instruction based upon these assessments serve to evaluate and refine instruction, curricula and assessments, professional development programs, administrative leadership strategies, and directions for overall school improvement in STEM areas. UMBC and BCPS collaboration is facilitated by the creation of the Center for Excellence in STEM Education, where UMBC faculty and BCPS teachers and administrators develop projects to serve the needs of the BCPS district and the university. At the center, faculty and teachers work together to simultaneously improve the university's STEM and teacher education departments and the teaching and learning culture in the BCPS.

One of the Targeted Partnership grants supports the Promoting Reflective Inquiry in Mathematics Education Partnership, which includes Black Hills State University, Technology and Innovations in Education (TIE) of the Black Hills Special Services Cooperative, and the Rapid City School District in South Dakota. The overall goal of the partnership is aimed at improving achievement in mathematics for all students in Rapid City schools, with a particular goal of reducing the achievement gap between Native American and non-Native American students. The project seeks to improve the professional capacity and sustain the quality of K-12 in-service teachers of mathematics in the Rapid City School District, and student teachers of mathematics from Black Hills State University in order to provide effective, inquiry-based mathematics instruction. Objectives include reducing the number of high school students taking non-college preparatory mathematics, increasing the number of students taking upper level mathematics, and increasing student performance on college entrance exams. To accomplish these goals, the project provides 100 hours of professional development in combination with content-based workshops at the district level, and building-based activities involving modeling of effective lessons, peer mentoring and coaching, and lesson study. Mathematics education and discipline faculty from Black Hills State University are involved in district-wide professional development activities. A cadre of building-based Mathematics Lead Teachers convenes learning teams composed of mathematics teachers, mathematics student teachers, school counselors, and building administrators to identify key issues in mathematics curriculum and instruction.

NSF Research Experiences for Undergraduates. The Research Experiences for Undergraduates (REU) program is the largest of the NSF STEM education programs that supports active research participation by *undergraduate* students. REU projects involve students in research through two avenues. REU Sites are based on independent proposals to initiate and conduct projects that engage a number of students in research. *REU Supplements* are requested for ongoing NSF-funded research projects or are included as a component of proposals for new or renewal NSF grants or cooperative agreements. REU projects may be based in a single discipline or academic department, or on interdisciplinary or multi-department research opportunities with a coherent intellectual theme. Undergraduate student participants in either Sites or Supplements must be citizens or permanent residents of the United States or its possessions. Students apply directly to REU Sites (rather that to the NSF) to participate in the program.

One of the grantees under this program is the REU Site in Microbiology at the University of Iowa. The goals of this project are to (1) recruit and select bright students, including women, individuals with diverse backgrounds with respect to geographic origin and ethnicity, and students from non-Ph.D.-granting institutions where research possibilities are limited; (2) involve students in basic, experimental research in microbiology; (3) expose students to a broad range of bioscience research; (4) develop each student's critical-thinking skills; and (5) develop each student's ability to record, analyze, and present scientific information. The student participants are integrated into faculty research programs and expected to perform like beginning graduate students. Informal faculty-student discussions and weekly seminars supplement laboratory research. Weekly informal lunches, two picnics, and a banquet facilitate social and scientific interactions. At the end of each summer's program, the students prepare oral presentations to be given at a Summer Program Symposium. Each student also prepares a written research report under the guidance of a mentor.

ED Science and Mathematics Access to Retain Talent Grants. The establishment of the Science and Mathematics Access to Retain Talent (SMART) Grants through the Deficit Reduction Act of 2005 (P.L. 109-17 1) nearly doubled the STEM education effort under ED. In its first year of funding, FY2006, the SMART Grants accounted for over half of ED's STEM education spending. The SMART Grant provides up to $4,000 for each of the third and fourth years of undergraduate study and is in addition to the student's Pell Grant award.

To be eligible to receive a SMART Grant a student must be a citizen, eligible to receive a Pell Grant, have a 3.0 cumulative grade point average, and enrolled as a full-time third or fourth year student in a science-related baccalaureate degree program.

ED's largest STEM program. The MSP is intended to increase the academic achievement of students in mathematics and science by enhancing the content knowledge and teaching skills of classroom teachers. These partnerships — between state education agencies, high-need school districts, and STEM faculty in institutions of higher education — are supported by state-administered formula grants and carried out in collaboration with the NSF-MSP program. Partnerships must use their grants for one or more of several specific activities. Among them are the following:

- professional development to improve math and science teachers' subject knowledge;
- activities to promote strong teaching skills among these teachers and teacher educators;
- math and science summer workshops or institutes with academic- year followup;
- recruitment of math, science, and engineering majors to teaching jobs through signing and performance incentives, stipends for alternative certification, and scholarships for advanced course work;
- development and redesign of more rigorous, standards-aligned math and science curricula;
- distance-learning programs for math and science teachers;
- and opportunities for math and science teachers to have contact with working mathematicians, scientists, and engineers.

A review of projects funded in FY2004 revealed that most grantees focus on math (as opposed to science) instruction in middle schools, and provide professional development to roughly 46 teachers over a period of about 21 months.[44] The survey found that most projects link content to state standards, and that algebra, geometry, and problem-solving are the top three math topics addressed by professional development activities. Most projects administer content knowledge tests to teachers, conduct observations, and make pre-and post-test comparisons. About half of the projects develop their own tests for teachers, and most rely on state tests of academic achievement to measure student knowledge.

RECOMMENDATIONS TO IMPROVE FEDERAL STEM EDUCATION POLICY

Many prominent reports from the scientific community have received serious consideration and their recommendations have been incorporated into legislative proposals that have ultimately gained passage. These recommendations concern every aspect of the educational pipeline. All of the recent reports issuing STEM education policy recommendations focus on five areas: improving elementary and secondary preparation in math and science, recruiting new elementary and secondary math and science teachers, retooling current math and science teachers, increasing the number of undergraduate STEM degrees awarded, and supporting graduate and early-career research.

As mentioned at the outset of this chapter, one report that has been of particular influence in the STEM debate is from the National Academy of Sciences (NAS) — *Rising Above the Gathering Storm*. This influence is perhaps due to the clear targets and concrete programs laid out in the report. The NAS report's five recommendations to improve STEM education are to

- quadruple middle- and high-school math and science course-taking by 2010,
- recruit 10,000 new math and science teachers per year,
- strengthen the skills of 250,000 current math and science teachers,

- increase the number of STEM baccalaureate degrees awarded, and
- support graduate and early-career research in STEM fields.

To *enlarge the pipeline* of future STEM degree recipients, NAS sets a goal of quadrupling the number of middle and high school students taking Advanced Placement (AP) or International Baccalaureate (IB) math or science courses, from the current 1.1 million to 4.5 million by 2010. NAS further sets a goal of increasing the number of students who pass either the AP or IB tests to 700,000 by 2010. To enlarge the pipeline, NAS also supports the expansion of programs such as *statewide specialty high schools* for STEM immersion and *inquiry-based learning* through laboratory experience, summer internships, and other research opportunities.

To *recruit 10,000 new STEM teachers*, NAS advocates the creation of a competitive grant program to award merit-based scholarships to obtain a four-year STEM degree in conjunction with certification as a K-12 mathematics or science teacher. These $10,000 to $20,000 awards could be used only for educational expenses and would require a five-year service commitment. An additional $10,000 annual bonus would be awarded to participating teachers in underserved schools in inner cities and rural areas. In further support of this scholarship program, NAS recommends that five-year, $1 million matching grants be awarded to postsecondary institutions to encourage the creation of programs that integrate the obtainment of a STEM bachelor's degree with teacher certification.

NAS proposes four approaches to achieving the goal of *strengthening the skills of 250,000 current STEM teachers*. First, NAS proposes that matching grants be awarded to support the establishment of state and regional summer institutes for STEM teachers modeled after the Merck Institute for Science Education. Second, NAS proposes that additional grants go to postsecondary institutions that support STEM master's degree programs for current STEM teachers (with or without STEM bachelor's degrees) modeled after the University of Pennsylvania Science Teachers Institute. Third, NAS proposes that programs be created to train current teachers to provide AP, IB, and pre-AP or pre-IB instruction modeled after the Advanced Placement Initiative and the Laying the Foundation programs. Fourth, NAS proposes the creation of a national panel to collect, evaluate, and develop rigorous K-12 STEM curricula modeled after Project Lead the Way.

To *increase STEM bachelor's degree attainment*, NAS proposes providing 25,000 new scholarships each year. These Undergraduate Scholar Awards in Science, Technology, Engineering, and Mathematics (USA-STEM) would be distributed to each state in proportion with its population, and awarded to students based on competitive national exams. The $20,000 scholarships could only go to U.S. citizens, and could only be used for the payment of tuition and fees in pursuit of a STEM degree at a U.S. postsecondary institution.

To *increase graduate study in areas of national need, including STEM*, NAS proposes the creation of 5,000 new fellowships each year to U.S. citizens pursuing doctoral degrees. The fellowships would be administered by the National Science Foundation, which would also draw on the advice of several federal agencies in determining the areas of need. An annual stipend of $30,000 would be accompanied by an additional $20,000 annually to cover the cost of tuition and fees. These fellowships would also be portable, so that students could choose to study at a particular institution without the influence of faculty research grants.

LEGISLATION ACTION ON STEM EDUCATION POLICY

In recent years, several pieces of legislation have been introduced with the purpose of improving STEM education in the United States. As has been noted, many of the proposals in these bills have been influenced by the recommendations of several reports recently issued by leading academic, scientific, and business organizations.[45] These recommendations, particularly those from the business community, are not limited to the educational system. This chapter does not discuss these non-educational policy recommendations (e.g., immigration policies that affect the supply of foreign workers to fill U.S. demand in STEM occupations or policies designed to incent private-sector research and development). Rather, this concluding section reviews proposals that have gained passage in the 109th and 110th Congresses that seek to improve the various STEM education outcomes discussed at the outset of this chapter.

Major Legislative Actions in the 109th Congress

Three bills containing STEM education-related proposals were passed in the 109th Congress and signed into law. The National Aeronautics and Space Administration Authorization Act of 2005 (P.L. 109-155) directed the Administrator to develop, expand, and evaluate educational outreach programs in science and space that serve elementary and secondary schools. The National Defense Authorization Act of 2006 (P.L. 109-163) made permanent the Science, Mathematics and Research for Transformation pilot program initiated by the Defense Act of 2005 to address deficiencies of scientists and engineers in the national security workforce. The Deficit Reduction Act of 2005 (P.L. 109-17 1) established the Academic Competitiveness Grants and the National Science and Mathematics Access to Retain Talent Grants programs, which supplement Pell Grants for students studying mathematics, technology, engineering, critical foreign languages, and physical, life, and computer sciences. The act also established the Academic Competitiveness Council, chaired by the Secretary of Education and charged with identifying and evaluating all federal STEM programs, and recommending reforms to improve program integration and coordination. The Council released the findings of its study in May 2007 (discussed earlier in this chapter).

The America COMPETES Act

The 110th Congress passed the America Creating Opportunities to Meaningfully Promote Excellence in Technology, Education, and Science Act (known as the America COMPETES Act) which was signed into law on August 9, 2007 (P.L. 110- 69). The act expands existing STEM education programs and establishes several new programs under the Department of Energy (DOE), Department of Education (ED), and the National Science Foundation (NSF). A brief discussion of the major provisions of the act follows.

Department of Energy. Title V of the act establishes several STEM education programs under the DOE. In an effort to draw middle and secondary school students into the STEM educational pipeline, the act creates (1) a pilot program that awards grants to states to help establish or expand statewide Specialty Schools for Mathematics and Science and (2) a program to provide internships to support Experiential-Based Learning Opportunities for middle and high-school students at the national labs, with priority given to students from high-needs schools. To improve K-12 teaching, the act creates (1) a program to establish a Center of Excellence in each national laboratory region in order to develop and disseminate best practices in STEM education and (2) a program to support Summer Institutes at the national labs and partner universities in order to improve the STEM content knowledge of current teachers. To encourage the pursuit of STEM fields among advanced students and young scholars, the act creates (1) grants to promote the establishment of Talent Expansion academic programs in nuclear and hydrocarbon studies, (2) PACE Graduate Fellowships for those studying a "mission area of the Department," and (3) Early Career Awards for new STEM research scientists. The act also appoints a new Director for STEM Education at the Department who would coordinate DOE education activities and serve as an interagency liaison for K-12 STEM education.

Education Department. Title VI of the act authorizes several new grant programs in ED to enhance STEM education. Subtitle A authorizes three new programs to improve K-12 teaching: (1) a Baccalaureate Degrees program that encourages STEM majors to concurrently obtain teaching certification, (2) a Master's Degrees program to upgrade the skills of current teachers through two to three years of part-time study or to support one-year programs to bring STEM professionals into teaching, and (3) a program to increase the number of Advanced Placement and International Baccalaureate teachers by 70,000. Subtitle B establishes three new programs specifically directed at improving students' math achievement. These programs award competitive grants to LEAs (through states) and include the Math Now program to improve math instruction at elementary schools with low math performance, the Summer Term Education program to provide additional instruction in high-need LEAs, and the Secondary School program that funds the hiring of math coaches. Subtitle D authorizes a new competitive state grant program to improve the Alignment of Secondary School Graduation Requirements with postsecondary and workforce demands and develop P-16 Data Systems. Subtitle E provides Mathematics and Science Partnership Bonus Grants for high-poverty elementary and secondary schools in each state.

National Science Foundation. Title VII of the act seeks to double spending on NSF STEM education programs in seven years. Most of these funds are directed at a number of existing STEM education programs at NSF. These programs include the Robert Noyce Teacher Scholarship program that recruits and trains math and science teachers, the Math and Science Education Partnerships program, the STEM Talent Expansion program to increase the number of students receiving associate or baccalaureate degrees, the Advanced Technological Education program to promote improvement in the education of science and engineering technicians at the undergraduate and secondary school levels, the Graduate Research Fellowship program that provides three years of support for graduate study in STEM fields leading to research-based master's or doctoral degrees, and the Integrative Graduate Education and Research Trainee ship program that supports collaborative research that transcends traditional disciplinary boundaries. The act amends the MSP program to add a new Teacher Institutes for the 21st Century program that provides additional professional development to STEM teachers in high-need schools and amends the Noyce Scholarship program to add a new Teaching Fellowships program that provides salary supplements. The act further creates a Laboratory Science Pilot program to award grants to improve laboratories at the secondary school level and a program to award grants to institutions of higher education to develop Professional Science Master's Degree programs.

End Notes

[1] In 2005 and early 2006, at least six major reports were released by highly respected U.S. academic, scientific, and business organizations on the need to improve science and mathematics education: The Education Commission of the States, *Keeping America Competitive: Five Strategies To Improve Mathematics and Science Education*, July 2005; The Association of American Universities, *National Defense Education and Innovation Initiative, Meeting America's Economic and Security Challenges in the 21st Century*, January 2006; The National Academy of Sciences, Committee on Science, Engineering, and Public Policy, *Rising Above the Gathering Storm: Energizing and Employing America for a Brighter Economic Future*, February 2006; The National Summit on Competitiveness, *Statement of the National Summit on Competitiveness: Investing in U.S. Innovation*, December 2005; The Business Roundtable, *Tapping America's Potential: The Education for Innovation Initiative*, July 2005; the Center for Strategic and International Studies, *Waiting for Sputnik*, 2005.

[2] U.S. Government Accountability Office, *Federal Science, Technology, Engineering, and Mathematics Programs and Related Trends*, GAO-06-1 14, October 2005.

[3] The ACC was created by the Deficit Reduction Act of 2005 (P.L. 109-171) and charged with conducting a year-long study to identify all federal STEM education programs. U.S. Department of Education, *Report of the Academic Competitiveness Council*, Washington, D.C., 2007 [http://www.ed.gov/about/inits/ed/competitiveness

[4] U.S. Department of Education, *Report of the Academic Competitiveness Council*, Washington, D.C., 2007, p. 11.

[5] These points were reiterated by Cornelia M. Ashby, Director of GAO's Education, Workforce, and Income Security Team. Her testimony can be found on the GAO website at [http://www.gao.gov/new.items/d06702t.pdf].

[6] U.S. Department of Education, *Report of the Academic Competitiveness Council*, Washington, D.C., 2007, p. 3.

[7] Office of Science and Technology Policy, Domestic Policy Council, *American Competitiveness Initiative — Leading the World In Innovation*, February 2006.

[8] For more information on NAEP and other assessments, see CRS Report RL3 1407, *Educational Testing: Implementation of ESEA Title I-A Requirements Under the No Child Left Behind Act*, by Wayne C. Riddle.

[9] The National Assessment Governing Board is an independent, bipartisan group created by Congress in 1988 to set policy for the NAEP. More information on the board and NAEP achievement levels can be found at [http://www.nagb.org/].

[10] U.S. Department of Education, National Center for Education Statistics, *The Nation's Report Card: Mathematics 2005*, (NCES 2006-453), October 2005, p. 3.

[11] The 2005 mathematics framework for grade 12 introduced changes from the previous framework in order to reflect adjustments in curricular emphases and to ensure an appropriate balance of content. For further information on these changes, go to [http://nationsreportcard.gov/reading

[12] U.S. Department of Education, National Center for Education Statistics, *The Nation's Report Card: Science 2005* (NCES 2006-466) May 2006, Figures 4, 14, and 24.

[13] More information on the development of this assessment can be found in archived CRS Report 86-683, *Comparison of the Achievement of American Elementary and Secondary Pupils with Those Abroad — The Examinations Sponsored by the International Association for the Evaluation of Educational Achievement (IEA)*, by Wayne C. Riddle (available on request).

[14] Performance on the 1995 TIMSS assessment was normalized on a scale in which the average was set at 500 and the standard deviation at 100. Each country was weighted so that its students contributed equally to the mean and standard deviation of the scale. To provide trend estimates, subsequent TIMSS assessments are pegged to the 1995 average.

[15] All the TIMSS results in this chapter were taken from, Patrick Gonzales, Juan Carlos Guzmán, Lisette Partelow, Erin Pahlke, Leslie Jocelyn, David Kastberg, and Trevor Williams, *Highlights From the Trends in International Mathematics and Science Study (TIMSS) 2003* (NCES 2005 — 005), December 2004.

[16] Like the TIMSS, PISA results are normalized on a scale with 500 as the average score, and results are not reported in terms of achievement levels. In 2003, PISA assessments were administered in just over 40 countries.

[17] Michael B. Allen, *Eight Questions on Teacher Preparation: What Does the Research Say?*, Education Commission of the States, July 2003.

[18] The sample is drawn from the Department of Education Common Core of Data, which contains virtually every school in the country.

[19] U.S. Department of Education, *Digest of Education Statistics, 2004*, NCES 2005-025, October 2005, Table 67.

[20] CRS analysis of Schools and Staffing Survey data, March 29, 2006.

[21] U.S. Department of Education, *Qualifications of the Public School Teacher Workforce*, May 2002, Tables B-1 1 and B-12.

[22] Through various "completions" surveys of postsecondary institutions administered annually since 1960, ED enumerates the number of degrees earned in each field during the previous academic year.

[23] U.S. Department of Education, National Center for Education Statistics, *Digest of Education Statistics, 2004*, NCES 2005-025, October 2005, Table 169.

[24] Includes Ph.D., Ed.D., and comparable degrees at the doctoral level, but excludes first-professional degrees, such as M.D., D.D.S., and law degrees.

[25] National Science Board, *Science and Engineering Indicators, 2006*, (NSB 06-1). Arlington, VA: National Science Foundation, January 2006, p. O-15.

[26] For more information on issues related to foreign students and foreign technical workers, see the following: CRS Report 97-746, *Foreign Science and Engineering Presence in U.S. Institutions and the Labor Force*, by Christine M. Matthews; CRS Report RL3 1973, *Programs Funded by the H-1B Visa Education and Training Fee and Labor Market Conditions for Information Technology (IT) Workers*, by Linda Levine; and CRS Report RL3 0498, *Immigration: Legislative Issues on Nonimmigrant Professional Specialty (H-1B) Workers*, by Ruth Ellen Wasem.

[27] Organization for Economic Co-operation and Development, Education at a Glance, OECD Indicators 2005, Paris, France, September 2005. The OECD compiles annual data from national labor force surveys on educational attainment for the 30 OECD member countries, as well as 13 non-OECD countries that participate in the World Education Indicators (WEI) program. More information on sources and methods can be found at [http://www.oecd.org/ dataoecd/36/39/35324864.pdf].

[28] The World Bank, *Constructing Knowledge Societies: new challenges for tertiary education*, Washington, D.C., October 2002. Available at [http://siteresources.worldbank.org/EDUCATION/Resources/278200-1099079877269/547664-1099079956815/ ConstructingKnowledgeSocieties.pdf].

[29] Unlike the OECD data, which are based on labor-force surveys of households and individuals, the CID data are based on the United Nations Educational, Scientific and Cultural Organization (UNESCO) census and survey data of the entire population. Documentation describing methodology as well as data files for the CID data is available at [http://www.cid.harvard.edu/ciddata/ciddata.html].

[30] *First university* degrees are those designated Level 5A by the International Standard Classification of Education (ISCED 97), and usually require less than five years to complete. More information on this classification and the ISCED is available at [http://www.unesco. org/education/information/nfsunesco/doc/isced_1 997.htm].

[31] U.S. Government Accountability Office, *Federal Science, Technology, Engineering, and Mathematics Programs and Related Trends*, GAO-06-114, October 2005. The GAO study does not include programs in the Department of Defense because the department decided not to participate. Other programs were omitted from the report for various reasons; typically because they did not meet the GAO criteria for a STEM-related educational program (according to an April 26, 2006 conversation with the report's lead author, Tim Hall).

[32] Attrition rates among college students majoring in STEM fields combined with the growth of foreign students in U.S. graduate STEM programs suggest that pre-college STEM education may be a major source of the nation's difficulty in this area.

[33] U.S. Department of Education, *Report of the Academic Competitiveness Council*, Washington, D.C., 2007, at [http://www.ed.gov/about/inits/ed/competitiveness science/index.html].

[34] U.S. Department of Education, *Report of the Academic Competitiveness Council*, Washington, D.C., 2007, p. 11.

[35] These points were reiterated by Cornelia M. Ashby, Director of GAO's Education, Workforce, and Income Security Team. Her testimony can be found on the GAO website at [http://www.gao.gov/ new.items/d06702t.pdf].

[36] Ibid.

[37] Ibid, pp. 21-29.

[38] U.S. Department of Education, *Report of the Academic Competitiveness Council*, Washington, D.C., 2007, p. 3.

[39] Ibid, p. 26.

[40] Ibid, p. 28.

[41] Appendix III of the GAO report provides very brief descriptions of programs funded at $10 million or more and the ACC report briefly describes the five largest programs in its inventory.

[42] More information on the NRSA program is available at [http://grants.nih.gov/training/nrsa.htm].

[44] Analysts at the Brookings Institution conducted a survey of 266 winning MSP projects from 41 states. Results of the survey are available at [http://www.ed.gov/programs/mathsci/proposalreview.doc].

[45] The Education Commission of the States, *Keeping America Competitive: Five Strategies To Improve Mathematics and Science Education*, July 2005; The Association of American Universities, *National Defense Education and Innovation Initiative, Meeting America's Economic and Security Challenges in the 21st Century*, January 2006; The National Academy of Sciences, Committee on Science, Engineering, and Public Policy, *Rising Above the Gathering Storm: Energizing and Employing America for a Brighter Economic Future*, February 2006; The National Summit on Competitiveness, *Statement of the National Summit on Competitiveness: Investing in U.S. Innovation*, December 2005; The Business Roundtable, *Tapping America's Potential: The Education for Innovation Initiative*, July 2005; The Center for Strategic and International Studies, *Waiting for Sputnik*, 2005.

Chapter 3

MOVING FORWARD TO IMPROVE ENGINEERING EDUCATION

National Science Board, National Science Foundation

NATIONAL SCIENCE BOARD

November 19, 2007

Memorandum from the Chairman of the National Science Board Subject: *Moving Forward to Improve Engineering Education*

This chapter of the National Science Board (Board) lays out our findings and recommendations for the National Science Foundation (NSF) to support innovations in engineering education programs. The Board, established by Congress in 1950, provides oversight for, and establishes the policies of, NSF. It also serves as an independent body of advisors to the President and Congress on national policy issues related to science and engineering research and education.

In March 2005, the Board undertook an examination of recent recommendations addressing changes in engineering education and implications for the engineering workforce. This effort built upon the work of the National Academy of Engineering (NAE) in its report, *The Engineer of 2020: Visions of Engineering in the New Century*, as well as recent Board policy reports that identified issues of concern for the domestic engineering workforce.

Moving Forward to Improve Engineering Education synthesizes the results of two Board-sponsored workshops and significant Board deliberations. The first workshop was held at the Massachusetts Institute of Technology in October 2005 and included a range of experts representing broad interests in engineering education. For the second workshop, held at the Georgia Institute of Technology in November 2006, 23 leading deans of engineering (or equivalent) and the NSF Assistant Director for Engineering participated in discussions that identified needs for change in engineering education and model programs to address those needs.

Throughout the process, the Board maintained a dialogue with NAE and coordinated with the NAE "Engineer of 2020" project. Our recommendations in this final report address issues of public perception of engineering, retention of students in engineering majors, responsiveness of engineering education to change in the global environment, and needs for additional data to support policy and planning.

We hope that you will join the Board in supporting the critical national need for innovations in engineering education in order to both sustain a globally competitive engineering workforce and enhance career opportunities for our future engineers.

Steven C. Beering
Chairman National Science Board

ACKNOWLEDGMENTS

Those who contributed to this study are too numerous to mention individually. Invited participants in the two workshops that provided the bulk of the input to our findings and recommendations are included in Appendices I and II.

We are deeply grateful for the excellent cooperation of and dialogue with Dr. William Wulf, the immediate past President of the National Academy of Engineering (NAE), and Dr. Charles Vest, the current NAE President, throughout this project, as well as the special assistance provided by Mr. Richard Taber, Program Officer, NAE.

Others who played less visible but still vital roles include Ms. Frances Marrone, Senior Administrative Assistant to Dr. Daniel Hastings, who coordinated the arrangements for the first workshop at the Massachusetts Institute of Technology, and Dr. Sue Ann Allen, Executive Assistant to the President, and Dr. Don Giddens, Dean of the College of Engineering, who coordinated the arrangements for the second workshop at the Georgia Institute of Technology.

We are especially appreciative of the cooperation and efforts of the National Science Foundation (NSF) Assistant Directors for Engineering throughout this project, including Dr. John Brighton and his successor, Dr. Richard Buckius, who is the current Assistant Director. We also appreciate the special assistance provided by other NSF staff involved in engineering education, including Dr. Russell Pimmel, Program Director, Division of Undergraduate Education, Directorate for Education and Human Resources, and Ms. Susan Kemnitzer, Deputy Director, Division of Engineering Education and Centers, Directorate for Engineering, both of whom briefed Board Members on the history of NSF engineering education programs and prepared presentation materials for the second workshop.

The National Science Board Office provided excellent and essential support throughout this project. Especially deserving of recognition are: Ms. Clara Englert, Science Assistant, who provided the primary staff support for this effort; Ms. Ann Ferrante, Writer-Editor, for editorial and publishing support; and Ms. Jennifer Richards, Science Assistant, for preparation of the final report and distribution.

Dr. Michael Crosby, the Board's Executive Officer and Board Office Director, provided guidance and support to all aspects of the Board's effort.

PROCESS FOR PRODUCING THE REPORT

This study was initiated and led by several Members of the National Science Board's (Board's) Education and Human Resources (EHR) Committee – Drs. G. Wayne Clough, Daniel Hastings, and Louis Lanzerotti. The Charge from the Board to the EHR Committee, *Workshop on Engineering Workforce Issues and Engineering Education: What are the Linkages?* (NSB-05-4 1), was approved at the Board meeting on March 30, 2005.

The purpose of the initial workshop was to "focus on recent recommendations for changes in engineering education and implications for the engineering workforce . . . to move the national conversation on these issues forward in a productive way by calling attention to how engineering education must change in light of the changing workforce demographics and needs." The Charge further noted the opportunity to work in parallel with the National Academy of Engineering (NAE) "Engineer of 2020" project, which called for reform in engineering education. The Board's study included the following range of inputs.

- The Selected Bibliography includes published background materials for the study.
- Two well-attended public workshops were held at major academic institutions offering engineering degrees:
    - Massachusetts Institute of Technology, October 20, 2005: *Engineering Workforce Issues and Engineering Education: What are the Linkages?* The workshop focused on broad issues in engineering education, with faculty, students, and representatives from employers and engineering professional societies. (See: Appendices I and III)
    - Georgia Institute of Technology, November 7, 2006: *Moving Forward to Improve Engineering Education*. The workshop focused on the National Science Foundation's (NSF's) role in encouraging change in engineering education; 23 leading deans of engineering (or equivalent representative of their institution) and the NSF Assistant Director for Engineering participated in the discussion with Board Members. (See: Appendices II and IV)
- Board Members coordinated with the President of the NAE to consider how the Board's effort would complement that of the NAE "Engineer of 2020" project. They held informal discussions over the course of the study and a formal meeting on August 8, 2006.
- Board Members met with NSF senior staff of the Directorate for Engineering and other staff involved in engineering education on August 8, 2006 for a presentation on and discussion about NSF's history of involvement in engineering education, and a review of the success of its programs. The Board consulted with NSF senior management for the NSF Directorate for Engineering throughout the project.

INTRODUCTION

It is widely recognized that our economy, national security, and indeed our everyday lives are increasingly dependent on scientific and technical innovation. Engineering is a key component of innovation and our technological society. Changes on a global scale are rapidly occurring for engineering, and Federal leadership is needed to respond quickly and informatively. The National Science Board (Board) has issued several reports expressing concern about long-term trends that affect U.S. workforce capabilities in engineering, including the dependence on international students and workers; the declining interest on the part of U.S. citizens in engineering studies and careers; weakness in the K-12 science, technology, engineering, and mathematics (STEM) education system; and demographic trends that are unfavorable to increasing citizen participation rates in these fields.

There is a current high level of attention to engineering education from a variety of sources that have converged to make engineering education an especially timely topic for the Board to address. In addition to the Board itself, these sources include the National Academy of Engineering (NAE) reports, *The Engineer of 2020: Visions of Engineering in the New Century (2004)* and *Educating the Engineer of 2020: Adapting Engineering Education to the New Century (2005)*. They also include expressed concern of U.S. industry and the public sector in engineering capabilities in the workforce; and concern over the poor progress in broadening participation in engineering.

Based on the concerns expressed from these sources, the Board decided it was timely to focus on improving engineering education, particularly with regard to the National Science Foundation (NSF)'s unique role in engineering research and education. In fall 2005 and fall 2006, the Board sponsored two workshops **with the goal of moving forward the national conversation on engineering issues by calling attention to how engineering education *must* change in light of changing workforce demographics and needs.** The Board feels that a continuation of the *status quo* in engineering education in the U.S. is not sufficient in light of the pressing demands for change. The workshop participants included representatives from leading engineering schools, industry, government agencies, and engineering societies. The workshops focused on key challenges for engineering education, which include the changing global context for engineering education, perceptions and often misperceptions of engineering, and difficulty in attracting and retaining students in engineering. The workshops also identified many promising programs and strategies, including both successful NSF programs and innovative programs in engineering schools and elsewhere. This chapter focuses on the role of NSF in building on and disseminating these innovations in engineering education.

> The Board feels that a continuation of the *status quo* in engineering education in the U.S. is not sufficient in light of the pressing demands for change.

KEY CHALLENGES IN ENGINEERING EDUCATION

Three essential challenges for engineering education are to respond to the changing needs for engineers, to change the perception of engineering, and to retain top students.

Responding to the Changing Global Context of Engineering

Changes in the global environment require changes in engineering education. Markets, companies, and supply chains have become much more international and engineering services are often sourced to the countries that can provide the best value. Basic engineering skills (such as knowledge of the engineering fundamentals) have become commodities that can be provided by lower cost engineers in many countries, and some engineering jobs traditionally done in the U.S. are increasingly done overseas.

To respond to this changing context, U.S. engineers need new skill sets not easily replicated by low-wage overseas engineers. The problems that have driven engineering – even in recent years – are changing, as technology penetrates more of society. Systems have become more tightly coupled. Engineering thinking needs to be able to deal with complex interrelationships that include not only traditional engineering problems but also encompass human and environmental factors as major components. In addition to analytic skills, which are well provided by the current education system, companies want engineers with passion, some systems thinking, an ability to innovate, an ability to work in multicultural environments, an ability to understand the business context of engineering, interdisciplinary skills, communication skills, leadership skills, an ability to adapt to changing conditions, and an eagerness for lifelong learning. This is a different kind of engineer from the norm that is being produced now.

U.S. engineering students also need preparation for a wider set of career paths, including management and marketing. Many engineers spend a relatively short period of time – about 6 years – in engineering practice, after which they move to jobs, such as management, for which their engineering training has not prepared them well. Engineers need to be adaptive leaders, grounded in a broad understanding of the practice and concepts of engineering. Reforming engineering education along these lines is likely to improve job prospects for engineers, attract and retain highly qualified students from all U.S. demographic groups, and make them capable of addressing the complex engineering and social problems of the future.

Perceptions of Engineering

Engineering is not attracting enough people to the field, and often is not attracting the diversity of backgrounds needed. A central issue is the way that engineering is perceived by prospective students, teachers, guidance counselors, and parents.

Society at large does not have an accurate perception of the nature of engineering. Survey data indicate that the public associates engineers with economic growth and defense, but less so with improving health, the quality of life, and the environment. These perceptions persist despite the seminal contributions of engineers in the last century to providing widespread electrification and access to clean water, both with huge quality of life improvements. Such perceptions attract to engineering those individuals who are good in math and science and are interested in "things" rather than people, but not individuals who prefer to work with others on teams and who want to contribute to solving social problems. As a result, many students, especially women and minorities, cannot see themselves as engineers.

Engineers are commonly perceived as "nerds" without interpersonal skills, doing narrowly focused jobs that are prone to being outsourced. Most high school girls believe engineering is just for boys who love math and science. Students at historically black colleges and universities may see engineering as unfriendly, unaffordable, and requiring extra preparation. They do not see a direct benefit to their community and often believe they would have to leave their community to succeed in engineering. In part due to these perceptions, engineers remain underrepresented among women, African Americans, Hispanics, and Native Americans. Engineering also is seen as unattractive by many talented and creative people who could excel in engineering but are discouraged by the rigidity of the required studies and perceptions about uncertain career prospects.

In contrast to these common public perceptions, the Board believes that it is an exciting time to be in engineering and that there are enormous opportunities for the next generation of U.S. engineers. The next generation of engineers will be challenged to find holistic solutions to population, energy, environment, food, water, terrorism, housing, health, and transportation problems. New subfields of engineering continue to emerge, including nanotechnology, biotechnology, information technology, and logistics. An infinite range of exciting new technologies and products – the future iPods and GameCubes – await development by engineers. There will continue to be a strong demand for U.S. citizen engineers in the defense and homeland security sector, as well as in the public sector. In order to align the public perception of engineering with the reality of opportunities in engineering, a conscious and sustained effort is needed to convey the opportunities and excitement of engineering.

> ...it is an exciting time to be in engineering...The next generation of engineers will be challenged to find holistic solutions to population, energy, environment, food, water, terrorism, housing, health, and transportation problems.

Retention of Engineering Students

The third challenge for engineering education is to retain those students who are initially attracted to engineering. Attrition is substantial in engineering, particularly in the first year of college. About 60 percent of students who enter engineering majors obtain a degree within 6 years. Although this retention rate is comparable to some other fields, it is especially critical for engineering to retain the pool of entering students. As noted by the Board in its 2003 report, *The Science and Engineering Workforce – Realizing America's Potential (NSB-03-69),* the sequential acquisition of skills and inflexible coursework in engineering and similar scientific disciplines means that the movement of undergraduate students from one major to another is almost entirely out during the undergraduate program, with few compensating transfers into engineering. For this reason, retention of the students is an especially critical strategy for increasing the number of students earning engineering degrees.

Engineering students often develop little identity as engineers in their first 2 years of college because they take math and science courses and have little exposure to engineering practice. Students have expressed dissatisfaction with teaching and advising in the early years, perhaps for this reason. Also, course requirements may be too restrictive to accommodate students' varied interests, and students may perceive that friends in other majors are taking easier courses and having more fun.

Some of the students who leave engineering are among the best students; others leave because they performed poorly in their first math courses. Attrition is higher than average among women and minorities – the groups most likely to lack role models in engineering. Perceptions of a too competitive and uncaring environment, fear that engineering jobs may disappear due to offshore outsourcing, and increased tuition in public universities also contribute to the high rate of attrition in engineering. Retention of engineering students is a systems problem that begins before college and involves the whole university. The Board recommended in its 2003 report on the science and engineering workforce that "the Federal Government must direct substantial new support to students and institutions in order to improve success in S&E study by American undergraduates from all demographic groups."

We commend the bipartisan efforts of Members of Congress and President Bush to provide new Federal support for scholarships and fellowships for students undertaking the study of engineering. This type of program will have a positive impact, particularly for those qualified students whose financial circumstances are limited. The pre-college preparation of entering students, the difficulty of the engineering curriculum relative to other academic tracks, the affordability of an engineering degree program, and the social experience of engineering students within the whole university all affect retention.

The workshops identified many approaches to improving retention of engineering students: introducing students to the excitement and relevance of engineering early in the educational experience; exposing students to research early on; placing engineering in a social or business context; inviting practitioners and other engineers to speak about what they do; providing role models and mentoring; providing a comfortable social environment; making extra resources available to students who need math help; making more need-based scholarships available; and working with community colleges to pave pathways for less affluent students to enter engineering.

Leading engineering schools have also had success with a variety of curricular and non-curricular programs to attract and retain engineering students. These include out-ofclassroom experiences, such as undergraduate research, study-abroad programs, internships, and participation in student organizations and professional organizations; assignments to multidisciplinary and even multinational project teams; training for a diversity of career paths; hands-on engineering and integrative experiences in the first year; emphasis on social relevance, service learning, volunteer leadership, and collaboration; and systems content in addition to component-level content in courses.

Engineering schools may be able to learn from business and medical schools, both of which have succeeded in transforming their student bodies from predominantly male to a 50:50 male/female ratio, and have succeeded in attracting and retaining more minority students.

> Engineering schools may be able to learn from business and medical schools, both of which have succeeded in transforming their student bodies from predominantly male to a 50:50 male/female ratio, and have succeeded in attracting and retaining more minority students.

KEYSTONE RECOMMENDATION

The national science foundation should expand and reinvigorate its efforts to stimulate and disseminate innovation in engineering education

NSF has a unique and central role in engineering research and education and can play an increasing role in addressing the key challenges in engineering education. NSF supports innovation in engineering education, engineering research, and the STEM education that provides the pipeline of students for engineering. It is uniquely qualified to support innovation in engineering thinking to address the increasingly broad set of problems with which engineers must engage.

Over the last two decades, NSF has made substantial investments in a wide range of activities to improve engineering education. These include investments in: curriculum improvement, Engineering Education Coalitions, Engineering Research Centers, Model Institutions of Excellence, and Centers for Learning and Teaching. Workshop participants commended especially the contributions of NSF's (1) Research Experiences for Undergraduates (REU) program, which encourages U.S. students to pursue graduate studies by engaging them in research activities as undergraduates; and (2) Research Experiences for Teachers (RET) program, which supports involvement of K-12 teachers and community college faculty in research activities at universities. Studies indicate that REU experiences increase interest in STEM careers and that RET experiences give teachers a better understanding of engineering and increase teacher motivation and confidence in teaching math and science. In addition, NSF addresses the issue of affordability through its graduate fellowship and traineeship programs, which include Integrative Graduate Education and Research Traineeships (IGERT), Graduate Teaching Fellows in K-12 Education (GK-12), and Graduate Research Fellowships.

Although these programs are generally viewed as being effective and helpful, they have not led to systematic changes in perceptions and retention of engineers. Moreover, best practices resulting from the programs are not readily disseminated throughout the engineering education community.

With its unique role in engineering education and research, crosscutting all educational levels and the workforce, NSF is perfectly situated to take on leadership in pursuing solutions to the issues raised at the two workshops. The Keystone Recommendation can be divided into five subsidiary recommendations. In each of these areas, there is also a need for evaluation of the programs to establish a causative relationship between funding and output.

GENERAL IMPLEMENTING RECOMMENDATIONS

NSF should build on its innovative programs that support engineering education. In particular:
- NSF should continue and expand its REU program to college freshmen and sophomores, as well as to community college and perhaps even high school students. NSF should also look forward to facilitate the transition of REU students to graduate school through fellowships. NSF should pursue additional REU partnerships with

Federal agencies, such as the National Aeronautics and Space Administration and the Departments of Energy, Transportation, and Agriculture.
- NSF should continue and expand its IGERT program to the undergraduate level. It should broaden IGERT to include research and education that integrates engineering with the arts, humanities, and social sciences to train well-rounded, dynamic engineers who can understand not only the technology but also the economic, political, and historical context for what they are learning.
- NSF should continue its ADVANCE program for Increasing the Participation and Advancement of Women in Academic Science and Engineering Careers, and consider creating a similar program focused on developing the minority professoriate.
- NSF should continue and expand its scholarship and fellowship programs, including the Graduate Research Fellowships and the GK-12 Fellows programs. In the face of rising tuitions, scholarships, and fellowships for engineering students are increasingly important, especially for less affluent students and disadvantaged minorities.
- NSF should continue and expand the RET program, and add a mechanism to keep K-12 teachers connected to the program after they return to their schools. RET can contribute in a major way to changing the perceptions K-12 students and parents have about engineering.

NSF should continue to support engineering education research and experimentation and expand dissemination of results. Successful models for attracting and retaining engineering students should be studied. Workshops could be held for sharing of practices in engineering education, such as how to mentor engineering students or how to incorporate non-technical skills (such as ethics) into technical courses. NSF should expand dissemination of best practices in engineering education through a database and Web site that provides details on successful programs and lessons learned. NSF should look into helping students make the transition to the next stage of their education; the transition from community college to engineering school deserves special attention.

NSF should support education that broadens the experiences of engineering students. NSF could provide support for programs that fund cross-disciplinary education and seminars, such as symposia that focus on the intersection of technology and the economy. NSF could support international programs by collecting data on universities with engineering programs overseas and providing support for students who otherwise would not have the resources to participate. NSF could support programs that provide global educational opportunities for undergraduate engineering students. More generally, NSF could support programs that experiment to produce different kinds of engineers.

NSF should increase its outreach efforts in order to combat public misperceptions about engineering. The NAE is supporting the development of themes to communicate a better image of engineering. NSF should work with the NAE to craft the messages it wants to convey to students, parents, counselors, and teachers. NSF should consider supporting industry-community-university partnerships that inform pre-college students and parents about engineering. NSF could sponsor workshops for guidance counselors and K-12 teachers so they understand the value of engineering, the different career options available in the field, and the opportunities in engineering for women and minorities. Minority-serving institutions could be approached for leadership in broadening participation. NSF should consider sponsoring a few highly visible "grand challenges" to attract the attention of engineers, the media, and the public, and to stimulate interest in engineering. NSF should also explore the role that industry can play in addressing instabilities in engineering employment that can lead to student concerns about career paths and therefore perceptions of engineering as a profession.

NSF should ask the National Research Council or the National Academy of Engineering to study how many and what kinds of engineers the United States must produce to be economically competitive. The Academies could examine goals for engineering education, such as a desired number of engineering graduates, percentage of graduates in engineering, demographic mix, or retention and graduation rates. It could also address the causes of the dearth of U.S.-born and -trained engineers and seek to better understand the cyclical nature of the demand for various engineering fields.

CONCLUSION

Worldwide, engineering is by far the largest major for first university degrees in science and engineering fields, reflecting the importance of the engineering workforce in national economic and social performance. It is therefore essential for the U.S. to attract, retain, and train American engineers from diverse backgrounds to meet domestic needs and the growing international competition in science and technology. Federal collaboration with the National Academy of Engineering, higher education, and the engineering communities is necessary to adapt engineering education to the new realities of the global workforce. In particular, NSF should reinvigorate its support for innovative engineering education to provide the leadership, knowledge, and resources to meet these challenges.

The Board's policy guidance for NSF must be implemented to ensure the adequacy and quality of the U.S. engineering workforce for the future. The Board is pleased to be able to join with our colleagues in the engineering communities to address the challenges and opportunities for engineering in the new century.

SELECTED BIBLIOGRAPHY

[1] Center for the Advancement of Scholarship on Engineering Education (CASEE), *Progress and Accomplishments: Engineering Education Research and Development* (Washington, DC: National Academy of Engineering, 2005- 2006).

[2] Farrell, Diana et al., *The Emerging Global Labor Market*, Executive Summaries (McKinsey Global Institute, McKinsey and Company, June 2005).

[3] Hoffer, Thomas and Vincent Welch, Jr., SRS Infobrief: *"Time to Degree of U.S. Research Recipients,"* NSF 06- 312 (Arlington, VA: National Science Foundation, Directorate for Social, Behavioral, and Economic Sciences, March 2006).

[4] Lattuca, Lisa, Patrick Terenzini, and J. Fredericks Volkwein, Center for the Study of Higher Education, The Pennsylvania State University, *Engineering Change: A Study of the Impact of EC2000*, Executive Summary (Baltimore, MD: ABET, Inc., 2006).

[5] Ed. Mary Mattis and John Sislin, *Enhancing the Community College Pathway to Engineering Careers* (Washington, DC: National Academy of Engineering and National Research Council, 2005).

[6] National Academy of Engineering, *The Bridge: Linking Engineering and Society*, Vol. 36, No. 2 (Washington, DC: National Academy of Engineering, Summer 2006).

[7] National Academy of Engineering, *Educating the Engineer of 2020: Adapting Engineering Education to the New Century* (Washington, DC: The National Academies Press, 2005).

[8] National Academy of Engineering, *Engineering Research and America's Future: Meeting the Challenges of a Global Economy*, Executive Summary (Washington, DC: National Academy of Engineering, 2005).

[9] National Academy of Engineering, *Enhancing the Community College Pathway to Engineering Careers* (Overview and Report Summary and Statistical Appendix) (Washington, DC: National Academy of Engineering, 2005).

[10] The National Academy of Sciences, National Academy of Engineering, and Institute of Medicine of the National Academies, *Rising Above the Gathering Storm: Energizing and Employing America for a Brighter Economic Future*, Executive Summary from Prepublication Copy (Washington, DC: The National Academies Press, 2005).

[11] National Science Board, *2020 Vision for the National Science Foundation (NSB-05-142)* (Arlington, VA: National Science Foundation, 2005).

[12] National Science Foundation, *Investing in America's Future: National Science Foundation Strategic Plan FY 2006-2011* (Arlington, VA: National Science Foundation, 2006).

[13] National Science Foundation, *Science and Engineering Indicators 2004 (NSB-04-07),* Appendix Tables 2-22 and 2-26 (Arlington, VA: National Science Foundation, 2004).

[14] Oliver, Julia, SRS Infobrief: *"First-Time S&E Graduate Enrollment of Foreign Students Drops for the Third Straight Year,"* NSF 06-32 1 (Arlington, VA: National Science Foundation, Directorate for Social, Behavioral, and Economic Sciences, July 2006).

[15] Parker, Linda, Engineering Workforce Project, *"The Education and Employment of Engineering Graduates"* (Arlington, VA: National Science Foundation, Division of Engineering Education and Centers, March 2004).

[16] Parker, Linda, Engineering Workforce Project, *"Engineers in the United States: An Overview of the Profession"* (Arlington, VA: National Science Foundation, Division of Engineering Education and Centers, June 2004).

[17] Tenner, Ed, *"Engineers and Political Power"* (TechnologyReview.com, April 2005).

[18] Tsapogas, John, SRS Infobrief: *"More Than One-Fifth of All Individuals Employed in Science and Engineering Occupations Have Less Than a Bachelor's Degree*

Education," NSF 04-333 (Arlington, VA: National Science Foundation, Directorate for Social, Behavioral, and Economic Sciences, August 2004).

[19] Tsapogas, John, SRS Infobrief: *"Recent Engineering and Computer Science Graduates Continue To Earn the Highest Salaries,"* NSF 06-303 (Arlington, VA: National Science Foundation, Directorate for Social, Behavioral, and Economic Sciences, December 2005).

APPENDIX I. WORKSHOP - ENGINEERING EMPLOYMENT AND ENGINEERING EDUCATION: WHAT ARE THE LINKAGES?

Summary Notes

The following summary notes of the discussions and presentations reflect the views and opinions of the participants and not necessarily the positions of the National Science Board.

Introduction

This chapter summarizes the key themes and suggestions resulting from the National Science Board-Sponsored Workshop on Engineering Workforce Issues and Engineering Education, held October 20, 2005 at the Massachusetts Institute of Technology. The workshop focused on recommendations for changes in engineering education and implications for the engineering workforce presented in the recent National Academy of Engineering reports, *The Engineer of 2020: Visions of Engineering in the New Century*, and *Educating the Engineer of 2020: Adapting Engineering Education to the New Century*, and NSB[1] reports that identified troublesome trends in the number of domestic engineering students, with potential impacts to U.S. preeminence in S &E based innovation and discovery.

The major workshop objective was to move the national conversation on these issues forward in a productive way by calling attention to how engineering education must change in light of the changing workforce demographics and needs. A key output was suggestions for how NSF could help enable the appropriate changes in education through data collection and research. The workshop involved leading engineering educators as well as representatives of industry, government agencies, and engineering societies. It included panels on "Aspirations for Engineering Education," "Engineering Education - Present and Future," and "Engineering Employment – Present and Future." The workshop addressed such topics as alternative scenarios for engineering workforce and engineering education; the roles of the different stakeholders (professional societies, universities, working engineers, and employers); broadening participation in engineering; the role of foreign students and engineers; the need for engineering education to prepare students more broadly for employment in the public, nonprofit, academic, and industry sectors; and how to attract the best and the brightest students to engineering studies and careers.

Central themes of the workshop were that the current standard engineering education appears neither to provide the full set of skills that engineers are likely to need in the future nor to attract the right numbers or types of people to engineering. Workforce opportunities for engineers and skill needs vary greatly among employers. Likewise, no one approach is most effective for achieving a broader base of participation by the "best and brightest" students, and a variety of successful models should be employed. Engineering education reforms can help attract and retain highly qualified students from all U.S. demographic groups, and prepare them to be adaptive leaders, capable of addressing complex problems for the engineering jobs of the future. Speakers in the workshop felt that the present is the time for leadership in U.S. engineering education since one of the economic battlefields of the future will be over the global redistribution of engineering talent.

Key Themes

There are exciting opportunities in engineering. There continue to be exciting new subfields of engineering, including nanotechnology, biotechnology, information technology, and logistics. The next generation of engineers will be challenged to find solutions to population, energy, environment, food, water, terrorism, housing, health, and transportation problems. These problems require multidisciplinary knowledge, systems thinking, and an understanding of social issues.

The context of engineering education is changing. Markets have become more international. Other countries have a competitive advantage in low cost manufacturing and services. In some countries, excellent engineers are available at one-fifth of the cost of a U.S.-educated engineer. Supply chains are increasingly integrated across companies and nations, requiring a different set of communication and cultural skills. Other countries, especially India and China, have greatly increased their production of engineers. Conventional engineering work from conceptual design through manufacturing is increasingly outsourced to lower cost countries. The speed of change means that any set of technical skills may quickly become obsolete. To prosper, U.S. engineers need to provide high value and excel at high-level design, systems integration, innovation, and leadership.

There is uncertainty about the number of U.S. engineers required in the future. This is in part due to uncertainty about the effects of outsourcing and the role of foreign-born engineers in the United States. The United States has historically used foreign-born engineers to meet needs, but there is concern that the U.S. will not be able to attract these as well in the future. Other countries, particularly in Europe, are beginning to compete for the world pool of science and engineering talent, and more students from India, China, and other countries may choose to return home because of the expanding economic opportunities in their home countries. There was widespread agreement among workshop participants, however, that:

- Career opportunities are likely to be much greater for engineers who have a broader set of skills (described below) than for more narrowly trained engineers, whose skill set can be easily replicated by low-wage overseas engineers.
- The United States must continue to attract the "best and brightest" (broadly defined) to engineering.

- There will continue to be a demand for U.S. citizen engineers in the defense and homeland security sector, and in the public sector.
- Regardless of the number of U.S. engineers needed, the United States needs a more technologically literate workforce.
- Many in industry want to partner with the K-12 schools and universities to attract more of the nation's talent into contributing to engineering.

Engineering is not succeeding in attracting and keeping many of the right students. Students appear to be making rational, well-informed decisions when they choose not to pursue engineering. Engineering is unattractive to many people who could excel in engineering, due to the rigidity of the required studies and perceptions about uncertain career prospects. Talented students feel they can make more money and have greater job security through other careers. Many engineers spend a relatively short period of time (i.e., 6 years) in engineering practice, after which they move to jobs, such as management, for which their engineering training has not prepared them well. Negative images of engineering also make it less attractive. Dissatisfaction with teaching and advising in undergraduate engineering colleges also leads many students to transfer from engineering to another undergraduate major. Poor retention rates for students who study engineering can often be attributed to issues with teaching and advising in the first and second years, a time when the students are taking service courses, some in large sections, and when there may be little contact with engineering. Attention is needed to improving teaching, advising, and support for the students during this time. Many students who are not retained in engineering are the students who are more comfortable working in cross-disciplinary environments. It is important to attract and retain students who are creative and have leadership and communication skills, not just math and science skills.

Engineers remain very underrepresented among women, African Americans, Hispanics, and Native Americans who together constitute the majority of the U.S. population. Groups that are under-represented in engineering are growing as a percentage of the U.S. population. Focus groups with women and underrepresented minorities have shown that they want more collaborative approaches to school and work, and want a greater focus on engineering to address socially important problems. Linear progress in attracting women and minority students into engineering is no longer sufficient.

Engineers of the future need a new set of skills. If engineering in the U.S. is to help the U.S. succeed in this century, it will need to attract students who not only have basic math and science skills, but also those who exhibit common sense, an interest in commerce and innovation, an understanding of culture, a willingness to interact with people, and a desire to help humanity and life on the planet. Through their native abilities and the shaping of an education that is updated to reflect new circumstances, an engineer will emerge who can be differentiated from those educated abroad. In addition to analytic skills, which are well provided by the current education system, companies want engineers with passion; life long learning skills; systems thinking; an ability to innovate; an ability to work in multicultural environments; an ability to understand the business context of engineering; interdisciplinary skills; communication skills; leadership skills; and an ability to change. The public sector especially needs engineers with a sophisticated understanding of the social environment within which their activity takes place, a systems understanding, and an ability to communicate with stakeholders.

Engineers should be educated with a wider set of career paths, including management and marketing, in mind. Engineers should be adaptive leaders, grounded in a broad understanding of the practice and concepts of engineering. Reforming engineering along these lines is likely to improve job prospects for engineers and the attractiveness of engineering as a profession.

There are many innovations in engineering education taking place. A wide variety of experiences with innovative approaches to engineering education were presented, including those of several NSF programs (Engineering Education Coalitions, Research Experiences for Undergraduates programs, Research Experience for Teachers programs, and the Engineering Research Centers) and several universities and colleges (Olin School of Engineering, MIT, Drexel, Georgia Tech, Smith College, University of California, Purdue, and others). Suggested approaches discussed include:

- Redefining the core engineering curriculum to free up time for other learning.
- Using content modules instead of courses to allow greater customization of curriculum.
- Focusing on threads of knowledge that connect different pieces of the engineering curriculum.
- Using student involvement in the design of the curriculum.
- Providing more diversity in types of engineering training, appropriate for different career goals.
- Using out-of-the-classroom experiences, such as undergraduate research, study-abroad programs, internships, and participation in student organizations and professional organizations, to broaden the experiences of engineers.
- Providing first year students with hands-on engineering and integrative experiences that involve design, imagination, and communication.
- Emphasizing social relevance, collaboration, and problem solving in the curriculum.
- Focusing on courses with some systems content in addition to component level content.
- Providing sophomore engineering students with internships to expose them to the practical world of engineering, including creating and marketing products.
- Putting students on multidisciplinary and even multinational project teams.
- Using more independent inquiry and open source learning.
- Providing master's degree programs in engineering management, manufacturing leadership, and system design and management.

There are some significant barriers to changing engineering education. Cost is one barrier -many of the proposed changes to engineering education involve investments in new curricula and more faculty-student interaction. Not all of the proposed changes need to be expensive, indeed several are not, but it was agreed that proposed changes need to have a business plan. Several of the engineering deans suggested that it was important that the changes to engineering education be scalable to larger numbers of students. Another barrier is that the engineering curriculum is already very tight, and adding more courses requires taking out other courses or increasing the length of the degree. Taking material out of the curriculum leads to concern that the traditional curriculum is being watered down, and there are concerns about how employers would react. Many of the proposed changes may require more faculty time in teaching, potentially detracting from research. Engineering education reforms need to come from the bottom up, but also need strong leadership and support from the top down. It was also pointed out by some of the industry representatives that education does not stop at graduation and collectively industry and academia need to think about lifelong learning.

Suggestions for Actions

The workshop generated a wide number of suggestions for future actions. These are suggestions for topics to be examined in more depth, not necessarily a consensus of the workshop participants. The suggestions pertain to pre-college education, university/college education, the engineering workforce, the image of engineering, and data/research needs.

Pre-College Education
There were suggestions to provide greater exposure to engineering in K-12 education. There should be a K12 engineering curriculum standard to complement, enhance, and enrich the curriculum in math and science.

Exposure to engineering could help to stimulate interest in K-12 math and science. It is especially important to begin engaging the interest of minorities and women as early as grades 4-6, and to continue to work with these students all the way through school. Parents and the general public also need to be engaged more through a variety of outreach and activities. It was suggested that industry and academia should interact more with K-12 schools to project a positive image of engineering into the schools. There are NSF programs in this arena, and it may be possible to strengthen them.

University/College Education
A wide variety of suggestions were focused on university/college engineering education. Engineering schools should:

- Engage students in engineering in their first year and help students to establish an early identity as an engineer through exposure to engineering coursework, early research experiences, experiential learning, and the context of engineering.
- Address poor teaching (some in non-engineering courses) and advising that is cited by many of the students leaving engineering.
- Provide opportunities to work for the public good, to take advantage of student interest in public service.
- Develop more active learning approaches to engineering and science, as well as practical exposure to broadening engineering education, through university-government-industry partnerships.
- Rethink the curriculum to include not just knowledge, but also skills and attitudes. There should be a focus on building an understanding of what it means to be a lifelong learner and building the related skills.

- Consider offering engineering courses to non-engineers.
- Reintroduce the history of engineering into the engineering curriculum. They should teach, for example, not only the Laplace transform but also teach who Laplace was and how he influenced math, engineering, and philosophy.

NSF should:

- Use teaching evaluation scores as part of the evaluation of research proposals.
- Increase the incentives for interdisciplinary work among engineering faculty.

Universities should:

- Create and support professional graduate programs in engineering and science leadership as an analog to professional programs in business, law, and medicine.
- Create skunk works (organizations free of institutional barriers) for reinventing engineering.
- Consider developing support systems for engineering students to help them learn to manage their time and meet social needs. Providing group housing for incoming engineering students is an option.

Community colleges should:

- Be included in the discussions of engineering education. Community colleges are an important pathway to the associate degree in engineering and then to four-year degrees; their role needs to be looked at more closely.

Universities and industry should consider:

- More joint programs between universities and industry, such as research consortia and grants for personnel exchanges between industry and universities.

Engineering Workforce

Several suggestions addressed policy changes to expand the pool of engineering talent:

- Congress should create a national innovation act, with 5,000 government-sponsored portable fellowships for U.S. students in math, science, and engineering.
- Congress should expand engineering traineeships for U.S. citizens.
- Congress should change laws to provide green cards to foreign citizens who graduate in the U.S. with a Ph.D. (or master's) degree. The U.S. must retain the best and brightest of the foreign nationals who study in this country.
- NSF/NSB should expand industrial participation in this discussion of engineering education.
- With respect to lifelong learning, universities should provide courses covering recent advances in science in order to refresh engineers' education.

Public Image of Engineering

There were several suggestions to improve the public image of engineering:

- NSF could support more ways to celebrate math, science, and engineering that young people find exciting and inspiring.
- The television and movie industry, perhaps with NSF/foundations' support, could develop popular television shows or movies highlighting the role of engineers -- "Detroit Manufacturing" or "Route 128 Engineering" in a similar vein as "L.A. Law" and "Boston Legal."
- NSF could sponsor a few highly visible "grand challenges" to attract the attention of engineers, the media, and the public. For example, DARPA is sponsoring a grand challenge about robotic vehicles, and a private foundation is sponsoring the X-Prize for a private team building an efficient craft for space tourism.
- The engineering community should find a Carl Sagan-quality spokesman for engineering.

Research and Data Collection

There were several suggestions to expand research and data collection related to engineering education:

- NSF and others should fund research on problem-based learning approaches to determine if they are effective.
- The U.S. government should develop better information about outsourcing, engineering labor markets, and engineering careers, including market signals such as job openings.
- NSF should fund research and data collection on the impact of engineering research.
- NSF should study models that have worked for attracting and retaining engineering students.

Future Workshops

Several suggestions were also made for possible future workshops. It was suggested that there should be greater participation from industry, including representation from more diverse industry sectors. It was also suggested that community colleges should be included, because of the important role they play both as a stepping-stone to college degrees and in lifelong learning. In addition, it would be good to expand the dialogue to include engineering deans and faculty other than those who have been at the forefront of innovation in engineering education.

Massachusetts Institute of Technology (MIT)

Wednesday, October 19, 2005

   7:00 p.m.   **Reception and Registration**

Boston Marriott Cambridge
Two Cambridge Center
Kendall Square (Broadway and Third Street)

Thursday, October 20, 2005

	NSB Workshop
	MIT Faculty Club
	Alfred P. Sloan Building
	E52-6th Floor – Dining 5 and 6
8:00 a.m.	**Continental Breakfast**
	Dining 5
8:25 a.m.	Welcome
	Warren M. Washington*, Chairman, National Science Board
8:30 a.m.	**Panel 1: Aspirations for Engineering Education**

	Opening Remarks	Daniel Hastings*
		National Science Board
	National Academy of Engineering	G. Wayne Clough*
	The Engineer of 2020, Phases I & II	National Science Board
	Data, trends, and outlooks	Richard Buckius
		National Science Foundation
	NSF activities in engineering	Arden L. Bement*
		National Science Foundation

9:10 a.m.	Group Discussion among Workshop Participants
9:20 a.m.	Questions and Comments from the Audience
9:30 a.m.	**Panel 2: Engineering Education – Present and Future**
	Moderator: Daniel Hastings, National Science Board

	Alice Agogino*	Eli Fromm*
	University of California, Berkeley	Drexel University
	Richard Miller*	Tom Magnanti*
	Olin College of Engineering	MIT
	Linda Katehi*	Purdue University

10:30 a.m.	Group Discussion among Workshop Participants
11:15 a.m.	Questions and Comments from the Audience
11:30 a.m.	**Break**
11:45 a.m.	**Lunch with MIT Engineering Council and Selected Engineering Students**
	By Invitation Only
	Susan Hockfield*, President, MIT
	John H. Marburger, III*, Science Advisor to the President Director, Office of Science and Technology Policy (OSTP)
12:45 p.m.	**Break**
1:00 p.m.	**Panel 3: Engineering Employment – Present and Future**
	Moderator: Louis L. Lanzerotti*, National Science Board

	Peter Pao*	Jim Miller*
	Raytheon Company	Cisco Systems, Inc.
	Ron Hira*	Gloria Jeff*
	IEEE-USA	Michigan Department of Transportation
2:00 p.m.	Group Discussion among Workshop Participants	
2:45 p.m.	Questions and Comments from the Audience	
3:00 p.m.	**Breakout Sessions to Address the Question: How do we ensure that the best and the brightest students pursue engineering studies and careers, and that their education quality, content, and teaching are of the highest caliber?**	
	Location: Dining 3, Dining 5, and Dining 6	
	Session Chairs: G. Wayne Clough, Louis L. Lanzerotti, Daniel Hastings	
4:30 p.m.	**Report Out and Wrap-Up**	
	Moderator: Daniel Hastings*	
5:00 p.m.	**Reception**	
	MIT Engineering Systems Division (ESD)	
	Building E40-298	

* Confirmed speaker/moderator

Invited Workshop Participants

Participant	Affiliation
	National Science Board
Dr. Warren Washington*	NSB Chairman
Dr. Dan Arvizu	NSB Member
Dr. G. Wayne Clough*	NSB Member
Dr. Daniel Hastings*	NSB Member
Dr. Elizabeth Hoffman	NSB Member
Dr. Louis Lanzerotti*	NSB Member
Dr. Jon Strauss	NSB Member
Dr. Michael Crosby	NSB Executive Officer
	National Science Foundation
Dr. Arden Bement*	NSF Director
Dr. Richard Buckius	NSF Interim Assistant Director for Engineering
Dr. Donald Thompson	NSF Interim Assistant Director for Education and Human Resources
	Participants
Dr. Alice Agogino*	UC-Berkeley, Professor of Mechanical Engineering
Dr. Sue Ann Bidstrup Allen	Georgia Tech, Executive Assistant to the President
Mr. Richard Anderson	ABET, President

Dr. Robert Armstrong	MIT, Head of the Department of Chemical Engineering
Dr. Joseph Bordogna	University of Pennsylvania, Professor of Engineering (formerly NSF Deputy Director and Chief Operating Officer)
Dr. John Brighton*	Iowa State University, Vice Provost for Research (formerly NSF Assistant Director for Engineering)
Dr. Judith Cardell	Smith College, Assistant Professor of Computer Engineering
Dr. José Cruz	Ohio State University, Professor of Electrical and Computer Engineering
Dr. Ruth David	Analytic Services Inc., President and CEO
Dr. Eli Fromm*	Drexel University, Director of the Center for Educational Research in the College of Engineering, and Professor of Electrical and Computer Engineering
Dr. Kent Fuchs	Cornell University, Dean of Engineering
Dr. Don Giddens	Georgia Institute of Technology, Dean of the College of Engineering
Dr. Mary Good	University of Arkansas (Little Rock), Dean of the Donaghey College of Information Science and Systems Engineering
Dr. Jack Hansen	Florida Institute for Human and Machine Cognition, Associate Director
Dr. John Harwood	Pennsylvania State University, Senior Director of Teaching and Learning with Technology, and Associate Professor of Information Sciences and Technology
Dr. Ron Hira*	IEEE-USA, Vice President of Career Activities Rochester Institute of Technology, Assistant Professor of Public Policy
Dr. Susan Hockfield*	MIT, President
Mr. William Howard	CDM, Chief Technical Officer and Executive Vice President for Quality and Client Service
Dr. Leah Jamieson	Purdue University, Associate Dean of Engineering for Undergraduate Education, and Professor of Electrical and Computer Engineering
Ms. Gloria Jeff*	Michigan Department of Transportation, Director
Dr. Gretchen Kalonji	University of Washington, Professor of Materials Science and Engineering
Dr. Linda Katehi*	Purdue University, Dean of Engineering
Dr. Richard Larson	MIT, Professor of Civil and Environmental Engineering and Engineering Systems
Dr. Tod Laursen	Duke University, Senior Associate Dean for Education, Pratt School of Engineering

Dr. Thomas Litzinger	Pennsylvania State University, Professor of Mechanical Engineering, and Director of the Leonhard Center for the Enhancement of Engineering Education
Dr. Thomas Magnanti*	MIT, Dean of the School of Engineering
Dr. John H. Marburger III*	Office of Science and Technology Policy, Director, and Science Advisor to the President of the United States
Mr. Ray Mellado	HENAAC, Chair and CEO
Mr. James Miller*	Cisco, Vice President of Manufacturing Operations
Dr. Richard Miller*	Franklin W. Olin College of Engineering, President
Dr. Wendy Newstetter	Georgia Tech, Director of Learning Sciences Research in the Department of Biomedical Engineering
Dr. Peter Pao*	Raytheon Company, Corporate Vice President and Chief Technology Officer
Dr. Rassa Rassai	Northern Virginia Community College System, Professor of Engineering/ Electronics
Dr. Joseph Sussman	MIT, Professor of Civil and Environmental Engineering and Engineering Systems
Dr. Sophie Vandebroek	Xerox Corporation, Chief Engineer and Vice President of the Xerox Engineering Center

* Speaker/Moderator

APPENDIX II. WORKSHOP - MOVING FORWARD TO IMPROVE ENGINEERING EDUCATION.
GEORGIA INSTITUTE OF TECHNOLOGY, NOVEMBER 7, 2006

Summary Notes

The following summary notes of the discussions and presentations reflect the views and opinions of the participants and not necessarily the positions of the National Science Board.

Introduction

This chapter summarizes the key themes and suggestions resulting from the National Science Board (the Board)- sponsored workshop *Moving Forward to Improve Engineering Education*, held November 7, 2006 at the Georgia Institute of Technology (Georgia Tech). The 2006 Workshop followed the *initial* workshop held October 20, 2006 at the Massachusetts Institute of Technology *(*MIT*)*, entitled: *Engineering Workforce Issues and Engineering Education: What are the Linkages?* The 2006 Workshop engaged leading deans of engineering in elaborating on the issues and conclusions raised at MIT, and examined how programs and activities at the National Science Foundation (NSF) may specifically address the issues raised by the National Academy of Engineering (NAE) report, *Educating the Engineer of 2020*.[2]

The special focus of the second workshop on the role of NSF for engineering education addressed pressing issues in engineering education that included:

- Retention rates for students who enter universities to study engineering.
- Educational experience for engineering students that will prepare more well-rounded graduates who have skill sets to compete in a "flat world" economy.
- What the data on international engineering schools and graduates mean for American engineering programs, research, and careers, and how NSF can further develop cooperative research and joint programs between American and international universities.
- What NSF can contribute to an understanding of the social perceptions, the societal trends, and industrial practices that may discourage students from pursuing engineering.
- The role of the Foundation in preparing the faculty of the future, particularly given the need to educate engineering students more broadly and to address the challenges caused by rapid changes in technology.
- How the Foundation can facilitate the perspectives of industry in engineering education and encourage the support of industry for innovative approaches to engineering education.

To prepare for this second Workshop, Board Members met with NAE President, Dr. William A. Wulf, in August 2006 to discuss and understand NAE plans for following up on the Engineer of 2020 activity. The NAE will focus on the hard issues of curriculum reform across engineering education. It was agreed that the NSB can contribute with the NAE to a "tipping point" in engineering education by focusing on complimentary issues. Board Members also met with the leadership of the NSF Engineering Directorate in August to discuss NSF's current and potential role in engineering education and to consider possible issues for discussion at the workshop.

Key Themes

Several key themes emerged at the Georgia Tech workshop. First, NSF has made substantial investment in programs to improve engineering education over the last 2 decades, but these investments have been small relative to the overall scope of the challenge. There have been many successful programs and substantial local change, but not systematic change.

Second, retention of students in engineering, especially in the first year, is a critical issue. Many groups are analyzing the issue and trying to address it. It is necessary to approach the retention issue as a systems problem. That is, one has to include the pipeline as well as the cultural perceptions of engineering, from scientists to the public. The pre-college preparation of entering students affects retention, as does the difficulty of the engineering curriculum relative to other academic tracks especially relative to the perceived value. Some steps to improve engineering retention in the first year may make it more difficult for students to transfer into engineering in their second or third year. Differential minority retention is a problem requiring special attention. There are no simple solutions and hard work is needed in several areas, but a variety of approaches and NSF programs can help.

Third, there are many examples of programs in engineering schools that make engineering more attractive to students and provide the broader education (including international experience, engineering practice, leadership, and service) that is needed. A barrier is the limited amount of faculty time and faculty culture. Adjustments in the reward system for faculty and other changes, such as greater involvement of industrial fellows or greater support staff, can help.

Fourth, the problems regarding the perception – or misperception – of engineering are very serious. The public perception of engineering must change in order to attract more students to engineering. Over the last 20 years, medicine and law have wrestled with changing the public attitudes toward these fields and in attracting women and underrepresented minorities to pursue degrees and careers in these fields. Similar changes need to occur in engineering, but much hard work will be required to convey the proper image and value of engineering to students, parents, guidance counselors, and others.

The following sections summarize the key points that were made with respect to each of these themes.

Summary of Key Points and Suggestions

Review of Previous and Current National Science Foundation Programs
NSF has supported a wide range of activities that contribute to engineering education. These include:

- Engineering Education Coalitions focused on broad reforms. Coalition members obtained local improvements, such as improved retention rates for first-year students and underrepresented groups. The coalitions, however, did not lead to the comprehensive and systematic new models for engineering reform that were expected.
- Engineering's department-level reform program supported departments to comprehensively reform curricula.
- Investments in curriculum improvement, with both planning and implementation grants.
- Engineering Research Centers, leading to many new degree programs and curricula, and to graduates whom companies recognize as better prepared for the practice of engineering.
- Model Institutions of Excellence focused on increasing the number of undergraduate minorities graduating in all areas of science, math, and engineering. The program has increased grade point averages (GPAs) and graduation rates of minority students.
- Centers for Teaching and Learning address learning and teaching across the fields of science, math, and engineering, and how to prepare future faculty.

- Graduate Fellowships and Traineeships include a variety of different fellowships and training programs, including Integrative Graduate Education and Research Traineeship (IGERT), Graduate Teaching Fellows in K-12 Education (GK-12), and Graduate Research Fellowships.
- Research Experiences for Undergraduates (REU) encourages U.S. students to pursue doctoral studies by engaging them in research activities as undergraduates. Studies have shown that REU experiences increase interest in science, technology, engineering, and mathematics (STEM) careers.
- Research Experiences of Teachers (RET) supports K-12 teachers and community college faculty to be involved in research activities at universities. Studies indicate that RET experiences increase teacher motivation and confidence in teaching math and science, and that teachers gain a better understanding of engineering.

In summary, NSF has made significant investments in activities related to engineering education, and many of these programs show positive results and change at institutions. However, the complexity of the system does not allow for quick and easy solutions. Still, greater success is needed to increase U.S. citizen participation in engineering studies and careers.

Retention

There was widespread agreement among workshop participants that retention of engineering students is a key issue. There is substantial attrition in engineering, especially in the first year. Most of the students who leave engineering continue in college but change their major. Attrition is higher among women and traditionally underrepresented minorities.

Reasons Why Engineering Students Leave

Some of the students who leave engineering are among the best students, with high grades. That is, it is not the case in general that students who leave engineering could not have made it. Those with high verbal SATs are more likely to leave than those with lower verbal scores, perhaps because they have more options. Also, women with good grades drop out at a higher rate than men. There are many reasons why students drop out of engineering. Some of the key reasons discussed at the workshop are:

- Poor teaching – which when combined with a lack of exposure to engineering in the first and second years can lead to discouragement and departure from engineering.
- Poor performance in the first math courses.
- Poor advising from faculty who see their role as weeding people out of engineering.
- Lack of connection between what students study and what they perceive as exciting engineering practice.
- Fear that engineering jobs may disappear in the United States due to offshore outsourcing.
- Perception that friends in other majors are having easier classes and more fun.
- Coursework too restrictive for students' more varied interests.
- Lack of a comfortable social environment in engineering classes.
- Perception of engineering as a competitive and uncaring field.

- Lack of role models, especially for women and underrepresented minority engineers. Many students see women and underrepresented minority faculty as overworked because of the challenges they face as pioneers. Thus, students do not find models of what they want to be.
- Rising cost of education – tuition, fees, room and board – which has a disproportionate impact on students from low income families.
- A feeling of isolation from the rest of the university due to amount of the workload. Engineering students without cross-disciplinary education may not see themselves as part of the university.

Participants in discussion of these issues recognized the need for caution in interpreting the reasons that students give for leaving engineering. For example, poor math performance has diverse causes. Some students are under- prepared when they enter college. Others are rusty in their basic math skills because they take advanced math earlier in high school, and may not take math in their last year of high school. Some students are overconfident, and are either placed in a college math course that is too advanced or skip classes because they think they know the math. Students may not be willing to admit they are leaving because they do not have the talent for engineering or do not want to work hard. Students do not perceive the value of working hard in engineering classes.

Programs That Improve Retention

Getting students through the first year is critical. To do this, it is important to approach retention as a systems problem. Addressing the issue requires starting with students before they come to campus and then engaging the whole university.

A major strategy for improving retention is to design a curriculum that offers the excitement and relevance of engineering early in the student's experience and, therefore, accelerates the student's ability to identify with the profession of engineering. There are many successful approaches:

- Moving design and systems courses and practical engineering laboratories earlier in the curriculum rather than waiting until the junior or senior year, by which time many students have already left engineering. This of course means changes in the traditional cumulative practice of engineering education.
- Offering a socially relevant curriculum that emphasizes service learning; a strategy especially attractive to underrepresented groups and women.
- Providing a first-year seminar on what engineering is, with examples from each discipline and discussions of engineering problems and applications led by invited engineering practitioners.
- Having a weekly symposium with speakers from industry.
- Inviting industry partners to work on team projects.
- Developing multi-year team-based projects that involve participants from other disciplines (sciences, humanities, social sciences).
- Working with math and physics professors to add engineering context to math and physics courses.
- Introducing undergraduate research experience as early as possible to students.

- Financial aid for students who have demonstrated need.
- Cooperative education.
- Intervention programs that address academic preparation and performance issues.

To address the problems associated with poor math preparation, it is important to do early assessment in math courses and to make available extra resources for students who need them – the University of Texas, El Paso (UTEP) was mentioned as a model, including math diagnostics, remediation, and clustering students in classes and study groups. It was noted that a successful strategy in computer programming separates students with no prior programming background from those with extensive programming background.

Workshop participants emphasized the importance of working with other units in the university to improve the educational and social environment for engineering. The sciences are responsible for teaching many of the fundamental courses in the engineering curriculum; interaction between faculty in engineering and faculty in the arts and social sciences can help put engineering in a social or business context. In addition, it is important that engineering students do not become isolated from the rest of the university. They need exposure to different disciplines to help them decide their major and career path or to give them the necessary career clarity.

To address issues of affordability, more need-based scholarships were considered necessary. Moreover, universities should develop and maintain good partnerships with community colleges to ensure their courses provide the right preparation for engineering. Two-year colleges provide a pathway for less affluent students to enter engineering and can help increase minority participation in engineering. Transfer students from community colleges have a good record of completing degrees after transferring to an engineering school.

Flexibility in the curriculum is important for people to transfer into engineering after the freshman year. It was cautioned that if more engineering courses are moved into the first and second years of a university engineering program, it might be more difficult for transferring students, either from community colleges or from other majors.

Diverse role models and mentoring have been effective in improving retention. Student organizations can play a part by bringing in role models as speakers or mentors. Peer-to-peer advising (pairing upper division students with new students) also has been especially helpful.

Research experiences too can help improve retention; it would be beneficial to provide more exposure to research in the earlier years. Research experiences expose students to the challenge of solving ambiguous problems in a setting where they interact with a faculty member.

The Educational Experience of Engineering Students

Workshop participants described a wide range of programs that enhance the educational experiences of students, especially with regard to preparing students for the "flat world paradigm" in which the research, design, and production of goods and services are often sourced around the world in response to market forces. These programs are intended to prepare engineering students to be aware of the world, technically grounded, creative, innovative, and versatile; to develop leadership skills; and to work effectively in teams.

Approaches

Since traditional curricula are so full, it is difficult to add traditional courses to the curriculum. Thus it may be necessary instead to integrate experiences throughout the curriculum and extracurricular activities. Experiential learning can take place in many forms (in the curriculum, non-curricular activities, coop programs, and internships); can motivate student learning in the fundamentals; and can create opportunities to bring design and analysis together, rather than segregating design and analysis. There is also a need to create long-term experiences, such as projects that span years and make connections between different skills and applications. Students working on open-ended projects under expert mentoring will learn unanticipated things. Another topic is how to modify the educational experience to provide global educational opportunities.

Participants identified a range of programs or extracurricular activities to provide international experiences:

- Study abroad programs, which are increasingly recognized as valuable for engineering.
- Classes with an international focus, such as an "engineering in China" seminar.
- A global design course, in which students interact on teams with students from other countries for a semester.
- A course on innovative design, entrepreneurship, and leadership, co-taught by industry practitioners, and involving cross-national teams with international clients.
- A global engineering internship program that places students in other countries for the summer.

Some programs change the traditional paradigm and put design at the center of the curriculum and applied science around the edge, rather than vice versa. Design courses serve to identify gaps in student knowledge and in the curriculum. Other programs emphasize service learning, such as volunteer leadership. One example is an engineering leadership development minor. Other programs focus on entrepreneurship. Some schools have an engineering entrepreneurship minor while others have entrepreneurship embedded throughout the curriculum and extracurricular activities. Kauffman Foundation programs in entrepreneurship provide examples of weaving entrepreneurship throughout the entire curriculum rather than narrowly embedding it in the business school.

Research experiences for undergraduates, including freshmen and sophomores, was also recognized as an effective program for getting students to understand the joys of engineering while broadening their education. These experiences also bring the students into contact with the faculty.

Professional societies, such as student chapters of the Institute of Electrical and Electronics Engineers, Inc. (IEEE), and other student activities are also important. They can build on relations with industry to provide lecturers, mentors, internships, and award programs.

Challenges

Participants identified a number of challenges for reform of engineering education. One challenge is assessment – how does one measure the learning that occurs in nontraditional settings where each student's experience is different? For example, how does one assure that leadership training is effective? Engineering schools may need to adopt a portfolio approach to assessment, which is common in the arts but not in engineering.

Another challenge relates to accreditation and professional engineering (PE) licensing. It is not possible to teach everything that students need to learn. A key issue is: What do students need to know, and what can be pared back to make room for new material? How will accrediting and licensing bodies view such changes? Professional engineering exams may need to be modified.

Concern was expressed about proposals to require additional credit hours beyond the BS degree before an individual can take the PE exam, with potential negative impacts on attracting students to engineering if certification requires a master's degree.

Another challenge is the increased burden that many of the activities for enriching the engineering education experience would place on faculty. Faculty members have a finite amount of time, and if they devote more time to these kinds of activities, what can get dropped from their workload? The issue is the culture of academic engineering which emphasizes research, teaching, and service, in that order. Workshop participants offered several suggestions for addressing the issue of faculty time:

- Get industry involved to provide advisors on a pro bono basis.
- Use engineers recently retired from industry as "Professors of Practice."
- Use upper-class students for assistance in classes and extracurricular activities.
- Hire facilitators/assistants to complete administrative work that faculty do not need to do.
- Conduct a review of how faculty spend their time to see if time can be freed up.
- Submit proposals for funding to do innovative things.
- Ask the college administration to define goals for each department, but let the department decide how to meet the goals – by distributing research, teaching, and service activities among the faculty, considering faculty members' interests and priorities at different stages of their careers.

Engineering Perceptions

Common Perceptions of Engineering

Engineering loses students because they cannot see themselves as engineers. There are major problems with the way engineering is perceived. Survey data indicate that the public associates engineers with economic growth and defense, but less so with social concerns such as improving health, the quality of life, or the environment. Outside of academic institutions, engineers are commonly perceived as nerds without personal skills, doing narrowly focused jobs that are prone to being outsourced. A recent widely circulated Dilbert cartoon emphasized the notion that engineers are without social skill. In addition, students do not understand or appreciate the use of an engineering education as a springboard into other fields.

High school girls believe engineering is just for people who love math and science, and just for guys. They do not have an understanding of what engineering is or show an interest in the field. At historically black colleges and universities (HBCUs), students see engineering as unfriendly, hard, difficult to afford, and requiring extra preparation. They may not see a direct benefit to their community and may believe that they would have to leave their community to succeed in an engineering career.

Such perceptions attract to engineering the people who are good in math and science and are interested in "things" rather than people, but not people with creativity who like to work with others on teams and who want to contribute to solving social problems. The current perceptions of engineering make it difficult to attract women and minority students, in particular, to the field. It has been shown, however, that when students learn more about engineering, especially its historical contributions as well as its social relevance, they react more positively about the field.

Solutions

Engineering needs a marketing facelift. There is a need to craft messages that will attract students, parents, counselors, and teachers. The messages should emphasize that engineers work in teams, create jobs and value, are global innovators and leaders, and start companies like Intel, Yahoo!, and Google as well as Boeing and Hewlett Packard. Engineering graduates succeed in many fields, from investment banking to medicine, and engineers will play a role in addressing the world's biggest problems, from global warming to poverty to nuclear proliferation. Engineers create cool devices like Xboxes and iPods. Opportunities to learn from business schools and medical schools were acknowledged. Business schools have a fully integrated project-based learning program. Both medical schools and business schools have succeeded in transforming their culture from 100 percent male to 50:50 male/female.

The NAE is supporting the development of themes to communicate the role, importance, and career potential of engineering to a variety of audiences. Some sample themes being tested include:

- Limitless imagination – engineers imagine things and see possibilities.
- Freedom to explore – engineers are never bored; they are constantly being challenged.
- Ideas in action.
- Life involves engineering, from medical equipment to safer water to microchips.

The messages should be targeted to specific fields. Concerns about offshore outsourcing mostly affect computer science. Some fields of engineering, such as bioengineering and environmental engineering, already attract many women, whereas other fields have a dearth of female engineering students.

Workshop participants offered a variety of concrete suggestions that could help improve the image of engineering:

- Work with the Nobel Prize committee to create a Nobel Prize for engineering. While there are existing large prizes for engineering (such as the NAE's Charles Stark Draper Prize), none as yet have the visibility of the Nobel Prizes or the Oscars.
- Work with Fortune 500 CEOs who are engineering graduates to put together ad campaigns that will affect both perceptions of the engineering community and their company.

- Support industry-community-university partnerships that inform pre-college students and parents about engineering. K-12 schools are a particularly important venue for changing the views of students about engineering. The Research Experiences for Teachers (RET) program can contribute much to changing perceptions.
- Have college engineering students do internships in K-12 that will provide role models for K-12 kids.
- Teach engineering in high school. The high school engineering curriculum developed through the Infinity project at Southern Michigan University (http://vab.infinity-project.org/home.html) and coursework developed by the Boston Museum of Science have been successful. Some concern was expressed, though, that high school engineering classes may not meet the current science requirements for entrance to college engineering courses.
- Develop more movies (e.g., "October Sky") and TV shows to present engineering in a positive light. Shows like "Pimp My Ride" on MTV provide ways to talk about engineering to students.
- Find spokespersons to whom high school students can relate.

Suggestions for NSF

The workshop generated a large number of specific suggestions for NSF. Many of these involved support for continuing and expanding existing programs. These include:

- Substantially expand the REU program to make it more available to college freshmen and sophomores, as well as to community college and even high school students. (A few REU sites are already open to college freshmen and sophomores and to community college students.)
- Explore expanding REU to include support from additional Federal agencies. There is already a partnership with the Department of Defense (DoD), which supports REU Sites in DoD-relevant research areas. This could be expanded to the National Aeronautics and Space Administration (NASA), the Departments of Energy, Transportation, Agriculture, and others.
- Provide a path for REU students to get fellowships for graduate school. Tie this to strong mentoring in this direction.
- Expand the RET program. Provide opportunities to keep teachers connected to the program.
- Expand support for the GK-12 program.
- Expand the Integrative Graduate Education and Research Traineeship (IGERT) concept to the undergraduate level with a focus on integrative engineering.
- Build on IGERT to create a broader program "ISEAHSS" (Interdisciplinary Studies in Engineering, Arts, and Humanities and Social Sciences) to train well-rounded dynamic engineers who can understand not only the technology, but also the economic, political, and historical context for what they are learning.

- Continue the ADVANCE program (Increasing the Participation and Advancement of Women in Academic Science and Engineering Careers),[3] and create a similar program focused on developing the minority professoriate.
- Expand full-ride scholarships, which are important to all students but especially minority students.
- Continue to support engineering education research and experimentation, in order to create a scholarship of engineering education. NSF should also expand dissemination of engineering education best practices through a database and Web site that would provide details on successful programs and lessons learned.

There were also a variety of suggestions for new activities:

- NSF could examine and leverage the success of various design competition programs, such as the For Inspiration and Recognition of Science and Technology (FIRST) robotics competitions (www.usfirst.org) and the Sally Ride Science Toy Challenge (www.toychallenge.com). NSF could review these programs and determine if there is a role for NSF to help support them, expand them to allow broader participation, or fill gaps in the programs (such as making them relate to different types of engineering or appeal to different demographic groups).
- NSF could focus attention and programs on the complete U.S. engineering pipeline, K-12 through Ph.D., through research experiences, with an emphasis on helping students make the transition to the next stage. The community college-engineering school transition deserves special attention. The Facilitating Academic Careers in Engineering and Science (FACES) program at Georgia Tech, which supports students to continue to the next level, is a model.
- NSF could state national goals for engineering education, such as a desired number of engineering graduates, percentage of graduates in engineering, demographic mix, or retention and graduation rates. It was acknowledged, however, that this might be difficult to do and might invite blame to be put on NSF for engineering shortages or surpluses. However, NSF should be visible on this.
- The NSF Directorates of Education and Human Resources (EHR), Mathematics and Physical Sciences (MPS), and Engineering (ENG) could collaborate to introduce an application-oriented capstone math program with engineering connections for senior high school students.
- The Board Chairman should ask the Commission on 21st Century Education in STEM to address the role of engineering education in high school.
- NSF could sponsor workshops to heighten awareness, exchange ideas, encourage implementation, and share practices. Examples might include mentoring and how to incorporate non-technical skills, such as ethics, in technical courses. NSF could also sponsor workshops that draw together high school guidance counselors and math and science teachers to exchange information regarding the career messages they are providing to students. This allows high school counselors to be well-informed and provide better guidance.

- NSF should look to minority-serving institutions (MSI) for leadership in broadening participation. NSF should engage MSIs for research on recruitment, preparation, and retention.
- NSF could provide support for programs that fund cross-disciplinary education and seminars, such as symposia that would focus on the intersection of technology and the economy.
- NSF could support international programs in engineering schools by collecting data on universities with programs overseas, and perhaps providing support for students who otherwise would not have the resources to participate in such programs.
- NSF and industry can support educational programs to address the perceptions issues in engineering. These programs should deal with the realities of how industry handles jobs and career stability issues.

Summary and Conclusions

The workshop focused on the issues faced by deans of engineering in reforming engineering education, primarily in three areas: (1) retention rates in engineering undergraduate programs; (2) the educational experience of engineering students; and (3) the public perception of engineering.

Participants showed general agreement on the changing context of engineering and the challenges facing engineering education. There also seemed to be general agreement, or a least a lack of disagreement, on most of the points made regarding the benefits or effectiveness of most of the programs and solutions discussed. There was agreement on the importance of retention in the first year of college, but some disagreement on the reasons for high attrition from engineering. While students may state that they leave engineering because of poor teaching, participants noted that early courses are often taught in science and mathematics departments, rather than engineering. Some suggested that students may blame the teaching when the real reason may be that students do not have talent for engineering or do not want to work hard. Underlying disagreement about causes of attrition may be associated with disagreement about what skills and traits are necessary for engineers, e.g., are strength in math and science fundamental to success in engineering, or should students who are not as strong in math and science but are creative, socially engaged, and good communicators also be retained in engineering?

With regard to the educational experience of engineering students, workshop participants seemed to be in general agreement on the desirability of providing a broader engineering educational experience. Several alternative general approaches to this were discussed, including:

- Dropping some of the existing traditional engineering curriculum (e.g., Fourier transforms) in favor of material related to soft skills such as communication, leadership, and entrepreneurship, etc.. This would have to be done in concert with graduate schools and employers.
- Embedding social and global context, leadership, and other broader skills as themes throughout the curriculum.

- Developing extra skills through extracurricular activities, rather than through the curriculum.
- Completely revising the curriculum, with design and student engagement at the center.
- Adding courses to the curriculum to make, in effect, the master's degree become the professional degree.

Each approach was seen as having some drawbacks, and there was no consensus on a best approach. Revising the curriculum with design at the center and with a focus on student engagement was viewed as impractical for large schools. This approach, as well as adding extracurricular activities, was seen as putting a large burden on faculty time. While there seemed to be a benefit to having universities use different or multiple approaches, participants recognized that reforms must take into account standards set by accrediting and licensing organizations for engineers. With regard to a proposal to require a master's degree for professional certification, participants expressed great concern that the additional hurdle would result in a decline in student interest in engineering.

There seemed to be consensus on the problems with the way engineering is perceived. There also seemed to be widespread agreement on appropriate solutions, which involved developing and communicating new messages about the excitement and value of engineering to students, parents, counselors, and teachers. Ad campaigns, internship experiences for students and teachers, and the mass media could be helpful in spreading positive messages about and deepening public understanding of engineering. There was discussion about the need to target messages to focus on specific fields that are having greater difficulty than others in attracting underrepresented populations or because some of the concerns about engineering, such as offshore outsourcing, affect only specific fields.

Many suggestions were made to expand or add to NSF programs. Although participants did not prioritize proposals, expanding the REU and IGERT programs and extending to make these programs available to younger students, even in high school, received strong support, as well as modifying the RET program to provide a way to keep teachers connected to the program after they return to their schools. There also was strong support for expanding financial support for engineering students and continued engineering education research and experimentation, combined with a database and Web site that would be easy to access and provide details on successful programs and lessons learned. It was also recommended that NSF sponsor workshops to improve engineering education, including discipline-specific workshops on incorporating soft skills into technical coursework and to heighten awareness of the importance of mentoring, especially by students. NSF also could be effective in raising awareness of math and science teachers and guidance counselors about engineering education and careers to help change public perceptions. There also seemed to be wide support for NSF to explore ways to support or expand engineering design competitions as a way of exciting students about engineering. Participants acknowledged that NSF cannot have sufficient impact acting alone, and that the National Science Board might undertake a role to involve more Federal agencies that employ engineers to help expand successful programs.

In sum, participants agreed on the need for engineering education reform and on very broad cooperation to be successful. The NSF was seen in a supportive role, through leadership in the Federal sector, increased development and dissemination of research-based scholarship on engineering education, expanded student financial support, support for programs that involve students and teachers in research and in broader experiences outside the scope of traditional disciplinary education, and outreach activities to generate greater public and student understanding and excitement about engineering.

Georgia Institute of Technology

Monday, November 6, 2006
    7:00 p.m.   Reception and Registration

Tuesday, November 7, 2006
    8:30 a.m.   **Welcome**
                      Steven C. Beering, Chairman, National Science Board
                      G. Wayne Clough, President, Georgia Institute of Technology
    8:45 a.m.   **Overview of the Workshop and Self-Introductions of Participants**
                      Michael P. Crosby, Executive Officer, National Science Board
    9:00 a.m.   **Summary of the October 20, 2006 National Science Board sponsored workshop, Engineering Workforce Issues and Engineering Education: What are the Linkages?**
                      Daniel E. Hastings, National Science Board
    9:15 a.m.   **Review of Previous and Current National Science Foundation (NSF) Programs and Activities in Engineering Education**
                      Richard O. Buckius, National Science Foundation
    9:30 a.m.   **Panel 1: Retention Rates in Engineering Undergraduate Programs**
                      Moderator: Dr. Clough, National Science Board
                      What is the role of the Foundation in understanding the issues associated with retention of students who enter universities to study engineering and in developing approaches to address these challenges?
                      Ilesanmi Adesida Esin Gulari
                      University of Illinois at Urbana-Champaign Clemson University
                      Kristina M. Johnson Duke University
    10:00 a.m.   Group Discussion among Workshop Participants
    10:30 a.m.   Questions and Comments from the Audience
    10:45 a.m.   **Break**
    11:00 a.m.   **Panel 2: The Educational Experience of Engineering Students**
                      Moderator: Dr. Hastings, National Science Board
                      What is the best way to create an educational experience for an engineering student that will allow for more well rounded graduates who have skill sets that will allow them to compete in a "flat world" economy? How may co-op and internship programs, student professional societies, volunteer activities, student government, and/or study abroad programs contribute to the educational experience of engineering students? How may larger university

environments best leverage opportunities for engineering students? Is there a unique role for NSF in supporting the efforts of colleges and universities to enhance the educational experience of engineering students? How can larger university environments be used to leverage opportunities for engineering students?

Leah H. Jamieson	Richard Miller
Purdue University	Olin College of Engineering
David N. Wormley	
The Pennsylvania State University	

11:30 a.m.	Group Discussion among Workshop Participants
12:00 noon	Questions and Comments from the Audience
12:15 p.m.	**Lunch**
	Speaker: Bryan Moss, President, Gulfstream Aerospace 1:30 p.m.
	Panel 3: Engineering Perceptions
	Moderator: Louis J. Lanzerotti, National Science Board

What can NSF contribute to an understanding of the societal trends and industrial practices that may discourage students from pursuing engineering?

Don Giddens	Eric J. Sheppard
Georgia Tech	Hampton University
Belle Wei	
San Jose State University	

2:00 p.m.	Group Discussion among Workshop Participants
2:30 p.m.	Questions and Comments from the Audience
2:45 p.m.	**Break**
3:00 p.m.	**Breakout Sessions**
	Session Chairs: Drs. Clough, Hastings, and Lanzerotti
	How can NSF assist in moving the agenda forward on engineering education reform and address the issues of retention rates, educational experience, and engineering perceptions?
4:30 p.m.	**Reports From Breakout Groups**
4:45 p.m.	**Roundtable Discussion among Workshop Participants**
	Moderator: Dr. Hastings
5:15 p.m.	**Summary of Major Findings and Conclusions**

Invited Workshop Participants

Participant	Affiliation
	National Science Board
Dr. Steven C. Beering	NSB Chairman
Dr. G. Wayne Clough	NSB Member
Dr. Patricia D. Galloway	NSB Member
Dr. Daniel E. Hastings	NSB Member
Dr. Elizabeth Hoffman	NSB Member
Dr. Louis J. Lanzerotti	NSB Member

Dr. Michael P. Crosby	NSB Executive Officer
	National Science Foundation
Dr. Richard O. Buckius	NSF Assistant Director for Engineering
	Participants
Dr. Ilesanmi Adesida	University of Illinois at Urbana-Champaign, Dean, College of Engineering
Dr. William Baeslack III	The Ohio State University, Dean, College of Engineering
Dr. Joseph Barba	The City College of New York, Dean, The Grove School of Engineering
Dr. P. Barry Butler	The University of Iowa, Dean, College of Engineering
Dr. Steven L. Crouch	University of Minnesota, Dean, Institute of Technology
Dr. Eugene M. DeLoatch	Morgan State University, Dean, School of Engineering
Dr. Don Giddens	Georgia Institute of Technology, Dean, College of Engineering
Dr. Esin Gulari	Clemson University, Dean of Engineering and Science
Dr. Laura Huenneke	Northern Arizona University, Dean, College of Engineering and Natural Sciences
Dr. Leah H. Jamieson	Purdue University, John A. Edwardson Dean of Engineering
Dr. Kristina M. Johnson	Duke University, Professor and Dean, Pratt School of Engineering
Dr. Richard K. Miller	Olin College, President
Dr. David C. Munson, Jr.	University of Michigan, Robert J. Vlasic Dean of Engineering
Dr. Kevin J. Parker	University of Rochester, Dean, School of Engineering and Applied Sciences
Dr. Paul S. Peercy	University of Wisconsin-Madison, Dean, College of Engineering
Dr. James D. Plummer	Stanford University, Frederick Emmons Terman Dean of the School of Engineering
Dr. John R. Schuring	New Jersey Institute of Technology, Dean, Newark College of Engineering
Dr. Eric J. Sheppard	Hampton University, Dean, School of Engineering and Technology
Dr. Stephen W. Stafford	The University of Texas at El Paso, Dean, College of Engineering
Dr. Ben G. Streetman	The University of Texas at Austin, Professor and Dean, College of Engineering
Dr. Satish S. Upda	Michigan State University, Dean, College of Engineering
Dr. Belle W. Y. Wei	San Jose State University, Dean, College of Engineering
Dr. David N. Wormley	Pennsylvania State University, Dean of Engineering
	Lunch Speaker
Mr. Bryan Moss	President, Gulfstream Aerospace

APPENDIX III. CHARGE FOR WORKSHOP I

Purpose

An initial, single day NSB-sponsored workshop is proposed to focus on recent recommendations for changes in engineering education and implications for the engineering workforce. A foundation for workshop discussions will include the cross cutting issues in the recent National Academy of Engineering report, *The Engineer of 2020: Visions of Engineering in the New Century,* as well as the NSB reports that identified troublesome trends in the number of domestic engineering students, with potential impacts to U.S. preeminence in S&E based innovation and discovery. The major workshop objective is to move the national conversation on these issues forward in a productive way by calling attention to how engineering education must change in light of the changing workforce demographics and needs. The National Academy of Engineering (NAE), which sponsored the Engineer of 2020 study, has undertaken a Phase II study. The proposed NSB workshop would be in parallel to these NAE efforts. The NSB workshop would focus more substantially on the issues of the current and desired future engineering workforce in light of the Engineer of 2020 report.

Statutory Basis

NATIONAL SCIENCE BOARD (42 U. S. C. Section 1863) SEC. 4 (j) (2) The Board shall render to the President for submission to the Congress reports on specific, individual policy matters related to science and engineering and education in science and engineering, as the Board, the President, or the Congress determines the need for such reports.

Link to National or NSF Policy Objective

It is widely recognized that our economy, national security, and indeed our everyday lives are increasingly dependent on scientific and technical innovation. Changes on a global scale are rapidly occurring for engineering, and Federal leadership is needed to respond quickly and informatively. The Board has issued several reports expressing concern about long-term trends that affect the U.S. workforce capabilities in engineering, including the dependence on international students and workers; the declining interest on the part of U.S. citizens in engineering studies and careers; weakness in the K-12 science, technology, engineering, and mathematics education system; and demographic trends that are unfavorable to increasing citizen participation rates in these fields. Engineers are the largest component of workers with college degrees in S&E occupations, with 39 percent of all S&E occupations in 1999. Almost half of S&Es in the labor force with bachelors' degrees as their highest-level degree are engineers. This field therefore has a huge impact on our national capabilities for S&T and deserves special attention.

There is a current high level of attention to engineering education from a variety of sources that converge to make engineering education an especially timely topic for the Board to address. These include the recent release of the National Academy of Engineering report, *The Engineer of 2020: Visions of Engineering in the New Century*, which calls for reform in engineering education; the National Science Board reports on unfavorable trends affecting longterm U.S. workforce capabilities in science and engineering and the need to address these trends along all points of the education pipeline; the concern of U.S. industry and the public sector in engineering capabilities in the workforce; and the poor progress in broadening participation in engineering.

Logistics

The NSB Office will be the focal point for providing all aspects of Board support in this NSB activity; coordinating NSF, other agencies and institutions involvement; and utilization of one or more NSB Office contractual agreement(s) to assist with meeting logistics. NSB/EHR will recommend full Board approval of the appointment of an *ad hoc* Task Group of EHR to provide oversight for, and actively engage in, this activity.

An agenda and a comprehensive list of potential participants in the event will be developed with input from Board Members, NSF management, contacts in other agencies, and the broader S&T research and industry community. Invitees would include young recently graduated engineers, more experienced engineers, a range of employers (spanning the range of engineering disciplines), university thought leaders on engineering, and experts on engineering demographics.

Timing: Fall/Winter 2005

Workshop Topics: A workshop on the linkages between workforce issues and engineering education would involve a large range of topics, such as:

1. What are different scenarios for engineering workforce development in the U.S.? What are the differences among engineering fields?
2. How successful have we been in predicting the engineering workforce needs in the past and what has happened to the engineers when we got it wrong?
3. What are the implications of the different scenarios for engineering education?
4. What are the roles of the different stakeholders in the development of the engineering workforce, particularly the professional societies, universities, working engineers (of differing ages) and employers?
5. What is a typical demographic for an engineer today, and what will it become? How do we broaden participation?
6. The past and future role of international students and engineers in the U.S. engineering workforce.
7. The changing role of engineering education in preparing for engineering workforce needs for the future, including graduate education and lifelong learning as career shifts occur, and the idea that engineering education might be to prepare students more broadly for employment in the public, nonprofit, academic, and industry sectors.

8. How do we ensure that the best and the brightest students pursue engineering studies and careers, and that their education quality, content, and teaching are of the highest caliber?

Workshop Product: The final output from the meeting will be a concise set of Board approved recommendations that tie back to what universities (with employers) and NSF can affect, published in paper and electronic formats.

Audiences: In addition to the President, Congress, and NSF:

- Engineering deans/departments/schools
- ABET
- Engineering thought leaders

Leaders in technical industry and the public sector that employ engineers.

APPENDIX IV. WORKPLAN FOR WORKSHOP II

Workplan for a National Science Board Sponsored Workshop on Engineering Education November 7, 2006

With the support of the National Science Board (the Board) Committee on Education and Human Resources (EHR), the ad hoc group composed of Drs. G. Wayne Clough, Daniel E. Hastings, and Louis J. Lanzerotti have moved forward with plans for a second engineering education workshop to follow-up on the workshop held October 20, 2006 at MIT, entitled: Engineering Workforce Issues and Engineering Education: What are the Linkages? This follow-up workshop, scheduled for November 7, 2006 at Georgia Institute of Technology, will engage leading deans of engineering and elaborate on the issues raised at MIT, and examine how programs and activities at the National Science Foundation (NSF) may specifically address the issues raised by the National Academy of Engineering (NAE) Educating the Engineer of 2020 report.

NSF is an important leadership agency for engineering education and needs to respond to pressing issues, including retention rates, the educational experience of engineering students, international education and workforce issues, the current perception of engineering, the faculty of the future, and the perspective of industry.

- *Retention Rates:* What is the role of the Foundation in understanding the issues associated with retention of students who enter universities to study engineering and in developing approaches to address these challenges?
- *Educational Experience:* What is the best way to create an educational experience for an engineering student that will allow for more well rounded graduates who have skill sets that will allow them to compete in a "flat world" economy? How may co-op and internship programs, student professional societies, volunteer activities, student government, and/or study abroad programs contribute to the educational experience

of engineering students? Is there a unique role for NSF in supporting the efforts of colleges and universities to enhance the educational experience of engineering students?
- *International Perspective:* In a broad sense, what do the data on international engineering schools and graduates mean for American engineering programs, research, and careers? How can NSF further develop cooperative research and joint programs between American and international universities?
- *Engineering Perceptions:* What can NSF contribute to an understanding of the societal trends and industrial practices that may discourage students from pursuing engineering?
- *Engineering Faculty:* What is the role of the Foundation in preparing the faculty of the future, particularly given the need to educate engineering students more broadly and to address the challenges caused by rapid changes in technology?
- *Industrial Perspective:* How can the Foundation facilitate the consideration of the perspective of industry, and to encourage the support of industry, for innovative approaches to engineering education?

To prepare for this second activity, the *ad hoc* engineering education group will meet with NAE President, Dr. William A. Wulf, in August to discuss what the Academy plans to do following the Engineer of 2020 activity. The *ad hoc* group will also meet with the leadership of the NSF Engineering Directorate in an informal roundtable discussion in August to discuss NSF's current and potential role in engineering education and consider possible issues for discussion at the fall workshop.

After this second workshop, the engineering education group plans to submit a draft report of both workshops, which could potentially be submitted to the full Board to consider issuing some recommendations to guide engineering education reform.

Cover Captions and Credits

1. Computational Fluid Dynamics

This graphic depicts the turbulent instability dynamics of large fire plumes, which have been modeled by Paul DesJardin, Department of Mechanical and Aerospace Engineering, on the University at Buffalo's Center for Computational Research (CCR) computers using Large

Eddy Simulation techniques. The research was supported by an NSF Career Award to Professor DesJardin. Instability dynamics are responsible for the unsteady heat transfer in fire environments, which have been observed experimentally. The mesh superimposed on the bottom of the plume is the underlying computational grid utilized to carry out the calculation. An improved understanding of instability dynamics will result in more accurate predictions of fire intensity and growth.

Credit: Paul DesJardin, Department of Mechanical and Aerospace Engineering, University at Buffalo; visualization by Adam Koniak, CCR, University at Buffalo

2. Systems-on-a-Chip for Powerful Prostheses

A novel, mixed-signal system on a chip as a platform for implantable prosthetic devices, developed at the University of Southern California's Center for Biomimetic MicroElectronic Systems (BMES) Engineering Research Center (ERC). Researchers at BMES ERC, an NSF centers program, are developing entire platforms for a range of implantable devices that could one day restore vision to the blind, reanimate paralyzed limbs, and overcome certain cognitive impairments.

Credit: University of Southern California, BMES ERC

3. PIE Institute

A "Playful Invention and Exploration (PIE) Institute" Mindfest visitor constructs automata using gears, Legos, found materials, and a Cricket computer. The PIE Institute is a 3-year project designed to increase the capacity of museum educators and exhibitors to design and implement technology-integrated inquiry activities for the public. The collaborators include the San Francisco Exploratorium, the Massachusetts Institute of Technology Media Lab, the Science Museum of Minnesota, the Fort Worth Museum of Science and History, and the Explora Science Center and the Children's Museum of Albuquerque. Participating centers and museums will receive technology-rich activities, professional development institutes, online educator resources, and a handbook of pedagogical design principles for museum educators. The project builds upon prior NSF-supported work that developed the PIE Network, which among other things developed the "cricket," an inexpensive computer that makes informal learning inquiry activities more compelling.

Credit: Karen Wilkinson, Exploratorium, San Francisco

4. BMES REU Program

Research Experiences for Undergraduates 2004 participant, Brittney Perry, at the Biomimetic MicroElectronic Systems (MBES) Engineering Research Center (ERC), with mentor Ashish Ahuja, is shown working in Armand Tanguay's laboratory at the University of Southern California, Los Angeles. BMES ERC offers a summer program for undergraduate students funded by NSF that allows students to contribute to the development of novel biomimetic microelectronic systems based on fundamental principles of biology in one of three testbeds: retinal prosthesis, neuromuscular prosthesis, and cortical prosthesis. BMES ERC invites talented undergraduates to participate in active research projects and work alongside world-renowned researchers and students.

Credit: University of Southern California, BMES ERC

5. *Mixing of Fluorescent Dye in Stirred Tank Reactor*

A fluorescent dye injected into a tank of stirred liquid creates a pattern that resembles a green apple. The demonstration, conducted by Rutgers University researchers from the NSF Engineering Research Center on Structured Organic Composites (C-SOC) shows how liquids mix in a typical pharmaceutical manufacturing operation. Engineers will use such studies to help drug makers improve product uniformity. In this view, a four- blade impeller attached at the bottom of the vertical shaft, visible at the center of the image, draws fluid from above and creates outgoing ripples in the flow. Dye injected from above is rapidly advected around a toroidal shell, but penetrates slowly into the interior: this separation between the outside and the inside of mixing regions represents a bottleneck to processing and a challenge to the generation of reproducible product uniformity. The NSF Engineering Research Centers (ERC) program established C-SOC to study the nature of finely ground granular materials and other substances that form the core of drug tablets, processed foods, agricultural chemicals, and other "composite organic" products. In addition to improving the quality and consistency of such materials, the center will develop more consistent and cost-effective manufacturing techniques than methods based largely on trial and error.

Credit: M. M. Alvarez, T. Shinbrot, F. J. Muzzio, Rutgers University, Center for Structured Organic Composites

6. *"Torus II"*

This image, from the Eric J. Heller Gallery, is a three-dimensional image (plotted in two dimensions) of a four- dimensional object. When classical motion of particles is not chaotic, it is integrable; it can be confined to the surface of donut-shaped objects or "tori," which live in four or more dimensions. The torus appears to intersect itself, because the viewer pretends it exists in three dimensions. In the four-dimension space, it does not intersect. The surface of the torus was made partially transparent to reveal the structure within. Heller's work was included in the exhibit "Approaching Chaos," shown at NSF, as part of "The Art of Science Project."

Credit: Eric J. Heller, Harvard University

7. *Robotics Competition*

Students from "McKinley Robotics - Team Kika Mana" at President William McKinley High School in Honolulu, Hawaii. Pictured from left to right are: Iat Ieong (co-captain), Jinny Park (co-captain), Calvin Ing, and James Park. The robot is "Hot Lava," and was part of the 2007 Robotics Competition called "Rack 'n Roll."

Credit: National Science Board Office

In: U.S. Science, Technology, Engineering and Mathematics… ISBN: 978-1-61122-549-5
Editor: Catherine L. Grover © 2011 Nova Science Publishers, Inc.

Chapter 4

NATIONAL ACTION PLAN FOR ADDRESSING THE CRITICAL NEEDS OF THE U.S. SCIENCE, TECHNOLOGY, ENGINEERING AND MATHEMATICS EDUCATION SYSTEM

National Science Board, National Science Foundation

NATIONAL SCIENCE BOARD

Steven C. Beering, *Chairman,* President Emeritus, Purdue University, West Lafayette

Kathryn D. Sullivan, *Vice Chairman*, Director, Battelle Center for Mathematics and Science Education Policy, John Glenn School of Public Affairs, Ohio State University, Columbus

Mark R. Abbott, Dean and Professor, College of Oceanic and Atmospheric Sciences, Oregon State University **Dan E. Arvizu**, Director and Chief Executive, National Renewable Energy Laboratory, Golden, Colorado **Barry C. Barish**, Maxine and Ronald Linde Professor of Physics Emeritus and Director, LIGO Laboratory, California Institute of Technology

Camilla P. Benbow, Patricia and Rodes Hart Dean of Education and Human Development, Peabody College, Vanderbilt University

Ray M. Bowen, President Emeritus, Texas A&M University, College Station

John T. Bruer, President, The James S. McDonnell Foundation, St. Louis

G. Wayne Clough, President, Georgia Institute of Technology

Kelvin K. Droegemeier, Associate Vice President for Research, Regents' Professor of Meteorology and Weathernews Chair, University of Oklahoma, Norman

Kenneth M. Ford, Director and Chief Executive Officer, Institute for Human and Machine Cognition, Pensacola **Patricia D. Galloway**, Chief Executive Offi cer, The Nielsen-Wurster Group, Inc., Seattle

José-Marie Griffiths, Dean, School of Information and Library Science, University of North Carolina, Chapel Hill

Daniel Hastings, Dean for Undergraduate Education and Professor, Aeronautics & Astronautics and Engineering Systems, Massachusetts Institute of Technology

Karl Hess, Professor of Advanced Study Emeritus and Swanlund Chair, University of Illinois, Urbana-Champaign **Elizabeth Hoff man**, Executive Vice President and Provost, Iowa State University, Ames

Louis J. Lanzerotti, Distinguished Research Professor of Physics, Center for Solar-Terrestrial Research, New Jersey Institute of Technology

Alan Leshner, Chief Executive Officer and Executive Publisher, *Science*, American Association for the Advancement of Science, Washington, DC

Douglas D. Randall, Professor and Th omas Jefferson Fellow and Director, Interdisciplinary Plant Group, University of Missouri-Columbia

Arthur K. Reilly, Senior Director, Strategic Technology Policy, Cisco Systems, Inc., Ocean, New Jersey **Jon C. Strauss**, President Emeritus, Harvey Mudd College

Thomas N. Taylor, Roy A. Roberts Distinguished Professor, Department of Ecology and Evolutionary Biology, Curator of Paleobotany in the Natural History Museum and Biodiversity Research Center, The University of Kansas, Lawrence **Richard F. ~ompson**, Keck Professor of Psychology and Biological Sciences, University of Southern California

Jo Anne Vasquez, Director of Professional Development, Policy and Outreach, Center for Research on Education in Science, Mathematics, Engineering, and Technology, Arizona State University, Tempe

Member *ex officio*
Arden L. Bement, Jr., Director, National Science Foundation
~ ~ ~ ~ ~
Michael P. Crosby, Executive Officer, National Science Board, and National Science Board Offi ce Director

The National Science Board consists of 24 members plus the Director of the National Science Foundation. Appointed by the President, the Board serves as the policy-making body of the Foundation and provides advice to the President and Congress on matters of national science and engineering policy.

MEMORANDUM FROM THE CHAIRMAN
OF THE NATIONAL SCIENCE BOARD

Subject: *A National Action Plan for Addressing the Critical Needs of the U.S. Science, Technology, Engineering, and Mathematics Education System*

The National Science Board (Board) is pleased to present a national action plan to address pressing issues in U.S. science, technology, engineering, and mathematics (STEM) education. In this action plan the Board identifies priority actions that should be taken by all stakeholders, working together cooperatively, to achieve measurable improvements in the Nation's STEM education system.

The Board believes that the Nation is failing to meet the STEM education needs of U.S. students, with serious implications for our scientific and engineering workforce in the 21st century. Addressing this issue is absolutely essential for the continued economic success of the Nation and its national security. All American citizens must have the basic scientific, technological, and mathematical knowledge to make informed personal choices, to be educated voters, and to thrive in the increasingly technological global marketplace.

The Board, established by Congress in 1950, provides oversight for, and establishes the policies of, the National Science Foundation (NSF). It also serves as an independent body of advisors to the President and Congress on national policy issues related to science and engineering research and education.

The Board undertook this project in response to both of these responsibilities and with the urging of Congress. Some portions of the action plan are directed to NSF, and other portions to the Nation as a whole.

This action plan was developed by the Board over nearly 2 years, with input from leaders in STEM education at a series of Board-sponsored hearings, a Board-established advisory committee – the Commission on 21st Century Education in Science, Technology, Engineering, and Mathematics – and the findings of previous reports, panels, task forces, and commissions that have called for a major transformation of STEM education in the United States.

The Board formally unveiled this action plan at the U.S. Capitol Building with Members of Congress, stakeholder groups, and the public in attendance on October 3, 2007. Fittingly, this was on the eve of the 50th anniversary of the launch of the Soviet satellite Sputnik – an event that shocked the world and spurred the American people to take dramatic action to improve STEM research and education. Today we face an equally daunting challenge in the potential economic threats and opportunities posed by globalization. We urge all Americans to recommit to ensuring our STEM education system prepares our children to sustain U.S. preeminence in science and technology for the future.

Steven C. Beering
Chairman National Science Board

ACKNOWLEDGMENTS

The National Science Board (Board) thanks the many members of the science, technology, engineering, and mathematics (STEM) education, research, and policy communities who generously contributed their time and intellect to the development of this action plan. Those who contributed to this action plan are too numerous to mention individually. Participants in the Board-sponsored public Hearings on 21st Century Education in Science, Mathematics, and Technology are listed in Appendix C. Those who submitted written comments on a draft of the action plan during August 2007 are listed in Appendix G.

The Board is particularly grateful to the members of its Commission on 21st Century Education in Science, Technology, Engineering, and Mathematics (Commission) who provided valuable insight from a broad range of expertise and perspectives in STEM education. Commission members

Dr. Leon Lederman (Co-Chairman), Dr. Shirley Malcom (Co-Chairman), Dr. Jo Anne Vasquez (Vice-Chairman), The Honorable Nancy Kassebaum Baker, Dr. George Boggs, Mr. Ronald Bullock, Dr. Karen Symms Gallagher, Dr. James Gentile, Dr. Dudley Herschbach, Ms. María Alicia LópezFreeman, Dr. Maritza Macdonald, Mr. Timothy McCollum, Dr. Cindy Moss, Mr. Larry Prichard, and The Honorable Louis Stokes all devoted considerable time and intellectual energy to the work of the Commission. The Board recognizes and appreciates their invaluable contributions. Commission meeting participants and working group members are acknowledged within Appendix F.

Dr. Elizabeth Strickland, Sigma Xi-National Science Board Fellow, who spearheaded this project and served as Executive Secretary of the Commission deserves special recognition for her tireless and significant contributions to the formulation of this national action plan. Those staff also deserving recognition are: Ms. Sarah Cana, Ms. Clara Englert, Ms. Ann Ferrante, Ms. Jean Pomeroy,

Ms. Jennifer Richards, Ms. Cara Rooney, Ms. Tami Tamashiro, and Ms. Amy Hoang Wrona. The Board's Executive Director, Dr. Michael Crosby, provided leadership and guidance for all Board Office activities related to the effort.

We wish to acknowledge the special contributions of several former and current Board Members who provided essential leadership in the development of this action plan. Former Board Chairman Dr. Warren Washington led the launch of this Board activity and guided the establishment and empanelling of the Commission. Dr. Elizabeth Hoffman, Chairman of the Committee on Education and Human Resources (EHR), shepherded the plan through the EHR Committee in the final stages of its development. Finally, Dr. Jo Anne Vasquez served as the Board's champion and advocate for this effort in her capacity as Commission Vice-Chairman and Member of the Board. Her career as a STEM educator and teacher and as a leader in the preK-12 STEM education community provided her with the unique ability to contribute significantly to the core essence of this national action plan.

EXECUTIVE SUMMARY

The United States possesses the most innovative, technologically capable economy in the world, and yet its science, technology, engineering, and mathematics (STEM) education system is failing to ensure that *all* American students receive the skills and knowledge required for success in the 21st century workforce. The Nation faces two central challenges to constructing a strong, coordinated STEM education system:

- Ensuring coherence in STEM learning, and
- Ensuring an adequate supply of well-prepared and highly effective STEM teachers.

In order to direct attention to pressing issues and concerns in STEM education and to coordinate and enhance STEM education across local, State, and Federal programs, the National Science Board (Board) recommends the following:

- The U.S. Congress should pass, and the President should sign into law, an act chartering a new, independent, non-Federal *National Council for STEM Education* to coordinate and facilitate STEM programs and initiatives throughout the Nation, as well as to inform policymakers and the public on the state of STEM education in the United States.
- The President's *Office of Science and Technology Policy* should create a standing Committee on STEM Education within the National Science and Technology Council with the responsibility to coordinate all Federal STEM education programs.
- The *Department of Education* should create a new Assistant Secretary of Education position charged with coordinating the Department's efforts in STEM education and interacting with stakeholders outside the Department.
- The *National Science Foundation* should lead an effort to create a national road map to improve pre-kindergarten to college and beyond (P-16/P-20) STEM education, drawing on its national standing in the science and engineering communities and its expertise in science and engineering research and education.

In recognition of the lead role of local and state jurisdictions in the Nation's P-1 2 education system, the Board recommends that all stakeholders work together, using the National Council for STEM Education as the focal point, to provide *horizontal* coordination of STEM education among states by:

- Facilitating a strategy to define national STEM content guidelines that would outline the essential knowledge and skills needed at each grade level,
- Developing metrics to assess student performance that are aligned with national content guidelines,
- Ensuring that assessments under No Child Left Behind promote STEM learning, and
- Providing a forum to share and disseminate information on best practices in STEM teaching and learning.

The Board also recommends that all stakeholders promote *vertical* alignment of STEM education across grade levels – from pre-K through the first years of higher education by:

- Improving the linkage between high school and higher education and/or the workforce,
- Creating or strengthening STEM education-focused P-1 6 or P-20 councils in each state, and
- Encouraging alignment of STEM content throughout the P-1 2 education system.

Finally, the Board recommends actions that ensure students are taught by well-prepared and highly effective STEM teachers. These include strategies for increasing the number of such teachers and improving the quality of their preparation by:

- Developing strategies for compensating STEM teachers at market rates,
- Providing resources for the preparation of future STEM teachers,

- Increasing STEM teacher mobility between districts by creating national STEM teacher certification standards, and
- Preparing STEM teachers to teach STEM content effectively.

This action plan lays out a structure that will allow stakeholders from local, State, and Federal governments, as well as nongovernmental STEM education stakeholder groups, to work together to coordinate and enhance the Nation's ability to produce a numerate and scientifically and technologically literate society and to increase and improve the current STEM education workforce. Strategies for producing the next generation of innovators are not explicitly addressed in this action plan and will require subsequent study. A coherent system of STEM education is essential to the Nation's economy and well-being.

INTRODUCTION

American ingenuity, built on a foundation of science and engineering, has led our country to the forefront of innovation and discovery in the 19th and 20th centuries and has changed the basis of our economy. In the 21st century, scientific and technological innovations have become increasingly important as we face the benefits and challenges of both globalization and a knowledge-based economy. To succeed in this new information-based and highly technological society, all students need to develop their capabilities in STEM to levels much beyond what was considered acceptable in the past. A particular need exists for an increased emphasis on technology and engineering at all levels in our Nation's education system.

> To succeed in this new information-based and highly technological society, all students need to develop their capabilities in STEM to levels much beyond what was considered acceptable in the past.

Business and industry leaders, governors, policy makers, educators, higher education officials, and our national defense and security agencies have repeatedly stated the need for efforts to reform the teaching of STEM disciplines in the Nation so that the United States will continue to be competitive in the global, knowledge-based economy. Many reports have spoken to this growing crisis over the past 25 years. One of the more recent and most influential is the National Academies' report, *Rising Above the Gathering Storm*, which makes several recommendations for improvements in U.S. STEM teacher quality and student education based on their importance to global competitiveness.[1] Although the recommendations in past reports have been widely praised, their importance and implications have not been appropriately recognized and understood. As a consequence, they have not been fully implemented.

Although the National Science Board (Board) has long been concerned with quality P-20 education in STEM fields, this action plan has its genesis during the development of the 2006 *Science and Engineering Indicators*. The Board noted worrisome trends in STEM education and commented on these in the *Indicators* companion piece, *America's Pressing Challenge – Building a Stronger Foundation*. As a result of its observations and a request from Congress,[2] the Board began to consider developing a national action plan to address the Nation's need for improvements in STEM education. The Board held a series of hearings around the U.S. to gather expert testimony from leaders in STEM education in 2005 and 2006 (see Appendix C).[3] Subsequently, the Board established an advisory Commission on 21st Century Education in Science, Technology, Engineering, and Mathematics (Commission) to provide advice for a bold new action plan to implement the findings of previous reports, panels, task forces, and commissions that have called for a major transformation of STEM education in the United States (see Appendices D and E). The Commission provided its advice to the Board in March 2007 (included as Appendix F). In addition to the Commission's input and the testimony given at the Board's hearings, the Board itself also reviewed the findings of previous panels, task forces, and commissions.

The Board has prepared this action plan based on all the input described above with the goal to improve the Nation's STEM education system. The actions recommended here are not the only possible positive actions that could be taken, but rather are actions that the Board has determined to be priorities nationally. It has long been recognized that to develop the next generation of innovators, the Nation must provide a broad pool of students with the opportunity to acquire a basic understanding of STEM.[4] Thus, this action plan focuses on raising the base level of scientific, technological, and mathematical capacity of *all* students. In FY2008, the Board will begin an effort to focus on the additional specialized needs of preparing the next generation of innovators.

The recommendations in this national action plan, taken together, will be an important first step in the transformation of STEM teaching and learning in the United States. A coherent, coordinated system of STEM education provided by well-prepared and highly effective STEM teachers is essential to the future prosperity and security of our Nation.[5]

> Almost 30 percent of students in their first year of college are forced to take remedial science and math classes because they are not prepared to take college-level courses.

CONTEXT OF THE ACTION PLAN

Current Status of the U.S. STEM Education System

Within the current education system, U.S. students are not obtaining the STEM knowledge they need to succeed. As *Rising Above the Gathering Storm* notes, "The danger exists that Americans may not know enough about science, technology, or mathematics to contribute significantly to, or fully benefit from, the knowledge-based economy that is already taking shape around us."[6] Almost 30 percent of students in their first year of college are forced to take remedial science and math classes because they are not prepared to take college-level courses.[7] International benchmarks, such as the Programme for International Student Assessment (PISA) test,[8] show that U.S. students are behind students in other industrialized nations in STEM critical thinking skills (see Table).

Table. United States Falls Behind Many OECD* Countries in Science Literacy of 15 Year Olds

Country	Score	Rank
Finland	548	1
Japan	548	1
South Korea	538	3
Australia	525	4
Netherlands	524	5
Czech Republic	523	6
New Zealand	521	7
Canada	519	8
Switzerland	513	9
France	511	10
Belgium	509	11
Sweden	506	12
Ireland	505	13
Hungary	503	13
Germany	502	15
Poland	498	16
Iceland	495	17
Slovak Republic	495	17
United States	**491**	**19**
Austria	491	19
Italy	487	21
Spain	487	21
Norway	484	23
Luxembourg	483	24
Greece	481	25
Denmark	475	26
Portugal	468	27
Turkey	434	28
Mexico	405	29

Source: M. Lemke, A. Sen, E. Pahlke, L. Partelow, D. Miller, T. Williams, D. Kastberg, and L. Jocelyn, *International Outcomes of Learning in Mathematics Literacy and Problem Solving: PISA 2003 Results From the U.S. Perspective: Highlights*. U.S. Department of Education, Center for Education Statistics

* OECD refers to Organisation for Economic Co-operation and Development

In order to provide American students with the STEM knowledge they require, two challenges must be addressed. First, current STEM education in the Nation is not coordinated horizontally among states nor aligned vertically through grade levels. *Horizontally,* STEM content standards and the sequence in which content is taught vary greatly among school systems, as do the expectations for and indicators of success. Because states have no consensus on what key concepts students should master and should be included in the curriculum at a certain grade level or within a specific content area, textbooks often cover too many topics at too superficial a level,[9] rather than focus on a few key topics in-depth. In our highly mobile society, students who move from one school system to another often miss exposure to critical fundamental concepts in one school and never have a subsequent opportunity to master those concepts.[10] Likewise, state assessments of student achievement vary widely.[11] *Vertically,* little or no alignment of STEM learning occurs during students' progression through school. Students do not always obtain mastery of key concepts at the elementary and middle school levels, thus limiting academic success at the high school level. In addition, many high schools provide a curriculum that is uninspiring, poorly aligned, outdated, lacking in rigor, and fraught with low expectations. The net result is that almost 30 percent of high school graduates enter college unprepared for first-year coursework[12] or arrive at the workplace without the mathematical, scientific, and technical skills that employers require.[13,14] Today, possessing a high school diploma too often does not signify that a young person will be able to thrive in the global, knowledge-based economy.

Second, the Nation faces a chronic shortage of qualified teachers who are adequately prepared and supported to teach STEM disciplines eff ectively.[15] Local school systems encounter many barriers to recruiting and retaining high-quality STEM teachers. STEM-trained professionals often do not choose to teach, and too few educators acquire STEM training.[16] Teachers, particularly at the elementary and middle school levels, often do not acquire sufficient STEM content knowledge or skills for teaching this content during their pre-service preparation. Once on the job, many teachers neither receive adequate support during the critical first few years in the classroom, nor adequate mentoring and/or continued professional development opportunities. For STEM-trained professionals, the current job market offers non-teaching career opportunities with substantially higher salaries[17] and often better working conditions than those professionals would receive in teaching careers. Lack of flexibility in teacher compensation restricts[18] how local education agencies compete for and retain qualifi ed candidates.[19] The problem of recruiting and retaining high-quality

STEM teachers is often compounded by a lack of adequate facilities and resources needed for effective teaching.

Direct and Indirect Stakeholder Involvement and Coordination

In the United States, education is primarily a local and state responsibility. More than 14,000 local school boards[20] determine local education policy across the Nation, and state governors play a central role in overseeing the education systems in their states. Th erefore, any effective strategy for nationwide improvements to STEM education must balance local and state implementation of education policy with a nationally shared aspiration of world-class achievement for all students.

STEM education initiatives and programs presently reside in a variety of state and Federal agencies and the informal learning community, and span pre-K through institutions of higher education. Within the Federal Government alone at least a dozen offices, departments, and agencies contain STEM education programs (see Figure 1),[21] but no consistent Executive Branch forum coordinates these programs.[22] Furthermore, no single entity currently exists to provide critical coordination for STEM education among all those who have a direct role (such as local education agencies and school boards, state boards of education, state governors, and the Federal Government) and those who have an indirect role (such as institutions of higher education, business and industry, teacher unions, the informal STEM learning community, and private foundations).

Precedent for Embracing Change

Substantial improvements in STEM education in the Nation today will require a commitment of leadership at the local, state, and Federal levels and effective communication and coordination among these levels of government. This type of commitment and coordination is not unprecedented. Two key examples illustrate the way in which restructuring Federal policy can yield improvements in education.

The shock effect of the Soviet's successful launch of Sputnik in 1957 jarred the United States into taking appropriate actions to win the space race. Within a year, the National Aeronautics and Space Administration (NASA) was established by Congress to oversee the development of a successful U.S. space program, and the science advisory system to the President was established to provide continuous scientific and technical advice. Precedent-shattering Federal assistance to education was provided via the National Defense Education Act (NDEA) to the Department of Defense, the National Science Foundation (NSF), and other Federal agencies. New curricula in mathematics and science were researched, field-tested, and implemented, and a unified national movement to improve the teaching and learning of these core disciplines emerged. The number of qualified graduates in STEM fields surged.[23]

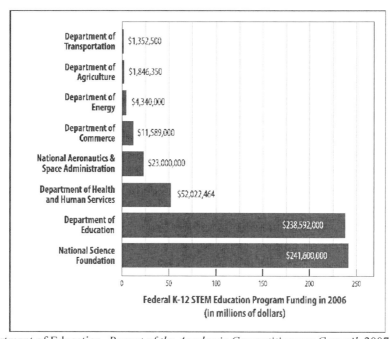

Source: Department of Education, *Report of the Academic Competitiveness Council*, 2007

Figure 1. Federal K-12 STEM Education Program Funding in 2006

Another instructive example is the transformation in the education of children with special needs. Since the early 1970s, substantial improvements have been made nationwide.[24] Th is transformation was prompted by changes in Federal policy and occurred down to the level of each local education agency. It was achieved through a combination of Federal legislation, court decrees, and Federal funding that required local and state adoption of Federal standards and guidelines.

Substantial improvements in STEM education in the Nation today will require the same type of commitment of leadership at the local, state, and Federal levels and eff ective communication and coordination among these levels of government. Currently, many of the Nation's governors are leading new state initiatives to address STEM education needs, and the Federal agencies are beginning to take stock of existing diverse and disparate Federal STEM education programs. Congress is drafting and passing numerous pieces of legislation related to STEM education. The window of national opportunity is open for implementing this bold new action plan to move STEM education into the 21st century – the time for all in the Nation to act together to make this a reality is now.

RECOMMENDATIONS

The Board is cognizant that local and state governments bear the ultimate responsibility in the Nation's system of public education. Its recommendations do not challenge the appropriateness of that responsibility. Rather, this national action plan is meant to support and enhance efforts by local and state governments to improve STEM education in their districts and states.[25] The Board is also aware of the difficulty of coordinating many diff erent parties to eff ect unified change. It is convinced, however, that coordination must occur among all stakeholders in order to ensure long-term improvements in STEM education and bring U.S. students to world-class levels.

> **Therefore, the Board makes the following two priority recommendations to the Nation. First, ensure coherence in the Nation's STEM education system, and second, ensure that students are taught by well-prepared and highly eff ective teachers.**

The Board feels both recommendations address significant issues and are of equal importance.

Priority Recommendation A: Ensure Coherence in the Nation's STEM Education System

To meet the Nation's demands for a numerate and technologically and scientifi cally literate workforce, the U.S. needs a nationally coherent STEM education system. Coherence in STEM education means coordination of what, when, and to whom STEM subjects are taught – both horizontally among states and vertically across grade levels from pre-K through the first years of college or vocational school. To ensure this coherence, the Board recommends the nationwide dissemination and implementation of best educational practices based on world-class research and national experience.

The impact of a coherent STEM education system would be widespread. Coordination of STEM content among states and across grade levels would ensure that classes focus on depth of understanding, not just coverage of topics. Thoughtfully sequenced classes would be structured to balance students' acquisition of content knowledge with their development of analytical, critical thinking, and problem-solving skills. They also would foster in students the ability to make connections among ideas and build a capacity for life-long learning.

The Board recommends the following specific actions to achieve coherence in STEM education:

A.1. Actions for Coordination of Key Stakeholders

The Board proposes a new infrastructure and set of activities to provide the necessary coordination among various stakeholders in order to achieve coherence in STEM education. The structural changes recommended in this section will not alone solve all the problems in STEM education. The proposed changes, however, are intended to increase communication and to bring together Federal and non-Federal parties in a forum where meaningful actions can be discussed and implemented. These parties should work together to implement the many excellent recommendations outlined in the Commission's report to the Board and in the many other reports written by expert panels.

1. The National Council for STEM Education

The Board recommends that Congress pass and the President sign into law an act chartering a new, independent, and non-Federal National Council for STEM Education (Council). The Council's central responsibilities would be to coordinate and facilitate STEM education initiatives across the Nation, as well as to inform policymakers and the public on the state of STEM education across the United States. As part of the Council's charter, Congress should require Federal STEM education programs[26] to be coordinated with state and local education agencies through the Council.

> The National Council for STEM Education's central responsibilities would be to coordinate and facilitate STEM education initiatives across the Nation, as well as to inform policymakers and the public on the state of STEM education across the United States.

Key local and state governmental agencies and non-governmental organizations would comprise the voting membership of the Council (see Figure 2). Non-voting seats would be reserved for the Federal Government through the National Science and Technology Council (NSTC) of the Office of Science and Technology Policy in the Executive Office of the President and congressional representatives. Congress would specify the representation of the Council's seats in its charter. The Board recommends that Congress appoint the initial members and co-chairs of the Council and that the initial Council members agree upon an orderly process to appoint subsequent members and co-chairs.

National Action Plan for Addressing the Critical Needs of the U.S. Science... 113

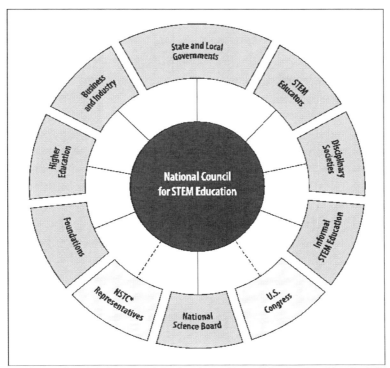

* NSTC refers to the National Science and Technology Council in the President's Offi ce of Science and Technology Policy

Figure 2. Potential Membership of the National Council for STEM Education

The Board recommends that the Council have approximately twenty-five members. Some seats should be permanently allocated to key stakeholder groups of such importance that they should always be represented on the Council. These seats would be filled by two State Governors, two chief state school officers, a representative of a local school board or government, two representatives from higher education, (including one representing community colleges), a practicing STEM classroom teacher, a school administrator, and a representative from the National Science Board.[27] The remaining seats should rotate among stakeholder groups and be filled by members such as STEM educators at all levels, informal STEM educators, and officials from local and state education and governmental organizations, higher education associations, business and industry, private foundations, and STEM disciplinary societies. The Board recommends that the initial co-chairs of the Council be a state governor and a chief state school officer. A list of potential Council members is provided in Appendix A.

The Board suggests that Congress provide funding for an initial period of 5 years for operating expenses (including a small professional staff) to determine the Council's effectiveness (see Appendix B). In the long term, funding for the Council's basic operations and special projects would transition to voluntary contributions from the Council's various stakeholder groups. A successful model for this funding scheme is the Transportation Research Board of the National Academies,[28] where states and other stakeholders have found this body valuable enough to allocate funding to support it.

The core mission of the Council would be to provide guidance as well as to coordinate and facilitate the flow of STEM education information among the various stakeholders.

The core mission of the Council would be to provide guidance as well as to coordinate and facilitate the flow of STEM education information among the various stakeholders. The Council would provide leadership by identifying critical deficiencies in the Nation's STEM education system and proposing strategies for its members to collaborate to address these shortcomings. It would also serve as a primary focal point for Federal agencies to improve their coordination with local and state school systems, per a key recommendation in the report of the Academic Competitiveness Council (ACC).[29] The Council could provide an effective forum for working towards the National Governors Association's goal for states to "identify best practices in STEM education and bring them to scale."[30] In line with this general framework, the Council would:

- Issue a regular report that highlights the status of STEM education in states and the Nation. This could complement the Board's biennial *Science and Engineering Indicators*.
- Evaluate progress toward the goals laid out in this action plan on a regular and sustained basis, including the effectiveness of the NSTC Committee on STEM Education's efforts to coordinate Federal K-12 STEM education programs.
- Serve as a national resource by disseminating to local and state education agencies information on research on teaching and learning, including best educational practices and models for effective STEM teaching and learning, P-1 6 alignment of STEM education, and scaling up of effective, proven programs.
- Coordinate and assist with the development of national STEM content guidelines for pre-K-12. These would draw on the considerable work already accomplished by various groups and disciplinary societies.
- Work with the Department of Education and the National Assessment Governing Board (NAGB)[31] to ensure that the National Assessment of Educational Progress (NAEP)[32] is aligned with the new STEM content guidelines to be developed.
- Help states establish or strengthen existing P-16 or P-20 councils[33] and serve as a technical resource center for P-16/P-20 councils.
- Work with all stakeholders to address: (a) the removal of barriers that exist throughout the Nation to compensating STEM educators at market rates; and (b) the removal of barriers imposed by school district wage guides on the movement of STEM educators between districts both within and across state borders.
- Work to coordinate the development of national standards for STEM teacher certification.
- Propose models for effective teacher professional development.

The Council might also consider developing programs to:

- Coordinate the development and maintenance of integrated data management systems to consolidate and share information among states on STEM educational practices, research, and outcomes, including, for example, student assessment results, teacher quality measures, and high school graduation requirements;

- Launch and sustain a public education initiative to raise awareness that STEM education is essential for the Nation's success – both domestically and globally;
- Assemble a database of opportunities for teachers interested in summer research in a STEM field in a government research laboratory, institution of higher education, or STEM-related business or industry; and
- Assemble a database of grants and other funding opportunities for STEM classroom resources to be used by teachers and local school districts.

2. Office of Science and Technology Policy – NSTC

The Board recommends that the President's Office of Science and Technology Policy[34] create a standing Committee on STEM Education within the National Science and Technology Council (NSTC)[35] with the responsibility of coordinating STEM education across all Federal agencies. Although the NSTC Committee on Science currently has a Subcommittee on Education and Workforce Development,[36] the critical importance of STEM education to the Nation merits attention at the full committee level. Both the Board's own Commission and the recent Academic Competitiveness Council report[37] from the Secretary of Education recommend that coordination of Federal agencies' STEM education efforts occur through the NSTC. Members of the NSTC Committee on STEM Education would include representatives from all Federal departments and agencies that play a role in STEM education, including the national laboratories. The Board recommends that the co-chairs of the Committee be representatives from the Department of Education and the National Science Foundation.

> Th e Board recommends that the President's Office of Science and Technology Policy create a standing Committee on STEM Education...with the responsibility of coordinating STEM education across all Federal agencies.

The NSTC Committee on STEM Education would:

- Coordinate among all Federal departments and agencies involved in STEM education research and programs to inventory and assess the effectiveness and coherence of Federally funded STEM education programs; and
- Represent all Federal agencies on the National Council for STEM Education and coordinate the STEM education efforts of the Federal agencies with local and state governments through the National Council for STEM Education.

3. The U.S. Department of Education

The Board recognizes the important role of the U.S. Department of Education in STEM education, particularly in providing funding for STEM education programs. Accordingly, the Board recommends that the Secretary of Education consider appointing an expert in STEM education as a new Assistant Secretary of Education or take other measures to ensure the outcomes described below. Th e office of this new Assistant Secretary could serve two functions. First, it could provide a central planning resource to strengthen existing and future STEM-related programs within the Department. Second, it could be a much-needed point of contact for states and other agencies across the Federal Government in eff orts to coordinate the Department's STEM education efforts with all stakeholders through the National Council for STEM Education. As part[38] of fulfilling these functions, the new Assistant Secretary for STEM Education could:

- Focus the Department of Education's efforts to use its funding capabilities to support quality, research-based STEM teacher professional development and to provide technical assistance to support STEM learning;
- Lead an effort for improvement and innovation in STEM-related education research and programs in all offices, bureaus, divisions, and centers within the Department of Education;
- Inform the Secretary of Education, policymakers, and STEM practitioners about the effectiveness of STEM-related education research and programs operated within the Department;
- Ensure that the Department of Education is coordinating with NSF and other agencies and groups to scale up peer-reviewed and research-based STEM education programs that have demonstrated effectiveness; and
- Marshal the resources of the Department of Education to support local and State governments and other stakeholders as they implement the recommendations for coherence in STEM education. Such support could include assistance with developing STEM content guidelines, aligning assessments with national STEM content guidelines, and aligning STEM learning across grade levels.

4. The National Science Foundation

Education is a core mission of the National Science Foundation (NSF), and NSF has exercised an important leadership role in STEM education at all levels for decades. Regarding STEM education at the K-12 level, the Board recommends that NSF focus its activities in three critical, interrelated areas: (1) research on learning and educational practice and the development of instructional materials; (2) development of human capital in STEM fields, including STEM teachers; and (3) improvement of public appreciation for and understanding of STEM (see Figure 3).

A clear framework for the NSF's role in STEM education is essential in order for NSF to set STEM education priorities and determine which activities merit a commitment of its resources. The development and funding of education programs should reflect the NSF's institutional priorities and not occur on a case-by-case basis. The Board believes that:

> NSF should develop a clear internal STEM education road map and an overarching set of priorities for its STEM education activities. NSF should report back to the Board with an interim report in early 2008 and a final STEM education road map for Board approval at the Board's May 2008 meeting. The goal of NSF should be to begin implementing these priority activities in FY2009 and fully incorporate the newly articulated STEM education road map priorities into its FY20 10 budget request.

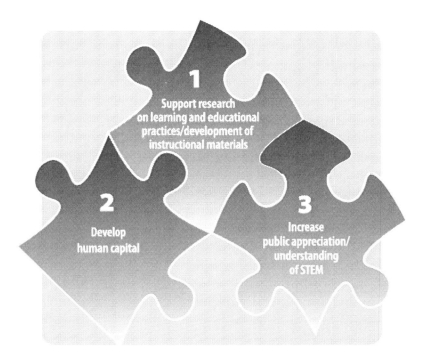

Figure 3. NSF K-12 Education Priorities

The following guidance can be the basis of this road map, which should be developed with the input of the Directorate for Education and Human Resources (EHR) Advisory Committee.

Since P-20 STEM education is a major institutional priority for NSF,[39] efforts to focus NSF's STEM education efforts should be agency-wide and not limited to the EHR Directorate.[40] The internal NSF STEM education road map should promote coherence of goals within the agency by addressing the cross-cutting areas between the EHR and Research and Related Activities (R&RA) Directorates[41] and among the scattered education activities in the R&RA Directorates and include all STEM disciplines within NSF.

Secondly, as NSF develops its institutional STEM priorities and internal STEM education road map, it should recognize that it occupies a unique position among the Federal agencies and within the STEM education community. NSF possesses a profound knowledge base in STEM disciplines, deep involvement with the scientifi c and engineering research communities, ongoing relationships with institutions of higher education, and a Congressional mandate to be involved in STEM education at all levels. No other Federal agency or organization is so well-situated to make informed contributions to the Nation's P-20 STEM education system, but NSF must be strategic in how it acts. NSF should leverage its assets in partnership with other Federal agencies, institutions of higher education, and the broader STEM education community in order to maximize its impact on P-20 student interest and achievement in STEM disciplines. The NSTC Committee on STEM Education and the National Council for STEM Education will provide contexts for forming and effectively utilizing partnerships; NSF should be an eager and proactive participant alongside other members of these bodies.

The NSF STEM education road map and strategic priorities should reflect the Foundation's responsibilities to:

(1) Support research on learning and educational practices and the development of instructional materials.

Among Federal agencies, NSF has the primary responsibility for research on teaching and learning in STEM disciplines. NSF currently performs many functions in STEM education, ranging from funding basic research on teaching, learning, and teacher education, to supporting applied research on the role and impact of educational innovations, to evaluating the implementation of new programs. NSF also plays a critical role in the development of instructional materials. The Board previously addressed the importance of quality instructional materials in its 1999 report, *Preparing Our Children*.[42]

> Among Federal agencies, NSF has the primary responsibility for research on teaching and learning in STEM disciplines.

As NSF is developing a road map for its support of research on learning and educational practices and the development of instructional materials, several issues are critical to consider. These include how educational research areas are identified, how the results of NSF-supported education research are disseminated and made available to guide large-scale implementation efforts, how STEM education programs are evaluated, and how the role of cyberinfrastructure can support STEM education.

First, as NSF sets strategic priorities for its research on learning and educational practices, it should consider the value of projects from both the education research community and the world of practice. While continuing to support research initiated within the education research community and maintaining its longstanding tradition of excellence, NSF should also promote innovation in STEM education by supporting research that responds to critical needs from the field. NSF should ensure that mechanisms are in place to collect input from educators and policymakers on grand challenges from the field and to ensure that its research programs are meeting real-world needs and expectations. In this way, NSF could work to provide solutions and tools for addressing the challenges that teachers face in classrooms every day across the Nation.

Among areas that NSF should consider including as part of its educational research portfolio are:

- Infrastructure that can support large-scale change – such as centers of excellence to research and develop new curricula, effective teaching strategies, and professional development models;
- Programs that systematically study the role of technology and cyber-enabled teaching in facilitating learning; and
- Research on entire education systems, including field research components and the synthesis of research results from the entire field.

In addition to setting its own research priorities, NSF should lead an effort to develop a national road map for research to improve P-20 STEM education. Importantly, NSF should collaborate with the Department of Education and others, including local and state entities, on the identification, development, and dissemination of best practices in STEM education.

Second, a critical challenge NSF must meet is to develop better mechanisms for informing STEM researchers, the STEM education community, and policymakers of the beneficial results flowing from STEM education research and STEM education programs at NSF.

NSF should create mechanisms to scale up proven, peer-reviewed, research-based innovations so that they have maximum impact. In addition, in an era when private and corporate foundations are increasing their interest and investments in STEM education programs, NSF should provide a research base for them so that they are able to develop their programs based on proven practices.

Third, in the context of the Academic Competitiveness Council (ACC) report on spending on STEM education programs across Federal agencies and the need for rigorous evaluation of these programs,[43] NSF should build on its base of technical expertise in evaluation to provide assistance to agencies in defining rigorous evaluation criteria and conducting evaluations. While the ACC report identified randomized controlled trials as the strongest study design for determining the effectiveness or impact of educational innovations, educational researchers also recognize as valid other ways to compare innovations with the status quo. Evaluation criteria should include how to determine the effectiveness of programs and their potential impact. In a limited-resource context, criteria for determining which programs should be funded and scaled up must consider not only whether programs do what they are intended to do, but whether the outcome is worthwhile. NSF should provide a research base to guide states and other Federal agencies as they make those decisions. It should also apply this strategic thinking to the evaluation of its own education programs and make use of external evaluators.

Fourth, a specific area in which NSF could make significant contributions is in the development of cyberinfrastructure, including computer gaming and simulations, to bolster STEM teaching and learning.[44] Cyber-enabled technologies could allow:

- The development, collection, distribution, and curation of digital content such as animations, simulations, text, video, data sets, lesson plans, and curricula. (NSF's National Science Digital Library (NSDL)[45] can play a role here, as can other consortial efforts, especially those focused on open source software and open access content);
- Access to virtual laboratory facilities that can bring general and specialized laboratory experiences into nearly any classroom – regardless of geographical location – via the internet;
- Collaborations among STEM students, teachers, researchers, and those designing and developing digital teaching and learning resources;
- Acquisition by students of knowledge and skills essential to success in the technology- rich future; and
- Active engagement of the current, internet-accustomed pre-K-12 student population in STEM.

Finally, NSF should take the lead in nurturing and developing a community of researchers – both social scientists and educational researchers – qualified to perform research on effective educational practices in order to generate the desired research base. NSF should also support those who develop instructional materials and learning resources.

(2) Develop human capital

NSF should continue to play a critical role in developing human capital in STEM fields. The science and engineering workforce includes pre-college STEM teachers as well as those working in research, industry, and higher education. Developing a strong STEM teaching force would significantly strengthen STEM education across the Nation and bolster the science and engineering workforce. NSF can play a significant role in strengthening the STEM teaching force because it has a unique relationship with and ability to effect large-scale change in the higher education system. NSF should consider support for the following types of programs to strengthen pre-college STEM teaching:

- Develop and fund effective programs for STEM teacher preparation. This could include expansion of the Robert Noyce Scholarship program,[46] which targets college students aspiring to teach STEM at the high school level.
- Use its strong connections with higher education to encourage and provide tools to university faculty and administrators who are committed to providing effective STEM teacher preparation programs.
- Develop programs that encourage student interest in STEM fields at all grade levels. One possibility would be to develop programs that provide STEM experiences for high school students similar to those offered by the Research Experiences for Undergraduates (REU) program.[47]
- Use its research base in learning and educational practice to develop and disseminate effective in-service teacher professional development model programs or modules that can be implemented on the large scale.
- Continue to support and grow programs that build bridges between P-12 and higher education, such as its highly successful model Math and Science Partnership (MSP) Program. The NSF's MSP program has demonstrated success in improving both student mathematics and science performance in K-12 schools and the willingness of higher education STEM faculty to work with K-12 teachers.[48] The Board is on record with its strong support for this program at NSF.[49] Consideration should be given to expanding the program to include technology and engineering partnerships as well as math and science.
- Support STEM professionals who wish to pursue research on teaching and learning in their respective STEM fields, perhaps in collaboration with education researchers with complementary and supporting interests and skills.
- Expand financial support for programs that have an established record of improving the performance and persistence of minority students pursuing STEM careers, including STEM teaching, such as the Louis Stokes Alliance for Minority Participation (LSAMP).[50]
- Partner with secondary schools, institutions of higher education, business and industry, and government agencies to strengthen the technical workforce.
- Ensure that STEM teachers and students are aware of and familiar with the full range of opportunities provided by cyber-enabled teaching, discovery, and learning.

(3) Increase public appreciation for and understanding of science, technology, engineering, and mathematics.

NSF should continue to develop and fund programs that increase public appreciation for and understanding of STEM. NSF should consider how its STEM outreach portfolio can be modified to provide more coherent public outreach on STEM and STEM education issues.

> NSF should continue to develop and fund programs that increase public appreciation for and understanding of STEM.

NSF also should consider ways in which it can promote partnerships both within NSF and the broader scientific community to increase public appreciation for and understanding of STEM. Within NSF, collaboration should be encouraged among all NSF directorates and offices, including, in particular, the Office of Legislative and Public Affairs (OLPA), the Directorate for EHR, and the Directorate for Social, Behavioral, and Economic Sciences (SBE), which performs research on effective communication.

As NSF is developing a road map for its public outreach efforts, it should consider directing resources toward several areas. These include:

- STEM programming in broadcast media. Television and movies are both important sources of information for the public on STEM fields;[51]
- Web-based resources and facilities; and
- Museums and informal STEM education learning environments. In the interest of coherence, NSF should make efforts to coordinate the activities of the informal STEM education community with the formal STEM education system. NSF should assist these institutions in developing materials and programs that enhance standard classroom curricula and provide rigorous professional development for teachers.

Furthermore, the Board has previously pointed out the role that the Board itself can play in promoting a public understanding of science and has called for each individual Board Member to become a "'personal ambassador' of fundamental science and engineering."[52] The Board should take on the responsibility not only of promoting public appreciation for and understanding of STEM fields and ground-breaking research in STEM fields, but also of highlighting the absolute importance of P-20 STEM education to the Nation's continued capacity for innovation and global competitiveness.

A.2. Actions for Horizontal Coordination and Coherence

The Board recommends increased coordination of STEM education among states via the actions described below. Although local education agencies and states bear the ultimate responsibility for implementation, the Board puts forth the following recommendations to benefit students in all states.

1. Develop National STEM Content Guidelines

The National Council for STEM Education should facilitate a strategy to define voluntary national STEM content guidelines.[53,54] These guidelines should define the essential knowledge and skills needed at each grade level for each STEM discipline and emphasize critical thinking skills. The effort should consider pre-existing guidelines[55] and strive to be clear, specific, and articulated between each grade level,[56] to incorporate the cumulative development across grade levels and connections between ideas, and to refl ect international comparisons. Participants in the guideline development process should include representatives from STEM disciplinary societies, professional STEM teacher organizations, state education agencies, and schools of education. Local education agencies and states should be encouraged to voluntarily align their own STEM content standards to these national guidelines. A model for the development and voluntary adoption of content guidelines is the National Council of Teachers of Mathematics (NCTM) curriculum focal points.[57,58] A further example of a group of states voluntarily adopting mathematics content standards that reflect international comparisons has been successfully facilitated by Achieve, Inc. and its American Diploma Project.[59] STEM content guidelines should allow flexibility for local and state education agencies to choose curricula that best meet local needs in adhering to these guidelines while still promoting very high-quality STEM education.

2. Align the Metrics used for Assessment of Student Performance with National STEM Content Guidelines

The National Council for STEM Education should work with those who develop and administer assessments to construct consensus-based metrics for assessing student performance that are aligned with the new national STEM content guidelines.[60]

International benchmarks should be taken into account in this eff ort.[61] Once national STEM content guidelines are developed, the National Assessment Governing Board (NAGB) should investigate alignment of the National Assessment of Educational Progress (NAEP) tests utilizing these guidelines.

3. Ensure that Assessments under No Child Left Behind Promote STEM Learning

The Board supports science being considered part of adequate yearly progress (AYP) as defined by No Child Left Behind (NCLB).[62] The Board recommends that NCLB eventually align its expectations of states with the STEM content guidelines discussed above and that states utilize assessments that measure the knowledge, critical-thinking skills, and problem-solving abilities required to meet real-life challenges.

4. Communicate Best Practices

The National Council for STEM Education should serve as a forum for NSF and the Department of Education to gather and review inputs based on research and practical experience and disseminate information on best practices in STEM teaching and learning. The Council should serve as a central reference bank for information about existing research on teaching and learning and models for scaling up effective educational and teacher professional development programs. In order to maximize its effectiveness, the Council should partner with other relevant organizations to disseminate information about best educational practices. For instance, the Council might partner with the National Governors Association (NGA) Center for Best Practices to support the NGA's current initiative to help states establish state Science, Technology, Engineering, and Math Centers.[63] These centers will engage in redesigning K-12 STEM education in order to enhance their states' economies and innovation capacity. Another potential partner might be the NSF's National Science Digital Library.[64]

STEM content guidelines should be designed so that as students move from one grade level to the next, they cumulatively build the foundational skills and knowledge needed to succeed at the next grade level.

A.3. Actions for Vertical Alignment and Coherence

The Board recommends that STEM education be provided to students in a coherent system that is vertically aligned across grade levels from pre-K through the first years of higher education. STEM content guidelines should be designed so that as students move from one grade level to the next, they cumulatively build the foundational skills and knowledge needed to succeed at the next grade level (see Figure 4). The Board recommends that the following actions be taken to enhance vertical alignment among all levels of STEM education.

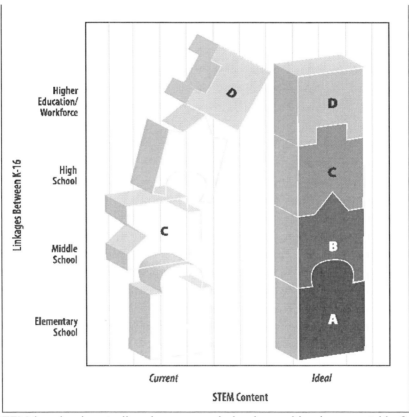

Currently STEM learning is not aligned among grade levels, resulting in an unstable foundation in STEM. Ideally, STEM learning should build cumulatively from one educational level to the next.

Figure 4. Vertical Integration a Key Component to Successful STEM Learning

1. Improve the Linkage between High School and Higher Education and/or the Workforce

All stakeholders should make a serious effort to minimize the current disconnect between high school graduation requirements and the skills and knowledge required to succeed in higher education and the workforce. The Board applauds efforts such as those of the American Diploma Project[65] and the National Governors Association Innovation America Initiative to "align state K-12 standards and assessments with postsecondary and workforce expectations for what high school graduates know and can do."[66] Career and technical education centers should be involved in these efforts.

2. Create or Strengthen Existing State P-16/P-20 Councils

The National Council for STEM Education should assist state governors in creating new or strengthening existing non-partisan and independent STEM education-focused P-16 or P20 councils in every state.[67] In some states, P-16/P-20 councils have already been effective

Priority Recommendation B: Ensure That Students Are Taught by Well-Prepared and Highly Effective STEM Teachers

Although this action plan has, thus far, concentrated on structural suggestions to ensure coherence in the Nation's STEM education system, the Board feels strongly that serious national attention must be focused on attracting, preparing, and retaining qualified and committed teaching candidates. STEM educators should be viewed as a valuable national resource, and the best and the brightest should be encouraged to consider pre-college STEM teaching as a profession.

> The Board feels strongly that serious national attention must be focused on attracting, preparing, and retaining qualified and committed teaching candidates.

The specific actions described below are meant to increase the number of STEM teachers entering the profession and ensure that thorough pre-service preparation is provided to STEM teachers. Equally, if not more importantly, however, are actions to support current STEM teachers so that they are able to be effective and are more likely to continue in the profession.[68] STEM educators should be provided with adequate mentoring during the critical first few years in the classroom,[69] proper instructional leadership and support while in the classroom, and opportunities for professional growth and enrichment of knowledge and skills. They also should have access to classroom resources that are required for effective STEM teaching and learning, including, for example, textbooks, supplies and equipment for laboratory and/or field experiences, and technology resources.

B.1. Actions for Increasing the Number of Well-Prepared and Highly Effective STEM Teachers in the Classroom

All possible promising strategies for increasing the number of well-prepared and highly effective STEM teachers should be utilized. All STEM stakeholders should work to increase the number of educators who acquire STEM training and the number of STEM- trained professionals who choose pre-college teaching as an occupation. Strategies include augmenting or increasing STEM teacher compensation for highly effective STEM teachers, lowering the barriers for the movement of STEM teachers from one school district or state to another, and providing incentives for the acquisition of STEM content knowledge by those who either aspire to become STEM teachers or are already pre-college teachers in other fields.

The Board recommends that the following actions be taken in order to increase the number of well-prepared and highly effective STEM teachers:

1. Provide Resources to Increase STEM Teacher Compensation

The Board is cognizant that teacher salaries are set and provided by local education agencies; however, local education agencies should be able to offer STEM teachers compensation more closely aligned with that available in other economic sectors.[70] Unless this issue is addressed, it will remain difficult to recruit an adequate number of qualified STEM teachers, particularly at the middle and secondary school levels. Stakeholders should work within the National Council for STEM Education to develop strategies for eliminating the barriers preventing local education agencies and states from increasing STEM teacher compensation. Beyond direct salary increases, stakeholders could consider incentives such as state or Federal tax credits for STEM teachers; pay supplements for increased student performance; pay supplements for obtaining specialized STEM teaching certifications that enhance teaching effectiveness; and augmentation of STEM teacher annual income through summer teacher professional development programs, research experiences, or applied STEM experiences.

2. Provide Resources for Future STEM Teacher Preparation

The National Council for STEM Education, in partnership with the Department of Education and NSF, should coordinate and disseminate information on models to attract and support talented students interested in STEM teaching careers. For example, the Council could promote the expansion of tuition and/or financial assistance programs for college students majoring in STEM content areas who commit to post-graduation careers in teaching. These students could complete a dual enrollment program enabling them to become certified STEM teachers with both content and pedagogy knowledge.[71] Similarly, the Department of Education, NSF, states, and other stakeholders could expand programs that provide loan forgiveness to students majoring in STEM content areas in return for service in teaching.[72]

3. Create and Endorse National STEM Teacher Certification Guidelines

The National Council for STEM Education should coordinate among its members – particularly state teacher credentialing agencies – to develop a mechanism to create and endorse national, rigorous STEM teacher certification guidelines for states to adopt voluntarily. These guidelines would facilitate a teacher's ability to continue teaching when they move from one district or state to another, and they would clarify the requirements for bringing STEM professionals from other occupations into pre-college teaching. Unlike the current National Board Certifi cation program,[73] the goal would not be to reward master teachers, but instead to expand the pool of potential STEM teachers, increase teacher mobility, and increase standards for all STEM teachers. The development of secondary school teacher certification guidelines in sub-specialties is also encouraged.

> STEM teachers should receive, at a minimum, STEM content knowledge that is aligned with what they are expected to teach.

B.2. Actions for Improving the Quality of STEM Teacher Preparation knowledge that is aligned with what they

All stakeholders and, in particular, teacher education programs at institutions of higher education, should make efforts to ensure that teachers are adequately prepared to teach STEM content. STEM teachers should receive, at a minimum, STEM content knowledge that is aligned with what they are expected to teach. Appropriate STEM content knowledge should be provided to elementary as well as secondary teachers. Although not emphasized here, ensuring that teachers remain current in STEM knowledge and pedagogy is a critical need. Public universities through their outreach efforts, STEM disciplinary societies, national laboratories, and informal STEM education institutions should make eff orts to address this need in collaboration with local and state education agencies.

1. Coordinate STEM Teacher Preparation with National Content Guidelines[74]

Teacher education programs at institutions of higher education should prepare their students to teach curricula aligned with national STEM content guidelines. The National Council for STEM Education, the Department of Education, NSF, higher education accrediting bodies, and teacher certification/licensure bodies should encourage institutions of higher education to ensure that their graduates are adequately prepared with STEM content knowledge, knowledge about how to teach STEM content in laboratory as well as traditional classrooms, and general teaching skills[75] prior to entering the classroom. Thorough preparation of STEM teachers should involve collaboration between the colleges of education and the colleges of arts and sciences and engineering to ensure that STEM content knowledge is acquired at sufficient depth to be useful in their future roles as teachers. STEM university faculty must take ownership and responsibility for the preparation of pre-college teachers by modifying their own teaching to engage and nurture these students. The STEM content knowledge acquired by future STEM teachers should be aligned with the knowledge and skills that their own students will need to succeed in college-level science and engineering courses and the workforce. Disciplinary societies, informal STEM education institutions, and national laboratories all provide STEM content expertise that could be effectively utilized to improve STEM teacher preparation.

2. Improve Articulation Agreements among Institutions of Higher Education

Institutions of higher education should make efforts to improve student and course transfer (articulation) agreements[76] so that students preparing to teach in STEM areas will not be slowed in earning degrees because course credits do not transfer between institutions.

CONCLUSION

Strengthening STEM education across the Nation is critical to maintaining a high quality of life for our citizens and ensuring that Americans remain competitive in international science and technology. Public awareness and action are critical to addressing this crisis. Jobs in the 21st century, even those outside STEM fields, will increasingly demand a technologically literate workforce. All citizens must have basic STEM literacy in order to be full and active participants in our increasingly technology-based democracy. If STEM education reform is not considered seriously now, the Nation is in danger of failing current and future generations. The recommendations in this action plan are essential to providing the Nation with a population that is numerate and scientifically and technologically literate. The recommendations that we have provided will ensure that all students have the skills and knowledge base to function successfully in our knowledge-based global economy. From this pool of students, some will become critically needed scientists, engineers, mathematicians, and STEM teachers. Ensuring that our education system will produce the next generation of brilliant innovators will require further action, and the Board will pursue this issue subsequently. The Nation must act now to address the critical needs of its science, technology, engineering, and mathematics education system; moving forward with the action plan presented here by the National Science Board should be the first step in launching this effort.

End Notes

[1] The National Academy of Sciences, National Academy of Engineering, and Institute of Medicine of the National Academies, *Rising Above the Gathering Storm: Energizing and Employing America for a Brighter Economic Future* (Washington, DC: National Academies Press, 2005). http://www.nap.edu/execsumm_pdf/11463.pdf

[2] The House Committee on Appropriations report that accompanied the FY2006 Science, State, Justice, Commerce and Related Agencies Appropriations Bill, included report language endorsing the establishment of the STEM Commission. The report states, "The Committee understands that the Board has taken steps to establish a commission to make recommendations for NSF and Federal Government action to achieve measurable improvements in the nation's science education at all levels. The Committee strongly endorses this effort." This chapter language was adopted in the final conference report for the Bill. Conference Committee, *Conference Report; Making Appropriations for Science, the Departments of State, Justice, and Commerce, and Related Agencies for the Fiscal Year Ending September 30, 2006, and for Other Purposes*, 109th Cong., 1st sess., 2005, H. Rep. 272, 184.

[3] National Science Board hearings on STEM education were held in December 2005 in Washington, DC, February 2006 in Boulder, CO, and March 2006 in Los Angeles, CA. Transcripts and video from these hearings are available at www.nsf.gov/nsb.

[4] See, for example, the argument made by Vannevar Bush in *Science – The Endless Frontier: A Report to the President*, (Washington, DC: U.S. Government Printing Office, 1945). http://www.nsf.gov/od/lpa/nsf50/vbush1945.htm

[5] The U.S. Commission on National Security/21st Century stated in its February 2001 Phase III Report that "In this Commission's view, the inadequacies of our systems of research and education pose a greater threat to U.S. national security over the next quarter century than any potential conventional war that we might imagine." The United States Commission on National Security/21st Century, Roadmap for National Security: Imperative for Change, (Washington, DC: U.S. Commission on National Security/21st Century, February 15, 2001). http://govinfo.library.unt.edu/nssg/PhaseIIIFR.pdf

[6] The National Academy of Sciences, National Academy of Engineering, and Institute of Medicine of the National Academies, Rising Above the Gathering Storm: Energizing and Employing *America for a Brighter Economic Future*, (Washington, DC: National Academies Press, 2005). http://www.nap.edu/execsumm_pdf/11463.pdf

[7] National Center for Education Statistics, *Remedial Education at Degree Granting Postsecondary Institutions in Fall 2000*, (Boston, MA: National Center for Education Statistics, 2000). http://nces.ed.gov/pubs2004/2004010.pdf

[8] The Organisation for Economic Co-operation and Development (OECD) Programme for International Student Assessment (PISA) test emphasizes "students' ability to apply scientifi c and mathematical concepts and thinking skills to problems they may encounter, particularly in situations outside the classroom." In 2003, 20 out of 31 countries scored higher than the United States among 4th graders, 8th graders, and 15 year olds. National Science Foundation, Division of Science Resource Statistics, *Science and Engineering Indicators 2006*, (Arlington, VA: National Science Foundation, February, 2006) http://www.nsf.gov/statistics

[9] "As textbooks have to cover more and more topics, keywords and the like, they end up jumping from subject to subject, covering little material in depth." Thomas B. Fordham Institute Report, *The Mad, Mad World of Textbook Adoption*, (Washington, DC: Th e Thomas B. Fordham Institute, 2004). http://www.edexcellence.net/doc/Mad%20World_Test2.pdf

[10] The 2004 Annual Social and Economic Supplement to the U.S. Census found that 15 to 20 percent of school-aged children moved in the previous year." Bureau of the Census of the Bureau of Labor Statistics, *Current Population Survey, 2004 Annual Social and Economic Supplement*, (Washington DC: Bureau of the Census, 2004). http://www.census.gov/apsd/techdoc/cps/cpsmar04.pdf. According to a study conducted in 1994 by the U.S. General Accounting Office, one out of six children had attended three or more schools by the end of the 3rd grade. U.S. General Accounting Office, *Elementary School Children Many Change Schools Frequently Harming Their Education*, (Washington DC: General Accounting Office, 1994). http://archive.gao.gov/t2pbat4/150724.pdf

[11] National Center for Education Statistics, *Mapping 2005 State Profi ciency Standards Onto the NAEP Scales*, (Washington DC: U.S. Department of Education, 2007) http://nces.ed.gov/nationsreportcard/pdf/studies/2007482.pdf

[12] National Center for Education Statistics, *Remedial Education at Degree Granting Postsecondary Institutions in Fall 2000*, (Boston, MA: National Center for Education Statistics, 2000). http://nces.ed.gov/pubs2004/2004010.pdf

[13] "One-third of our high school graduates are not prepared to enter postsecondary education or the workforce." Council of Chief State School Officers, *Mathematics and Science Education Task Force. Report and Recommendations*, (Washington, DC: Council of Chief State School Offi cers, November, 2006). http://www.ccsso.org/content/pdfs/Math%20Science%20Recom%20FINAL%20lowrez.pdf

[14] The National Commission on Mathematics and Science Teaching for the 21st Century, *Before It's Too Late: A Report to the Nation*, (Jessup, MD: Education Publications Center, September 27, 2000). http://www.ed.gov/inits/Math/glenn/report.pdf

[15] Levine, Arthur, *Educating School Teachers*, (Washington, DC: The Education Schools Project, September, 2006). http://www.edschools.org/pdf/Educating_Teachers_Report.pdf

[16] For example, according to UNC system President Erskine Bowles "...in the past four years, our 15 schools of education at the University of North Carolina turned out a grand total of three physics teachers." Bowles, Erskine. "Inaugural Address." Inaugural address, UNC Presidential Inauguration, Greensboro, NC, April 12, 2006. Note: the number of teachers graduating from the UNC system with a broader science certification was much larger.

[17] In 2003 the median annual (school-year) salary of full-time high school mathematics and science teachers was $43,000 compared to a median annual salary of $72,000 for computer systems analysts, $61,000 for accountants, auditors, and other financial specialists, or $75,000 for engineers. National Science Foundation, Division of Science Resources Statistics, National Survey of College Graduates.

[18] The lockstep salary model is a form of determining teacher pay and is used in most public school systems within the United States. In general, this system has a series of pay ladders that are usually based on education levels, teacher certification, and seniority. Each year, a teacher's raise is determined based on the ladder they qualify for within the schedule.

[19] This has been noted before by the National Academy of Sciences, National Academy of Engineering, and Institute of Medicine of the National Academies' *Rising Above the Gathering Storm: Energizing and Employing America for a Brighter Economic Future* as well as in The Center for Teaching Quality's *Performance Pay for Teachers: Designing a System that Students Deserve*. (Hillsborough, NC: Center for Teaching Quality, 2007). http://www.teacherleaders.org/teachersolutions/TSreport.pdf

[20] "There are more than 91,000 public schools in the United States governed by 15,000 school districts in 50 states and the extra-state jurisdictions." National Forum on Education Statistics. *The Forum Voice: Spring 2002 (Volume 5, No. 1)*. (Washington, DC: National Forum on Education Statistics, 2002). http://nces.ed.gov/forum/v_spring_02.asp

[21] Federal agencies and departments with involvement in elementary and secondary STEM education include, but are not limited to: Department of Education (DoED), National Science Foundation (NSF), Office of Science and Technology Policy (OSTP), Department of Energy (DoE), National Aeronautics and Space Administration (NASA), National Oceanographic and Atmospheric Administration (NOAA), Department of

Defense (DoD), National Institute of Standards (NIST), Department of Agriculture (USDA), National Institutes of Health (NIH), Smithsonian Institution, and the United States Geological Survey (USGS). The U.S. Department of Education's *Report of the Academic Competitiveness Council* inventories all Federal STEM education programs. U.S. Department of Education, *Report of the Academic Competitiveness Council* (Washington, DC: U.S. Department of Education, May, 2007). http://www.ed.gov/about/inits/ed/competitiveness *report.pdf*

[22] One of the National Science and Technology Council's roles is to coordinate these stakeholders. However, as a cabinet-level Council in the Executive Office of the President, the NSTC's mission and focus varies according to the policy goals of the sitting Administration.

[23] The Space Race began in 1957 with the launch of Sputnik by the Soviet Union. Over the course of the next 12 years, the U.S. and Soviet Union competed to be the first country to conquer outer space. To achieve this, great emphasis was placed on scientific and mathematical skills. To meet this skills need, Congress passed the National Defense Education Act (NDEA) in 1958. The aim of this legislation was primarily to stimulate the advancement of education in the elementary and secondary levels in science, mathematics, and modern foreign languages, but it has also provided aid in other areas, including technical education, and English as a second language. Although the effects of this law are difficult to prove as a result of poor record keeping, the number of bachelor degrees awarded in education rose more sharply than in other fields following the law's passage. It can be said that in the first few years of operation, NDEA had a considerable influence on the growth of graduate education in a number of states which had produced no doctoral graduates or very few up to that time.

[24] In 1975, Congress passed the Education for All Handicapped Children Act (EHA), which required all public schools accepting Federal funds to provide equal access to education for children with physical and mental disabilities. Public schools were required to evaluate handicapped students and create an educational plan with parent input that would emulate as closely as possible the educational experience of non-disabled students. For more information visit: http://www.scn.org/~bk269/94-142.html

[25] Although the Board is focusing this chapter toward public education, it is cognizant that a portion of U.S. students are in private schools (about 10 percent of elementary and high school students in the 2003-2004 school year, according to the National Center for Education Statistics) or are home schooled (2.2 percent in 2003, according to the same source). Broughman, S.P. and Swaim, N.L., *Characteristics of Private Schools in the United States: Results from the 2003 -2004 Private School Universe Survey*, (Washington, DC: U.S. Department of Education, National Center for Education Statistics, 2006). http://nces.ed.gov/pubs2006/2006319.pdf and Princiotta, D. and Bielick, S. *Homeschooling in the United States: 2003*, (Washington, DC: U.S. Department of Education, National Center for Education Statistics, 2005). http://nces.ed.gov/pubs2006/2006042.pdf

[26] According to the GAO's report on Higher Education Federal Science, Technology, Engineering and Mathematics Programs and Related Trends, 13 civilian agencies reported spending about $2.8 billion in Fiscal Year 2004 for 207 education programs. United States Government Accountability Office. *Higher Education Federal Science, Technology, Engineering and Mathematics Programs and Related Trends*. (Washington, DC: U.S. Government Accountability Office, October 2005). http://www.gao.gov/new.items/d06114.pdf. It has also been noted in the U.S. Department of Education's Report of the Academic Competitiveness Council that there are 105 STEM education programs across 13 Federal agencies, which have spent approximately $3.12 billion in total funding for Fiscal Year 2006. U.S. Department of Education, *Report of the Academic Competitiveness Council*, (Washington, DC: U.S. Department of Education, May, 2007). http://www.ed.gov/about/inits/ed/competitiveness report.pdf.

[27] National Science Board representation on the Council is intended to demonstrate the Board's commitment to long-term, continued engagement with and support of P-16 STEM education.

[28] For example, the National Cooperative Highway Research Program (which is part of the Transportation Research Board) is funded by the state departments of transportation. Support is voluntary and funds are drawn from the states' Federal-Aid Highway apportionment of State Planning and Research (SPR) funds. Furthermore, the funds can be spent only for the administration of problems approved by at least two-thirds of the states. Each state's allocation amounts to 5 and 1/2 percent of its SPR apportionment. More information can be found at: http://www.trb.org/default.asp

[29] A similar recommendation was also made in the U.S. Department of Education, *Report of the Academic Competitiveness Council*, (Washington, DC: U.S. Department of Education, May, 2007). http://www.ed.gov/about/inits/ed/competitiveness. In the report they recommend that "Federal agencies should improve the coordination of their K-12 STEM education programs with states and local school systems."

[30] Recommended in the National Governors Association and Council on Competitiveness, *Innovation America: A Partnership*, (Washington, DC: National Governors Association, February 24, 2007). http://www.nga.org/Files/pdf/0702INNOVATIONPARTNERSHIP.PDF

[31] The National Assessment Governing Board (NAGB), appointed by the Secretary of Education but independent of the Department, sets policy for the National Assessment Education Program (NAEP) and is responsible for developing the framework and test specifications that serve as the blueprint for the assessments. NAGB is a

bipartisan group whose members include governors, state legislators, local and state school officials, educators, business representatives, and members of the general public. Congress created the 26-member Governing Board in 1988. More information can be found on their website: http://www.nagb.org/

[32] The National Assessment of Educational Progress (NAEP), also known as "the Nation's Report Card," is the only nationally representative and continuing assessment of what America's students know and can do in various subject areas. More information can be found on their website: http:// nces.ed.gov/nationsreportcard/about/

[33] P- 16 and P-20 Councils are bodies of education stakeholders at the state level including state and local policy makers, teachers, administrators, and parents designed to improve education and to address issues in its educational system.

[34] Congress established the Office of Science and Technology Policy (OSTP) in 1976 with a broad mandate to advise the President and others within the Executive Office of the President on the effects of science and technology on domestic and international affairs. Its primary charge is to serve as a source of scientific and technological analysis and judgment for the President with respect to major policies, plans, and programs of the Federal Government. More information can be found at http:// ostp.gov/index.html

[35] The National Science and Technology Council (NSTC) was established by Executive Order in 1993. This Cabinet-level Council is the principal means within the executive branch to coordinate science and technology policy across the diverse entities that make up the Federal research and development enterprise. A primary objective of NSTC is the establishment of clear national goals for Federal science and technology investments in a broad array of areas. The Council prepares research and development strategies that are coordinated across Federal agencies to form investment packages aimed at accomplishing multiple national goals. The work of NSTC is organized under four primary committees: Science, Technology, Environment and Natural Resources, and Homeland and National Security. More information can be found at: http://www.ostp.gov/nstc/index.html.

[36] The National Science and Technology Council Committee (NSTC) on Science Subcommittee on Education and Workforce has, for example, issued relevant reports such as a *Review and Appraisal of the Federal Investment in STEM Education Research*, (Washington, DC: Office of the President, October 2006). http://www.ostp.gov/nstc/html/ ReviewAppraisaloftheFederalInvestmentSTEMEducationResearchOctober06.pdf

[37] Also recommended in the U.S. Department of Education *Report of the Academic Competitiveness Council*, (Washington, DC: U.S. Department of Education, May 2007). http://www.ed.gov/about/ inits/ed/competitiveness/acc-mathscience/report.pdf

[38] ~is position could also potentially play an important role in developing programs for the next generation of innovators, the subject of a future National Science Board activity on STEM education.

[39] Although STEM education from pre-kindergarten through graduate education (P-20) is a priority for NSF, this Board action plan is focused on alignment of P-16 STEM teaching and learning and does not consider graduate education.

[40] The NSF Education and Human Resources Directorate is charged with achieving excellence in U.S. science, technology, engineering and mathematics (STEM) education at all levels and in all settings (both formal and informal) in order to support the development of a diverse and well-prepared workforce of scientists, technicians, engineers, mathematicians, and educators and a well-informed citizenry that have access to the ideas and tools of science and engineering. More information can be found at: http://www.nsf.gov/ehr/about.jsp

[41] ~e NSF Research and Related Activities Directorate is the overarching directorate within NSF that is involved in all research and development aspects and which receives funding from Congress to engage in research activities for all non-educational and non-training related programs.

[42] National Science Board, *Preparing Our Children: Math and Science Education in the National Interest*, (Arlington, VA: National Science Foundation, 1999). http://www.nsf.gov/pubs/1999/nsb9931/nsb9931.pdf

[43] See Recommendation 2 of the *Report of the Academic Competitiveness Council* which states that, "Agencies and the Federal government at large should foster knowledge of effective practices through improved evaluation and-or implementation of proven-effective, research-based instructional materials and methods." U.S. Department of Education. R*eport of the Academic Competitive Council*. (Jessup, MD: Education Publication Center, May 2007). http://www.ed.gov/about/inits/ed/competitiveness/

[44] See also *Cyberinfrastructure Vision for 21st Century Discovery* (Arlington, VA: National Science Foundation, February 2007). http://www.nsf.gov/pubs/2007/nsf0728/index.jsp

[45] To access the National Science Digital Library visit http://nsdl.org/

[46] ~e Robert Noyce Scholarship program seeks to encourage talented science, technology, engineering, and mathematics majors and professionals to become K-12 mathematics and science teachers. ~ e program provides funds to institutions of higher education to support scholarships, stipends, and programs for students who commit to teaching in high-need K-12 school districts. More information can be found by visiting: http://www.nsf.gov/funding

[47] The Research Experience for Undergraduates (REU) program supports active research participation by undergraduate students in any of the areas of research funded by the National Science Foundation. REU

projects involve students in meaningful ways in ongoing research programs or in research projects specifically designed for the REU program. More information can be found by visiting: http://www.nsf.gov/funding

[48] Data gathered through a variety of sources, including a specially developed online management information system, have shown a number of significant improvements, including a rise in profi ciency test scores in mathematics and science for students in the partnerships in 2002-2003, 2003-2004, and 2004-2005, as well as other measures. For more information read the National Science Foundation's Math and Science Partnership National Impact Report by visiting: http://www.nsf.gov/news/newsmedia/ msp_impact/fi nal_msp _impact_report.pdf

[49] National Science Board, *A Statement of the National Science Board: In Support of the Math and Science Partnership Program at the National Science Foundation*, (Arlington, VA: National Science Board, 2004). http://www.nsf.gov/nsb/documents/2004/nsb_msp_statement2.pdf. More information on the Math and Science Partnership Program can be found at http://www.nsf.gov/funding. jsp?pims_id=5756 and http://hub

[50] The Louis Stokes Alliances for Minority Participation Program (LSAMP) is aimed at increasing the quality and quantity of students successfully completing STEM baccalaureate degree programs, and increasing the number of students interested in, academically qualified for, and matriculated into programs of graduate study. LSAMP supports sustained and comprehensive approaches that facilitate achievement of the long-term goal of increasing the number of students who earn doctorates in STEM fields, particularly those from populations underrepresented in STEM fields. The program goals are accomplished through the formation of alliances. More information can be found at: http://www. nsf. gov/pubs/2003/nsf03520/nsf03520.htm

[51] According to the 2006 Science & Technology Public Attitudes and Understanding Indicators, most adults in the U.S. and other countries pick up information about science and technology primarily from watching television, including educational and nonfiction programs, newscasts and newsmagazines, and even entertainment programs. In addition, the internet is also playing a role in communicating science and technology news as the internet moved in 2004 to the second most popular source of news about science and technology. National Science Foundation, Division of Science Resource Statistics, *Science and Engineering Indicators 2006*, (Arlington, VA: National Science Foundation, February 2006). http://www.nsf.gov/statistics

[52] National Science Board, *Communicating Science and Technology in the Public Interest*, (Arlington, VA: National Science Board, August 3, 2000). http://www.nsf.gov/nsb/documents/2000/nsb0099/nsb0099. htm

[53] "Content guidelines" are defined here to mean descriptions of expected student knowledge in various subject areas.

[54] Several pieces of legislation from the 110th Congress include provisions to create STEM content standards. They include the following: H.R. 35, the *Science Accountability Act of 2007*, requires states to establish challenging academic content and student achievement standards in science. S. 164, the *SUCCESS Act*, requires the National Assessment of Educational Progress(NAEP) Board's national academic content and student achievement standards to be competitive with rigorous international standards and set at a level that prepares students for non-remedial higher education, participation in the 21st century workforce, and the Armed Forces. The NAEP Board would be required to provide assistance to any state that works to align its standards with those of the Board. S. 757, the *National Mathematics and Science Consistency Act*, directs the Secretary of Education to work with the National Academy of Sciences to convene a panel to develop voluntary national expectations for science and math education for grades K- 12 (the expectations are required to reflect core ideas in math and science education which are common to all states). Library of Congress, "Thomas; Legislation in Current Congress," http://thomas.loc.gov/ (accessed April 19, 2007).

[55] Th ese grade-specific standards should build upon pre-existing standards such as: National Council of Teachers of Mathematics, *Principles and Standards for School Mathematics*, (Reston, VA: NCTM, 2000); International Technology Education Association, *Standards for Technological Literacy* (Reston, VA: ITEA, 2000). http://standards.nctm.org/; American Association for the Advancement of Science, Benchmarks for Science Literacy (New York: Oxford University Press, 1993). http://www.project2061. org/publications/bsl/on line/bolintro.htm; National Research Council, National Science Education Standards (Washington, DC: National Academy Press, 1996); and Douglas Gorham, Pam Newberry, and Theodore Bickart, "Engineering Accreditation and Standards for Technological Literacy," *Journal of Engineering Education* 92 (Ashburn, VA: American Society for Engineering Education, 2003).

[56] Th e Third International Mathematics and Science Study (TIMSS) observed that mathematics and science curricula in U.S. high schools lack coherence, depth, and continuity and cover too many topics in a superficial way. Standards must emphasize depth of understanding over exhaustive coverage of content. National Center for Education Statistics, "Third International Mathematics and Science Study," *Institute of Education Sciences*, (Washington, DC: U.S. Department of Education, 2003). http://nces.ed.gov/timss/index.asp

[57] National Council of Teachers of Mathematics, *Curriculum Focal Points: From Pre-Kindergarten through Grade 8 Mathematics*, (Reston, VA: National Council of Teachers of Mathematics, 2006). http://www.nctmm edia.org/cfp/front_matter.pdf

[58] Although several individuals highlighted the important contributions made by the AAAS Project 2061 *Benchmarks for Science Literacy* (http://www.project2061.org/publications/bsl/) and Atlas of Science Literacy (http://www.project2061.org/publications/atlas/default.htm) during the public comment period, the

benchmarks need to be updated as they are now more than a decade old and are grade-span rather than grade-specific.

[59] "Created by the nation's governors and business leaders in 1996, Achieve, Inc., is a bipartisan, nonprofit organization that helps states raise academic standards, improve assessments and strengthen accountability to prepare all young people for postsecondary education, work, and citizenship. Achieve has helped more than half the states benchmark their academic standards, tests, and accountability systems against the best examples in the U.S. and around the world. It has developed benchmark standards that describe the specific math and English skills high school graduates must have if they are to succeed in postsecondary education and high-performance jobs. Achieve works with states to incorporate these expectations in state standards and assessments for high schools. Achieve has also developed grade-level math standards for kindergarten through grade 8." http://www.achieve.org/

[60] Also recommended in the National Science Board Commission on Precollege Education in Mathematics, Science and Technology, *Educating Americans for the 21st Century: A Plan of Action for Improving Mathematics, Science and Technology Education for All American Elementary and Secondary Students So That Their Achievement is the Best in the World by 1995*, (Arlington, VA: National Science Foundation, 1983); The National Science Board, *America's Pressing Challenge - Building a Stronger Foundation: A Companion to Science and Engineering Indicators*, (Washington DC: Government Printing Office, 2006). http://www.nsf.gov/statistics and the Domestic Policy Council of the Office of Science and Technology Policy. *America's Competitiveness Initiative; Leading the World in Innovation*, (Washington DC: Government Printing Office, 2006). http://www.whitehouse.gov/stateoftheunion/2006/aci/aci06-booklet.pdf

[61] As part of the National Governors Association (NGA) Innovation America initiative, funding for voluntary international benchmarking has been proposed and included as part of the STEM Center Grant Program. As part of this program, the NGA has encouraged states to participate in international assessments and align their standards and assessments with international benchmarks. More information can be found by visiting: http://www.nga.org/portal/site/nga/menuitem.751b186f65e10b568a278110501010a0/?vgnextoid=e34e2bad2b6dd010VgnVCM1000001a01010aRCRD&vgnextchannel=92ebc7df618a2010VgnVCM1000001a01010aRCRD

[62] Using such metrics as an added measure of AYP is reflected in H.R. 35, the *Science Accountability Act of 2007*. This act would amend the Elementary and Secondary Education Act of 1965 to require the use of science assessments in the calculation of adequate yearly progress. Library of Congress, "Thomas; Legislation in Current Congress," *http://thomas.loc.gov/* (accessed April 19, 2007).

[63] The STEM Center Grant Program is part of National Governors Association (NGA) Innovation American initiative. The grant program was designed to build off the success of the High School Honor States initiative. STEM centers will help state K-12 education systems ensure all students graduate from high school with essential competencies in STEM subjects. More information on the program can be found by visiting: http://www.nga.org/Files/pdf/0702INNOVATIONSTEMRFP.PDF

[64] To access the National Science Digital Library, visit http://nsdl.org/.

[65] The American Diploma Project (ADP) is a partnership of four national organizations (Achieve, The Education Trust, the National Alliance of Business, and the Fordham Foundation) and five states (Indiana, Kentucky, Massachusetts, Nevada, and Texas) that joined forces in a collaborative effort to strengthen ongoing standards-based reform efforts at the state level. Its goal is to ensure that American high school students have the knowledge and skills necessary for success following graduation, whether in college, the workplace or the armed services. The ADP also aims to develop and solidify demand for standards-based high school assessment data in admissions and hiring processes; assist states in revising and/or strengthening their current standards-based systems; and develop national high school graduation benchmarks in English language arts and mathematics that all states may use to calibrate the quality and rigor of their standards and assessments. More information can be found by going to: http://www.achieve.org/node/604

[66] National Governors Association and Council on Competitiveness, *Innovation America: A Partnership*, (Washington, DC: National Governors Association, February 24, 2007). http://www.nga.org/Files/pdf/0702INNOVATIONPARTNERSHIP.PDF

[67] Also recommended in Business-Higher Education Forum, *A Commitment to America's Future: Responding to the Crisis in Mathematics and Science Education*, (Washington, DC: Business-Higher Education Forum, January 2005). http://www.bhef.com/solutions/MathEduPamphlet_press.pdf; National Science Board, *America's Pressing Challenge – Building a Stronger Foundation*, Companion to *Science and Engineering Indicators 2006*, (Arlington, VA: National Science Foundation, 2006). http://www.nsf.gov/statistics National Science Board Commission on Precollege Education in Mathematics, Science and Technology, *Educating Americans for the 21st Century: A Plan of Action for Improving Mathematics, Science and Technology Education for All American Elementary and Secondary Students So That Their Achievement is the Best in the World by 1995*, (Arlington, VA: National Science Foundation, 1983); Domestic Policy Council of the Office of Science and Technology Policy *America's Competitiveness Initiative; Leading the World in Innovation* (Washington DC: Government Printing Office, 2006). http://www.whitehouse.gov/stateoftheunion/2006/aci/aci06-booklet.pdf; National Science Board, *Preparing Our Children: Math and Science Education in the National Interest*,

(Arlington, VA: National Science Foundation, 1999). http://www.nsf.gov/pubs/1999/nsb9931/nsb9931.pdf ; American Association for the Advancement of Science, *A System of Solutions: Every School, Every Student* (Washington, DC: American Association for the Advancement of Science, 2005). http://ehrweb.aaas.org/PDF/GEReport.pdf

[68] Based on data compiled from the Teacher Followup Survey, about half of all teachers who depart their jobs give as a reason either job dissatisfaction or the desire to pursue another job, in or out of education. Notably, math/science teachers are significantly more likely to move from or leave their teaching jobs because of job dissatisfaction than are other teachers (40 percent of math/science and 29 percent of all teachers). Of those who depart because of job dissatisfaction, the most common reasons given by math and science teachers are: low salaries (56.7%); a lack of support from the administration (45.9%); student discipline problems (29%); and a lack of student motivation (21.4%). Note that the percent of teachers giving various reasons for turnover each add up to more than 100 percent, because respondents could indicate up to three reasons for their departures. Ingersoll, R. *Turnover Among Math and Science Teachers in the U.S.* (Washington, DC: Department of Education, 2000). www.ed.gov/inits/Math/glenn/Ingersollp.doc

[69] According to data compiled by the National Center for Education Statistics as part of their Schools and Staffing Survey and the Teacher Followup Survey (TFS), 11 percent of teachers will leave the teaching profession altogether after only one year of teaching; 29 percent will leave after 3 years, and a full 39 percent will have left after 5 years. Data is based on surveys conducted during 1987-89; 1990- 92; and 1993-95. Ingersoll, R. *Turnover Among Math and Science Teachers in the U.S.* (Washington, DC: Department of Education/National Commission on Mathematics and Science Teaching for the 21st Century, 2000). www.ed.gov/inits/Math/glenn/Ingersollp.doc

[70] "To make precollege science and math teaching more competitive with other career opportunities, resources must be provided to compensate teachers of mathematics, science, and technology comparably to similarly trained S&E professionals in other economic sectors." National Science Board, *America's Pressing Challenge: Building a Stronger Foundation*, (Arlington, VA: National Science Foundation, February, 2006). http://www.nsf.gov/statistics

[71] This is in agreement with The National Academy of Sciences, National Academy of Engineering, and Institute of Medicine of the National Academies, *Rising Above the Gathering Storm: Energizing and Employing America for a Brighter Economic Future* (Washington, DC: National Academies Press, 2005). http://www.nap.edu/execsumm_pdf/11463.pdf.

[72] Legislation incorporating similar ideas passed both the House and Senate on August 2, 2007 in the form of H.R. 2272, the America Creating Opportunities to Meaningfully Promote Excellence in Technology, Education and Science Act (COMPETES).

[73] The National Board for Professional Teaching Standards (NBPTS) program off ers certificates in 24 subject and developmental teaching areas. National Board for Professional Teaching Standards, *http:// www.nbpts.org/* (accessed April 19, 2007).

[74] Also recommended in the National Science Board Commission on Precollege Education in Mathematics, Science and Technology, *Educating Americans for the 21st Century: A Plan of Action for Improving Mathematics, Science and Technology Education for All American Elementary and Secondary Students So That Their Achievement is the Best in the World by 1995*, (Arlington, VA: National Science Foundation, 1983); National Science Board, *Preparing Our Children: Math and Science Education in the National Interest*, (Arlington, VA: National Science Foundation, 1999). http:// www.nsf.gov/pubs/1999/nsb9931/nsb9931.pdf; Building Engineering Science Talent, *A Bridge for All: Higher Education Design Principles to Broaden Participation in Science, Technology, Engineering and Mathematics*, (San Diego, CA: Building Engineering and Science Talent, 2004). http://www. bestworkforce.org/PDFdocs/BEST_BridgeforAll_HighEdFINAL.pdf; and Business-Higher Education Forum, *A Commitment to America's Future: Responding to the Crisis in Mathematics and Science Education*, (Washington, DC: Business-Higher Education Forum, January 2005). http://www.bhef. com/solutions/MathEduPamphleçpress.pdf

[75] Critical teaching skills include behavior management and the ability to teach learners from diverse cultural backgrounds and with varying abilities.

[76] An articulation agreement is a policy that allows a student to apply credits earned in specifi c programs at one institution toward advanced standing, equal transfer, or direct entry into specifi c programs at another institution.

SELECTED ACRONYMS AND ABBREVIATIONS

ACC   Academic Competitiveness Council
AYP   Adequate Yearly Progress

EHR	NSF Education and Human Resources Directorate
K-12	Kindergarten – 12th grade
MSP	Math and Science Partnership Program
NAEP	National Assessment of Educational Progress
NCLB	No Child Left Behind legislation
NSF	National Science Foundation
NSTC	National Science and Technology Council
OSTP	Office of Science and Technology Policy
P-12	Pre-kindergarten – 12th grade
P-16	Pre-kindergarten – undergraduate education
P-20	Pre-kindergarten – graduate education
Pre-K	Pre-kindergarten
R&RA	NSF Research and Related Activities Directorates
STEM	Science, Technology, Engineering, and Mathematics

BIBLIOGRAPHY AND OTHER RELATED SOURCES

Abrahams, Camille, Bridget Curran and Theresa Clarke. *Solving Teacher Shortages Through License Reciprocity*. (Denver, CO: National Governors Association Center for Best Practices. February, 2001). http://www.sheeo.org/quality/mobility/reciprocity

ACT, Inc. Developing the STEM Education Pipeline. (Washington DC: ACT, 2006). http://www.act.org/path/policy/pdf/ACT_STEM_PolicyRpt.pdf

American Association of Colleges of Teacher Education. Preparing STEM Teachers: The Key to Global Competitiveness. (AACTE's Day on the Hill, June 20-21, 2007). http://www.aacte.org/Governmental_Relations/AACTE_STEM_Directory2007.pdf

American Association for the Advancement of Science. *Atlas of Science Literacy, Volume 1.* (Washington, DC: American Association for the Advancement of Science, 2001).

American Association for the Advancement of Science. Benchmarks for Science Literacy (New York: Oxford University Press, 1993). http://www.project2061.org/publications/bsl/

American Electronics Association. Losing the Competitive Advantage? The Challenge for Science and Technology in the United States. (Washington DC: American Electronics Association, 2005). http://www.aeanet.org/Publications/idjj_AeA_Competitiveness.asp

American Electronics Association. We are Still Losing the Competitive Advantage. Now is the Time to Act. (Washington DC: American Electronics Association, March, 2007). http://www.aeanet.org/publications/AeA_Competitiveness_2007.asp

The Asia Society. Math and Science Education in a Global Age: What the U.S. Can Learn from China. (New York: the Asia Society, May 2006). http://www.internationaled.org/mathsciencereport.pdf

Barnett, Lynn, Faith San Felice and Madeline Patton. *Teaching by Choice: Community College Science and Mathematics Preparation of K-12 Teachers*. (Washington, DC: American Association of Community College Press, 2005). http://www.nctaf.org/documents/Teaching_by_Choice_publication_000.pdf

Building Engineering Science Talent. A Bridge for All: Higher Education Design Principles to Broaden Participation in Science, Technology, Engineering and Mathematics.

(San Diego: BEST, 2004). http://www.bestworkforce.org/PDFdocs/BEST_BridgeforAll_HighEdFINAL.pdf

Business-Higher Education Forum. An American Imperative: Transforming the Recruitment, Retention and Renewal of Our Nation's Mathematics and Science Teaching Workforce. (Washington, DC: Business-Higher Education Forum, 2007). http://www.bhef.com/news/AnAmericanImperative.pdf

Business-Higher Education Forum. A Commitment to America's Future: Responding to the Crisis in Mathematics and Science Education. (Hagerstown: Business-Higher Education Forum, January 2005). http://www.bhef.com/publications/MathEduReport-press.pdf

Biological Sciences Curriculum Study (BSCS). A Decade of Action, Sustaining Global Competitiveness: A Synthesis of Recommendations from Business, Industry, and Government for a 21st-century Workforce. (Colorado Springs, CO: BSCS, 2007). http://www.bscs.org/pdf/ doafullreport.pdf

Bush, Vannevar. Science – The Endless Frontier. A Report to the President on a Program for Postwar Scientifi c Research. (Washington, DC: U.S. Government Printing Offi ce, 1945). http://www.nsf.gov/od/lpa/nsf50/vbush1945.htm

Carcieri, Donald L. The Governor's Blue Ribbon Panel on Mathematics & Science Education: An Action Plan for Rhode Island. (Providence, RI: Office of the Governor, October 2005). http://www.governor.ri.gov/documents/TEC_M&S_FA_LR.pdf

Carnegie Commission on Science, Technology and Government. In the National Interest: The Federal Government in the Reform of K-12 Math and Science Education. (New York: Carnegie Corporation, 1991). http://www.carnegie.org/sub/pubs/science_tech/educ.txt

The Center for Teaching Quality. Performance Pay for Teachers: Designing a System that Students Deserve. (Hillsborough, NC: Center for Teaching Quality, 2007). http://www.teacherleaders.org/teachersolutions/TSreport.pdf

The Commission on No Child Left Behind. Beyond NCLB: Fulfi lling the Promise to Our Nation's Children. (Washington, DC: Aspen Institute, 2007). http://www.aspeninstitute.org/atf/cf/%7BDEB6F227-659B-4EC8-8F84-8DF23CA704F5%7D/NCLB_Book.pdf

Committee for Economic Development. Learning for the Future: Changing the Culture of Math and Science Education to Ensure a Competitive Workforce. (Washington DC: CED, 2003). http://www.ced.org/docs/report/report_scientists.pdf

Committee on Science Learning, Kindergarten Through the Eighth Grade, Richard A. Duschl, Heidi A. Schweingruber, and Andrew W. Shouse, Editors. *Taking Science to School: Learning and Teaching Science in Grades K-8.* (Washington, DC: The National Academies Press, 2007). http://www.nap.edu/catalog.php?record_id=11625

Coppola, Ralph K., Joyce Malyn-Smith. Preparing for the Perfect Storm: A Report on the Forum Taking Action Together Developing a National Action Plan to Address the "T&E" of STEM. (Reston, VA: International Technology Education Association, November 2006). http://www.iteaconnect.org/Publications/Promos/NAE.pdf

The Council of Chief State School Officers Mathematics and Science Education Task Force. *Mathematics and Science Education Task Force Report and Recommendations.* (Washington DC: Council of Chief State School Offi cers, 2006). http://www.ccsso.org/content/pdfs/Math%20Science%20Recom%20FINAL%20lowrez.pdf

Domestic Policy Council of the Office of Science and Technology Policy. America's Competitiveness Initiative; Leading the World in Innovation. (Washington DC: Government Printing Offi ce, 2006). http://www.ostp.gov/html/ACIBooklet.pdf

The Education for Innovation Initiative. Tapping America's Potential: The Education for Innovation Initiative Building Public Support. (Washington DC: The Education for Innovation Initiative, 2005). http://www.tap2015.org/about/TAP_report2.pdf

Exxon Education Foundation. Science Education in the United States: Essential Steps for Achieving Fundamental Improvement. A Report on a Meeting of Educational Leaders Hosted by the Exxon Education Foundation. (New York, NY: Exxon Education Foundation, January 17-20, 1984).

Finn, Chester, Liam Julian and Michael J. Pertrilli. To Dream the Impossible Dream: Four Approaches to National Standards and Tests for America's Schools. (Washington, DC: Th omas B. Fordham Foundation, August 2006). http://www. edexcellence. net/doc/National%20Standar ds%20Final%20PDF.pdf

Friedman, Th omas. *The World Is Flat: A Brief History of the Twenty-fi rst Century.* (New York, NY: Farrar, Straus and Giroux, 2005).

Hirsch, Eric. Teacher Recruitment, Staffi ng Classrooms with Quality Teachers. (Denver, CO: National Conference of State Legislators, February 2001). http://www.sheeo.org/quality/mobility/recruitment.PDF

Hussar, W. Predicting the Need for Newly Hired Teachers in the United States to 2008-09. (Washington, DC: National Center for Education Statistics, Oct. 15, 1999). http://nces.ed.gov/pubs99/1999026.pdf

Hussar, W. Projections of Education Statistics to 2015, 34th Edition. (Washington, DC: National Center for Education Statistics Institute of Education Sciences, 2006). http://nces.ed.gov/pubs2006/2006084.pdf

Illinois Business Roundtable & Northern Illinois University. Keeping Illinois Competitive. (DeKalb, IL: Northern Illinois University, June 2006). http://www.ke epingillinoiscompetitive.niu.edu/ilstem/pdfs/STEM_ed_report.pdf

Ingersoll, R. Is There Really a Teacher Shortage? (Center for the Study of Teaching and Policy, 2003). http://depts.washington.edu/ctpmail/PDFs/Shortage-RI-09-2003.pdf

Ingersoll, R. *Turnover Among Math and Science Teachers in the U.S.* (Washington, DC: Department of Education/National Commission on Mathematics and Science Teaching for the 21st Century, 2000). http://www.ed.gov/inits/Math/glenn/Ingersollp.doc

International Technology Education Association. Standards for Technological Literacy: Content for the Study of Technology. (Reston, VA: International Technology Education Agency, 2000). http://www.iteaconnect.org/TAA/PDFs/xstnd.pdf

Levine, Arthur. Educating School Teachers. (Washington, DC: The Education Schools Project, September 2006). http://www.edschools.org/pdf/Educating_Teachers_Report.pdf

Malcolm, Shirley, Joan Abdallah, et al. A System of Solutions: Every School, Every Student. (Washington DC: American Association for the Advancement of Science, 2005). http://www.aaas.org/programs/centers/capacity/documents/GELongReport.pdf

National Academy of Sciences, National Academy of Engineering and Institute of Medicine of the National Academies. *Rising Above the Gathering Storm: Energizing and Employing America to a Brighter Economic Future.* (Washington DC: National Academies Press, October 2005). http://www.nap.edu/execsumm_pdf/11463.pdf

National Association of System Heads (NASH). Turning the Tide: Strategies for Producing the Mathematics and Science Teachers Our Schools Need. (Washington, DC: NASH, November 2006). http://www2.edtrust.org/NR/rdonlyres/7DCD6A7C-980C-4EA7-BE99- 80D0EA3734AF/0/Turning~ eTide.pdf

National Center on Education and the Economy. Tough Choices, Tough Times: ~e Report of the New Commission on the Skills of the American Workforce. (Washington, DC: National Center on Education and the Economy, 2007). http://skillscommission.org

National Council of Teachers of Mathematics. Curriculum Focal Points: From Pre-Kindergarten through Grade 8 Mathematics. (Reston, VA: National Council of Teachers of Mathematics, 2006). http://www.nctmmedia.org/cfp/front_matter.pdf

National Council of Teachers of Mathematics. *Principles and Standards for School Mathematics.* (Reston, VA: National Council of Teachers of Mathematics, 2000).

National Education Summit on High Schools. An Action Agenda for Improving America's High Schools. (Washington DC: Achieve, Inc and the National Governor's Association, 2005). http://www.nga.org/Files/pdf/0502ACTIONAGENDA.pdf

National Governors Association. *Innovation America Brochure.* (Washington, DC: National Governors Association, 2006). http://www.nga.org/Files/pdf/ 06NAPOLITANOBROCHURE.pdf

National Governors Association. Innovation America: Building a Science, Technology, Engineering and Math Agenda. (Washington, DC: National Governors Association, 2006). http://www.nga.org/Files/pdf/0702INNOVATIONSTEM.PDF

National Governors Association and The Council on Competitiveness. *Innovation America: A Partnership.* (Washington, DC: National Governors Association, February 24, 2007) http://www.nga.org/Files/pdf/0702INNOVATIONPARTNERSHIP.PDF

National Innovation Initiative. *Innovate America.* (Washington DC: Council on Competitiveness, March 2004). *http://www.compete.org/*

The National Research Council. National Science Education Standards. (Washington, DC: National Academies Press, 1996). http://www.nap.edu/openbook.php?isbn=0309053269

The National Science Board. America's Pressing Challenge - Building a Stronger Foundation; A Companion to Science and Engineering Indicators. (Arlington, VA: National Science Foundation, 2006). http://www.nsf.gov/statistics

The National Science Board. Communicating Science and Technology in the Public Interest. (Arlington, VA: National Science Foundation, August 3, 2000). http://www.nsf.gov/nsb/documents/2000/nsb0099/nsb0099.htm

The National Science Board. An Emerging and Critical Problem of the Science and Engineering Labor Force: A Companion to the Science and Engineering Indicators. (Arlington, VA: National Science Foundation, March 2004). http://www.nsf.gov/statistics.pdf

The National Science Board. Preparing Our Children: Math and Science Education in the National Interest. (Arlington, VA: National Science Foundation, March 1999). http://www.nsf.gov/pubs/1999/nsb9931/nsb9931.pdf

The National Science Board. *Undergraduate Science, Mathematics and Engineering Education.* (Arlington, VA: Government Printing Office, March 1986).

National Science Board Commission on Pre-college Education in Mathematics, Science and Technology. Educating Americans for the 21st Century: A Plan of action for improving mathematics, science and technology education for all American elementary and secondary students so that their achievement is the best in the world by 1995. (Washington DC: National Science Foundation, March 1983).

National Science and Technology Council Committee on Science Subcommittee on Education and Workforce. *Review and Appraisal of the Federal Investment in STEM Education Research.* (Washington, DC: Office of the President, October, 2006). http://www.ostp.gov/nstc/html/ReviewAppraisaloftheFederalInvestmentSTEMEducationResearchOctober06.pdf

President's Council of Advisors on Science and Technology. Sustaining the Nation's Innovation Ecosystem: Maintaining the Strength of Our Science and Engineering Capabilities. (Washington DC: Government Printing Offi ce, March 2004). http://www.ostp.gov/PCAST/FINALPCASTSECAPABILITIESPACKAGE.pdf

Princiotta, D. and Bielick, S. Homeschooling in the United States: 2003. (Washington, DC: U.S. Department of Education, National Center for Education Statistics, 2005). http://nces.ed.gov/pubs2006/2006042.pdf

Project Kaleidoscope. Report on Reports II. Transforming America's Scientifi c and Technological Infrastructure: Recommendations for Urgent Action. (Washington, DC: Project Kaleidoscope, 2006). http://www.pkal.org/documents/ReportOnReportsII.cfm

Ruppert, Sandra S. Improving Pension Portability for K-12 Teachers. (Denver, CO: Educational Systems Research, February, 2001). http://www.sheeo.org/ quality/mobility/pension. PDF

Skandera, Hanna and Richard Sousa. Mobility and the Achievement Gap. (Stanford, CA: Board of Trustees of Leland Stanford Junior University, 2007). http://www.hoover.org/publications/digest/4488356.html

The Task Force on the Future of American Innovation. The Knowledge Economy: Is the United States Losing its Competitive Edge? (Washington DC: Task Force on the Future of America's Innovation, 2005). http://futureofi nnovation.org/PDF/Benchmarks.pdf

The Teaching Commission. Teaching at Risk: A Call to Action. (Washington DC: Th e Teaching Commission, 2004). http://www.ecs.org/html/off site.asp?document=http %3A%2F%2 Fftp %2Eets%2Eorg%2Fpub%2Fcorp %2Fttcreport%2Epdf

The Technology CEO Council. Choose to Compete: How Innovation, Investment, and Productivity Can Grow U.S. Jobs and Ensure American Competitiveness in the 21st Century. (Washington, DC: Technology CEO Council, 2004). http://www.cspp.org/documents/choosetocompete.pdf

U.S. Chamber of Congress. Leaders and Laggards: A State-by-State Report Card on Educational Eff ectiveness. (Washington, DC: U.S. Chamber of Commerce, 2007). http://www.uschamber.com/icw/reportcard/default#top

The U.S. Commission for National Security/21st Century. Road Map for National Security: Imperative for Change" (Phase III). (Washington DC: Government Printing Offi ce, February 2001). http://cryptome.sabotage

U.S. Department of Education. Report of the Academic Competitiveness Council. (Washington, DC: U.S. Department of Education, 2007). http://www.ed.gov/about/inits/ed/competitiveness

U.S. Department of Education, Institute of Education Sciences, National Center for Education Statistics. *Mapping 2005 State Profi ciency Standards Onto the NAEP Scales Research and Development Report.* (Washington, DC: Department of Education, June 2007). http://nces.ed.gov/nationsreportcard/pdf/studies/2007482.pdf

U.S. Department of Education National Commission on Excellence in Education. *A Nation at Risk: The Imperative for Educational Reform.* (Washington, DC: Government Printing Office, 1983). http://www.ed.gov/pubs/NatAtRisk/index.html

U.S. Department of Education National Commission on Mathematics and Science Teaching. *Before It's Too Late: A Report to the Nation.* (Washington, DC: Government Printing Office, March 2000). http://www.ed.gov/inits/Math/glenn/report.pdf

APPENDIX A. PROPOSED NATIONAL COUNCIL FOR STEM EDUCATION MEMBERSHIP

The following list is meant to provide examples of the types of representatives who might sit on the National Council for STEM Education and is not meant to be either inclusive or exclusive. Those groups designated here as "permanent seats" with an asterisk are of such importance that the Board recommends that they always have a representative on the Council.

Non-Voting Seats

- *Federal Government* (2 permanent seats)
- All Federal agencies, including the national laboratories, are represented by the NSTC STEM Education Committee Co-Chairs
- *Congress* (8 permanent seats)
  - Senate Committee on Health, Education, Labor, and Pensions
  - Senate Committee on Commerce, Science and Transportation
  - House Committee on Education and Labor
  - House Committee on Science and Technology

Voting Seats

- State and Local Governments (6 seats total)
  - *State Governors (2 permanent seats)
  - *Chief state school officer (2 permanent seats)
  - *Local school board representative (1 permanent seat)
  - National Association of State Boards of Education (NASBE)
  - National School Boards Association (NSBA)
  - Education Commission of the States (ECS)
  - Council of Great City Schools
  - National League of Cities

  National Conference of State Legislatures (NCSL)
  National Alliance of State Science and Mathematics Coalitions (NASSMC)
- *National Science Board (1 permanent seat)
- *STEM Educators* (5 seats total)

- *Active classroom teacher (1 permanent seat) *School administrator (1 permanent seat)
- National Science Teachers Association (NSTA) National Council of Teachers of Mathematics (NCTM)
- International Technology Education Association (ITEA) American Association of Physics Teachers (AAPT) National Association of Biology Teachers (NABT) National Earth Science Teachers Association (NESTA) Council of State Science Supervisors (CSSS)
- Association of State Supervisors of Mathematics (ASSM) Association for Science Teacher Education (ASTE) Computer Science Teachers Association (CSTA)
- STEM education researchers
- Association for Career and Technical Education (ACTE)
- *Higher Education Associations* (3 seats total, 2 permanent seats total)
  - *American Association of Community Colleges (AACC) (1 permanent seat) Association of American Universities (AAU)
  - American Association of Colleges of Teacher Education (AACTE)
  - National Association of State Universities and Land Grant Colleges (NASULGC) American Association of State Colleges and Universities (AASCU)
  - National Association for Research in Science Teaching (NARST)
  - American Council on Education (ACE)
  - National Council for Accreditation of Teacher Education (NCATE)
- Business and Industry Associations (2 seats total)
  - Business Roundtable
  - Council on Competitiveness
  - Business Higher Education Forum (BHEF) U.S. Chamber of Commerce
  - National Association of Manufacturers (NAM)
- Private and Corporate Foundations (2 seats total)
  - Bill and Melinda Gates Foundation
  - The GE Foundation
  - National Math and Science Initiative (NMSI)
  - The Sloan Foundation
  - The Ford Foundation
  - Society of Manufacturing Engineers Education Foundation
- Informal STEM Education (2 seats total)
  - Public broadcast media such as Corporation for Public Broadcasting (CPB),
  - Public Broadcasting System (PBS), National Public Radio (NPR) Commercial broadcast media such as Discovery Channel, CBS, Fox Association of Science-Technology Centers (ASTC)
  - Museums
  - Internet-based informal STEM resources
- *STEM Disciplinary Societies* (2 seats total) The National Academies
  - American Association for the Advancement of Science (AAAS)
  - Sigma Xi

- American Chemical Society (ACS) American Meteorological Society (AMS) American Geological Institute (AGI) American Mathematical Society (AMS)
- Mathematical Association of America (MAA) American Physical Society (APS)
- Federation of American Societies for Experimental Biology (FASEB)
- Institute of Electrical and Electronics Engineers (IEEE)
- American Society of Mechanical Engineers (ASME)
- American Institute of Aeronautics and Astronautics (AIAA)
- American Geophysical Union (AGU) Materials Research Society (MRS)
- American Institute of Biological Sciences (AIBS) Association for Computing Machinery (ACM) Computing Research Association (CRA)

APPENDIX B. PROPOSED NATIONAL COUNCIL FOR STEM EDUCATION OPERATIONAL STAFF AND BUDGET

The scope of the Council as envisioned suggests the need for a small cadre of professional staff. The day-to-day operations of the Council could be staffed with one executive director, two professional staff, and two clerical staff.

Initial cost estimates suggest a needed yearly budget of $700,000-800,000 for operational costs to pay for personnel, office space, equipment, and travel.

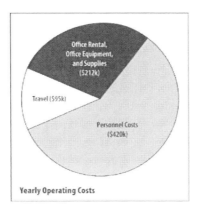

Appendix C. National Science Board Hearings on 21st Century Education in Science, Mathematics, and Technology

Hearing Participants

Hearing 1 December 7, 2005

Washington, DC	Cannon House Offi ce Building
Participant	**Affiliation***
	National Science Board
Dr. Warren Washington	NSB Chairman
	Senior Scientist and Section
	Head National Center for Atmospheric Research
Dr. Dan E. Arvizu	NSB Member
	Director,
	National Renewable Energy Laboratory
Dr. Steven C. Beering	NSB Member
	President Emeritus,
	Purdue University
Dr. Ray M. Bowen	NSB Member
	President Emeritus,
	Texas A&M University
Dr. Elizabeth Hoff man	NSB Member President Emerita,
	University of Colorado
Dr. Douglas D. Randall	NSB Member
	Professor of Biochemistry and Director,
Interdisciplinary	Program on Plant Biochemistry and Physiology,
	University of Missouri
Dr. Michael Crosby	NSB Executive Officer and Director,
	National Science Board Office
	Members of Congress
Congressman Sherwood Boehlert	Chairman, Committee on Science
Congressman John Abney	Culberson Subcommittee on Science, State, Justice, and Commerce, Committee on Appropriations

* Affiliation listed as at time of hearing.

Congressman Vernon J. Ehlers	Chairman, Subcommittee on Environment, Technology, and Standards, Committee on Science
Congressman Bart Gordon	Ranking Member, Committee on Science

Congresswoman Eddie Bernice Johnson	Committee on Science Congressman Frank Wolf Chairman, Subcommittee on Science, State, Justice, and Commerce, Committee on Appropriations

Department of Education and the National Science Foundation

Mr. Thomas Luce	Department of Education, Assistant Secretary, Office of Planning, Evaluation and Policy Development
Dr. Arden L. Bement, Jr.	Director, National Science Foundation
Dr. Donald Thompson	National Science Foundation, Directorate for Education and Human Resources, Acting Assistant Director

Other Participants

Ms. Mary Vermeer Andringa	President and COO, Vermeer ManufacturingCompany
Mr. William Archey	President and CEO, American Electronics Association
Mr. Alfred Berkeley	Chairman, Pipeline Trading Systems, LLC
Mr. Ronald Bullock	CEO, Bison Gear and Engineering
Dr. Raymond Cline	Vice President of Innovation Integration, EDS
Dr. Jack Collette	Senior Consultant, Delaware Foundation for Science and Mathematics
Dr. Cecily Cannan Selby	Affiliated Scholar, Steinhardt School of Education, New York University
Dr. David Shaw	Chairman, D. E. Shaw & Co., Inc.
Dr. Robert Tinker	President, The Concord Consortium
Dr. Gerald Wheeler	Executive Director, National Science Teachers Association (NSTA)

Hearing 2 February 10, 2006

Boulder, Colorado University of Colorado

Participant	**Affiliation**
	National Science Board
Dr. Warren M. Washington	NSB Chairman Senior Scientist and Section Head National Center for Atmospheric Research
Dr. Dan E. Arvizu	NSB Member Director, National Renewable Energy Laboratory
Dr. Steven C. Beering	NSB Member President Emeritus, Purdue University
Dr. Ray M. Bowen	NSB Member President Emeritus, Texas A&M University
Dr. Kelvin K. Droegemeier	NSB Member Regents' Professor & Roger and Sherry Teigen Presidential Professor; Weathernews Chair of Applied Meteorology; Director, Center for Analysis and Prediction of Storms; and Director, Sasaki Institute, University of Oklahoma

Dr. Kenneth M. Ford	NSB Member Director, Institute for Human and Machine Cognition, University of West Florida
Dr. Daniel E. Hastings	NSB Member Director, Engineering Systems Division and Professor, Aeronautics and Astronautics and Engineering Systems, Massachusetts Institute of Technology
Dr. Elizabeth Hoffman	NSB Member President Emerita, University of Colorado
Dr. Alan I. Leshner	NSB Member Chief Executive Officer, American Association for the Advancement of Science
Dr. Douglas D. Randall	NSB Member Professor of Biochemistry and Director, Interdisciplinary Program on Plant Biochemistry and Physiology, University of Missouri
Dr. Michael G. Rossman	NSB Member Hanley Distinguished Professor of Biological Sciences, Purdue University
Dr. Daniel Simberloff Nancy Gore Hunger	NSB Member Professor of Environmental Science, University of Tennessee
Dr. Jon C. Strauss	NSB Member President, Harvey Mudd College
Dr. Kathryn D. Sullivan	NSB Member Science Advisor, Center of Science and Industry (COSI)
Dr. Jo Anne Vasquez	NSB Member Mesa Public Schools (Retired) Gilbert, Arizona
Dr. Arden L. Bement, Jr.	NSB Member Ex Officio Director, National Science Foundation
Dr. Michael P. Crosby	NSB Executive Officer and Director, National Science Board Office

Members of Congress

Congressman Mark Udall	Ranking Member, Subcommittee on Space and Aeronautics, Committee on Science

Colorado Spokespersons

President Hank Brown	President, University of Colorado System
Mr. Randy DeHoff	Board Member, Colorado Department of Education, Colorado State Board of Education
Senator John Evans	Senator, Colorado General Assembly Senate Education Committee
Representative Keith King	Representative, Colorado General Assembly House Education Committee
Senator Susan Windels	Senator, Colorado General Assembly, and Chair, Senate Education Committee

Panelists

Dr. Michael Barnett	Senior Physicist and Educator, Lawrence Berkeley National Laboratory
Dr. Ruth David	President and CEO, Analytic Services, Inc.
Dr. Joseph Heppert	Chairman, Department of Chemistry, University of Kansas
Dr. Leon Lederman	Fermilab Director Emeritus and Chairman, Teachers Academy for Mathematics and Science
Dr. Shirley Malcom	Head, Directorate for Education, American Association for the Advancement of Science (AAAS)
Mr. Timothy McCollum	7-12 Science Teacher, Charleston Middle School, Charleston, Illinois
Mr. Michael Miravalle	President and CEO, Dolphin Technology, Inc.
Dr. Cindy Moss	Director of Science, K-12, Charlotte Mecklenburg Schools, Charlotte, North Carolina
Ms. Judith Sandler	Vice President, Education Development Center, Inc.
Dr. Thomas Smith	Professor, Chemistry and Microsystems Engineering Rochester Institute of Technology
Dr. Cindy Stevenson	Superintendent, Jefferson County Public Schools, Golden, Colorado
Mr. James Von Ehr	Founder, Chairman, and CEO, Zyvex Corp.
Dr. Karin Wiburg	Associate Dean for Research, New Mexico State University
Ms. Della Williams	President and CEO, Williams-Pyro, Inc.
Ms. Robin Willner	Vice President, Global Community Initiatives, IBM Corporation

Hearing 3, March 9, 2006

Los Angeles, California
University of Southern California

Participant	Affiliation
	National Science Board
Dr. Steven C. Beering	NSB Member President Emeritus, Purdue University
Dr. Elizabeth Hoffman	NSB Member President Emerita, University of Colorado
Dr. Jon C. Strauss	NSB Member President, Harvey Mudd College
Dr. Jo Anne Vasquez	NSB Member Mesa Public Schools (Retired) Gilbert, Arizona
Dr. Michael P. Crosby	NSB Executive Officer and Director, National Science Board Office

University of Southern California Spokespersons

Dr. C.L. Max Nikias	Provost, University of Southern California
President Steven B. Sample	President, University of Southern California
Dr. Karen Symms Gallagher	Dean, School of Education, University of Southern California

Panelists

Dr. Dennis Bartels	President, TERC Science and Math Learning
Chancellor Denice Denton	Chancellor, University of California, Santa Cruz
Dr. Eugene Garcia	Dean, School of Education, Arizona State University
Dr. James Gentile	President, Research Corporation
Dr. Dean Gilbert	President, California Science Teachers Association
Dr. Terry Joyner	Chief Academic Officer, Cincinnati Public Schools
Ms. Maria Alicia Lopez-Freeman	Executive Director, California Science Project
Dr. Lillian McDermott	Director, Physics Education Group, University of Washington
Dr. Willie Pearson, Jr.	Chair, School of History, Technology, and Society, Georgia Institute of Technology
Mr. Larry Prichard	Superintendent, Carter County, Kentucky
Dr. Jody Priselac	Director, Center X, University of California, Los Angeles
Dr. Rc Saravanabhavan	Dean, School of Education, Howard University
Mr. George Scalise	President, Semiconductor Industry Association
Dr. Robert Semper	Executive Director, Exploratorium
President Priscilla Slade	President, Texas Southern University
Dr. Elizabeth Stage	Director, Lawrence Hall of Science, University of California at Berkeley
Dr. Herbert Thier	Founding Director, Science Education for Public Understanding Program, University of California at Berkeley
Dr. Todd Ullah	K-12 Science Director, Los Angeles Unified School District
Dr. Jerry Valadez	K-12 Science Coordinator, Fresno Unified School District
Mr. Andrew Viterbi	President, Viterbi Group, LLC

APPENDIX D. CHARGE TO THE COMMISSION ON 21ST CENTURY EDUCATION IN SCIENCE, TECHNOLOGY, ENGINEERING, AND MATHEMATICS*

Background

Over the last two decades, numerous reports and statements from eminent bodies representing the broad range of national interests in science and technology literacy in U.S. society and skills in the U.S. workforce have sounded alarms concerning the condition of pre-K-16 education in science and technology areas. Nevertheless, our

Nation's education competitiveness continues to slip further behind the rest of the world. A number of spokespersons for the science and engineering education communities have urged the National Science Board (the Board) to undertake an effort similar to the 1982-1983 Board Commission on Pre-college Education in Mathematics, Science, and Technology. Congressional Appropriations Committee report language for FY 2006 stated that they strongly endorse the Board taking steps to "establish a commission to make recommendations for the National Science Foundation (NSF) and Federal Government action to achieve measurable improvements in the Nation's science education at all levels," and expects the Board to "report the commission's findings and recommendations to the Committee at the conclusion of the commission's work." Subsequently, the Board held three public hearings to explore the merit of establishing a special Commission on Education for the 21st Century. By approving this charge, the Board has decided to establish such a Commission to develop a national action plan addressing issues that have inhibited effective reform of U.S. science, technology, engineering, and mathematics (STEM) education.

Statutory Basis under the NSF Act

Under 42 U.S.C. § 1862 (d): "The Board and Director shall recommend and encourage the pursuit of national policies for the promotion of... education in science and engineering."

42 U.S.C. § 1863(h) authorizes the National Science Board "to establish such special commissions as it may from time to time deem necessary for the purposes of this chapter." The Board Commission on 21st Century Education in Science, Technology, Engineering, and Mathematics (the Commission) will conduct its activities according to the Federal Advisory Committee Act (FACA) and other authorities, including applicable conflict-ofinterest laws and regulations.

Objectives

The Commission will make recommendations to the Nation through the Board for a bold new action plan to address the Nation's needs, with recommendations for specific mechanisms to implement an effective, realistic, affordable, and politically acceptable long-

---

* *NSB-06-39*, March 30, 2006

term approach to the well-known problems and opportunities of U.S. pre-K-16 STEM education. The objective of a national action plan is to effectively employ Federal resources cooperatively with those of stakeholders from all sectors including but not limited to: Federal, State and local government agencies; parents, teachers and students; colleges – including community colleges; universities, museums and other agents of formal and informal education outside the K- 16 systems; industry; and professional, labor and public interest organizations to encourage and sustain reform of the national pre-K-16 STEM education system to achieve world class performance by U.S. students, prepare the U.S. workforce for 21st century skill needs, and ensure national literacy in science and mathematics for all U.S. citizens.

In developing a national action plan, the Commission will address the following issues and identify the specific role of NSF in each:

- Improving the quality of pre-K-16 education related to both general and pre-professional training in mathematics, engineering and the sciences, including, but not limited to: the availability of competent teachers; the adequacy and currency of curricula, materials, and facilities; standards and trends in performance, as well as promotion, graduation and higher-education entrance requirements; and comparison with performance and procedures of other countries.
- Identifying critical aspects in the entry, selection, education and exploitation of the full range of potential talents, with special attention to transition points during the educational career where loss of student interest is greatest; and recommend means to assure the most effective education for all U.S. students as well as future scientists, engineers and other technical personnel.
- Improving mathematics and science programs, curricula, and pedagogy to capitalize on the Nation's investment in educational research and development and appropriate models of exemplary education programs in other countries.
- Promulgating a set of principles, options and education strategies that can be employed by all concerned, nationwide, to improve the quality of secondary school mathematics and science education in the 21st century, as an agenda for promoting American economic strength, national security, employment opportunities, and social progress that will support U.S. pre-eminence in discovery and innovation.

Membership and Structure

The Board Commission will consist of up to fifteen (15) members appointed by the Chairman of the Board, in consultation with the full Board, the Executive Branch, Congress and other stakeholders. The Board Chairman will designate a Commission chairperson and vice chairperson from among the members. No more than three Commission members will be appointed from current Board membership. Commission members will be persons whose wisdom, knowledge, experience, vision or national stature can promote an objective examination of mathematics, science and technology education in the pre-K-16 system and develop a bold new national action plan for the 21st century.

A quorum of the Commission will be a majority of its members. Terms of service of members will end with the termination of the Commission. The Commission may establish such working groups, as it deems appropriate. At least one member of each working group shall be a member of the Commission. A Commission member will chair each working group, which will present to the Commission findings and recommendations for consideration by the Commission. Timely notification of the establishment of a working group and any change therein, including its charge, membership and frequency of meetings will be made in writing to the Executive Secretary or his/her designee. Management (including Executive Secretary and Designated Federal Official (DFO)) and staff services will be provided by the Board Office under the direct supervision of the Board's Executive Officer. Commission working groups will act under policies established by the Commission, in accordance with FACA and other applicable statutes and regulations.

Meetings

The Commission will meet as requested by the chairperson. Working groups will report to the full Commission and will meet as required at the call of their chairperson with the concurrence of the Commission chair. Meetings will be conducted, and records of proceedings will be kept, in accordance with applicable laws and regulations.

Expenses

Per diem and travel expenses will be paid in accordance to Federal Travel Regulations.

Reporting

The future action plan will especially focus on the appropriate role of NSF in collaboration and cooperation with other Federal agencies, State government, local school districts, gatekeepers, business and industry, informal STEM educational organizations, professional associations, scientific organizations, and parents and other citizens interested in improving education in mathematics, science and technology for our Nation's children. In addition to its final report, which is expected 12 months from the initial meeting, the Commission will submit to the Board periodic progress reports at least every 4 months. The Commission will develop an action plan that includes a plan for public dissemination and outreach for Commission activities, recommendations, and reports.

Warren M.
Washington Chairman

APPENDIX E. MEMBERS OF THE COMMISSION ON 21ST CENTURY EDUCATION IN SCIENCE, TECHNOLOGY, ENGINEERING, AND MATHEMATICS[*]

Dr. Leon M. Lederman, Commission Co-Chairman, Resident Scholar, Illinois Mathematics and Science Academy

Dr. Shirley M. Malcom, Commission Co-Chairman, Head, Directorate for Education and Human Resources Programs, American Association for the Advancement of Science (AAAS)

Dr. Jo Anne Vasquez, Commission Vice-Chairman, Member, National Science Board; Director of Policy and Outreach, Center for Research on Education in Science, Mathematics, Engineering and Technology, Arizona State University

The Honorable Nancy Kassebaum Baker, Former United States Senator (R-KS)

Dr. George R. Boggs, President and CEO, American Association of Community Colleges (AACC)

Mr. Ronald D. Bullock, Chairman and CEO, Bison Gear and Engineering, St. Charles, IL

Dr. Karen Symms Gallagher, Dean, Rossier School of Education, University of Southern California

Dr. James M. Gentile, President, Research Corporation, Tucson, AZ

Dr. Dudley R. Herschbach, Frank B. Baird, Jr., Research Professor of Science, Harvard University

Ms. María Alicia López-Freeman, Executive Director, California Science Project

Dr. Maritza B. Macdonald, Director of Professional Development, American Museum of Natural History, New York City

Mr. Timothy D. McCollum, Science Teacher, Charleston (IL) Middle School

Dr. Cindy Y. Moss, Director of K-12 Science, Charlotte/Mecklenburg (NC) Public Schools **Mr. Larry G. Prichard,** Superintendent, Carter County (KY) Schools

The Honorable Louis Stokes, Former United States Congressman (D-OH)

Dr. Elizabeth Strickland, Commission Executive Secretary

APPENDIX F.

Appendix F is the final draft report of the Commission on 21st Century Education in Science, Technology, Engineering, and Mathematics as submitted to the National Science Board on March 15, 2007. Although much of the Commission's advice was incorporated into the Board's action plan, the Commission's report to the Board does not necessarily represent either the work or views of the National Science Board.

---

[*] *NSB/STEMCOMM-06-1,* May 10, 2006, revised January 16, 2007

Draft Report of the Commission on 21st Century Education in Science, Technology, Engineering, and Mathematics

Introduction

In 2006, the National Science Board (the Board) established the Commission on 21st Century Education in Science, Technology, Engineering, and Mathematics (STEM) with the strong endorsement of Congressional Appropriations Committee language.[1] The Commission was charged with developing a bold, new action plan to implement the findings of the many previous panels, taskforces, commissions, and workshops that have called for a major transformation of STEM education in the United States (U.S.).

The Board's own report to Congress, *Science and Engineering Indicators 2006*, summarizes much of the data on education performance by U.S. students that compelled the Board to act. Numerous factors have informed this action plan including the high degree of attention directed toward STEM education; the growing concern from business and industry leaders, as well as from the nation's governors, regarding America's economic future; and the findings of the Board's recent education policy statement, *America's Pressing Challenge – Building a Stronger Foundation*.

The Commission has read and incorporated the work of previous groups in the preparation of this action plan and is mindful that many previous recommendations have never been implemented. Therefore, we set about to imagine the mechanisms, processes, structures, and metrics that would lead to implementation. In the report that follows, we present a set of actions that, taken together, would lead to the transformation of STEM education in the United States. Th ese actions necessarily depend on the good faith and the coherent and comprehensive efforts of many actors (i.e., local school systems, government at all levels, universities, community colleges, professional societies, Federal agencies, corporate sponsors, and accrediting bodies).

The Nation has successfully faced challenges to the STEM education system in the past - challenges that led us to re-examine our actions and chart a new path in STEM education and research. It is that history and our responses to it that we recall below.

The shock effect of the Soviet success in launching Sputnik in 1957 jarred the United States into taking a series of appropriate actions to win the space race. For example, in less than a year of Sputnik's launch, the United States Congress established the National Aeronautics and Space Administration (NASA) to oversee the task of developing a successful U.S. space program. The Defense Advanced Research Projects Agency (DARPA) was similarly established because the Department of Defense had no such ability to utilize up-to-the minute technology in support of national security. A science advisory system to the President was also established to provide the executive branch with scientifi c and technological advice. Furthermore, precedent-shattering Federal assistance to public education was established via the National Defense Education Act[2] (NDEA). Providing critical support and organizational infrastructure to the Nation's STEM development was deemed necessary to confronting the challenges of that day.

However, despite the importance of STEM fields to our Nation's economic development and competitiveness, today, almost 50 years after Sputnik, our Federal system has no entity specifically charged with and enabled to implement STEM education initiatives. These initiatives span across many Federal agencies, the vast K-12 education system, universities (including community colleges), and the informal learning community. As we studied the needs of our complex system, it became clear that a new structure is needed: a national, non-Federal entity to support more cohesive and research-based approaches to locally based reform.

We are mindful of the difficulty in orchestrating, facilitating, and coordinating the disparate efforts of many actors with responsibility for different components of a highly distributed education system. Thus, we are making a single recommendation to Congress:

> **Congress should charter a national body to implement, in partnership with the National Governors Association, a national system for 21st century science, technology, engineering, and mathematics education.**

The National Institute for STEM Educational Transformation

The National Institute for STEM Educational Transformation (NISET), the provisional name given to this body, would be chartered by Congress to work with the National Governors Association (NGA) and other organizations to facilitate, coordinate, and support implementation of the STEM education action plan outlined in this document. NISET would be modeled on the structure of the National Academy of Sciences (NAS).

The NAS was chartered by Congress in 1863 with the following mission: "The Academy shall, whenever called upon by any department of the government, investigate, examine, experiment and report upon any subject of science or art, the actual expense of such investigation to be paid from appropriation but the Academy shall receive no compensation whatever for any services to the Government of the United States." Thus, the Federal Government assured itself access to scientific advice at the highest level by creating an entity independent of the Federal structure. NAS has served this critical function over 140 years since its founding. Today, NAS is comprised of 600 members, many of whom are the most productive leaders in all fields of science in the nation. The original structure of the Academy was so successful that the National Academy of Engineering and the Institute of Medicine were later established to complement the work of the "parent" entity, and subsequently formed what we know today as the National Academies. The U.S. Government depends on the input and advice of the Academies for important tasks related to science, even though a number of Federal science agencies exist.

We propose that the newly chartered NISET operate under the same model as the National Academies. NISET should collaborate with other government agencies that handle STEM education activities and the NGA to focus and maintain national attention on STEM education in the nation. NISET would be composed of a number of outstanding persons capable of exercising national leadership in those domains relevant to STEM education: business, education, science, engineering, higher education, and public policy. Representation would be included from such agencies as the National Academies, NSF, the Department of Education (ED), state pre-K through graduate (P-20) education councils, the Council of Chief State School Officers (CCSSO), the Education Commission of the States, the National School Boards Association (NSBA), and others. This new entity would constitute a powerful consortium whose objectives would be to encourage and ensure the implementation and monitoring of STEM education initiatives in such a way as to generate a nationwide transformation.

The absence of management and oversight functions and the diversity of structure and membership should discourage the notion that the NISET is "just another layer of bureaucracy." Rather, the functions are to encourage the conduct and dissemination of the results of research and evaluation and to incubate innovative proposals that emerge from Commissions like this one. There will be future crises in our nation, which will call for new education initiatives. Since NISET would be a permanent addition to the array of national education entities, its implementation, coordination, and monitoring role - exercised in collaboration with the state education councils - would be available to all future Commissions.

NISET would also be expected to straddle and cross boundaries. To have legitimacy and appeal, it must be widely representative. Its value resides in its ability to facilitate, coordinate, support and monitor knowledge generating and knowledge sharing functions. It is designed as a beacon and an enabler rather than an enforcer. Agencies and departments would participate because their missions would be supported and their support leveraged. NISET could provide the "glue" that would bring state and local groups to the table.

Our vision of the value of this proposal is exciting. Like the National Academies, NISET is an intellectual structure now absent from our system but with far reaching possibilities and long lasting impact.

P-20 Councils

To complement the work of NISET, the Commission endorses the recommendation made in previous reports to encourage all states to form effective P-20 education councils. Approximately half of all U.S. states have already established P-20 councils. New education initiatives would be planned and marketed within these councils, and implementation would be supported. This is a logical place to begin discussing and enabling state-level, system-wide transformation of education in ways that support STEM education change. Supported by NISET, these state councils would facilitate the creation of local councils. The state councils would report to their respective governors and act as apolitical bodies in order to overcome partisan challenges. Council members would be highly respected for what they bring individually and collectively to deliberations: integrity, judgment, wisdom, political savvy, knowledge, and the vision to bring the United States from the present to the possible. Just as the presence of community members, business leaders, and local philanthropy representatives would be needed for external legitimacy, so too are representatives from various stakeholder groups needed, such as elected officials, boards of education, principals, superintendents, unions, parent groups, community college/university leaders, for achieving internal legitimacy.

P-20 councils would gain important information to benchmark their activities, share research and evaluation of promising practices, and be supported by NISET, the facilitating national entity responsible for disseminating information and providing assistance to inform local decision making. The councils would consider how the thoughtful and judicious use of technology in education might create new learning opportunities, help to build and extend capacity, link educational "haves and have-nots," expand the time for learning, and close the resource gaps that are found across systems. The larger STEM community would also need to be engaged at every level of dialogue and participation, including as members of councils, to guide the changes that they will need to make within their own community, to develop needed innovations in teaching and learning, as well as to assist others in their efforts. For example, the councils would need to consider STEM teacher recruitment and retention and how salary levels can be raised to respond to market forces for such highly skilled professionals. The councils would need also to focus on how well the system is serving *all* students, including those with disabilities, English language learners, girls and boys of all racial/ethnic groups, rural and urban schools and so on, as called for under No Child Left Behind (NCLB) legislation. They would also need to consider and advise on the relative value of investing early, such as in pre-school programs, where research suggests a high payoff for enhancing school readiness, especially for students most likely otherwise to be left behind. Th ey may consider other issues related to "time for learning," such as extension or modification of the school day, week or year. Whatever innovation is put in place should be well evaluated for effectiveness. Whatever is adapted from others should be formatted for local success and be widely shared. This will ensure that the councils, in coordination with NISET, collectively become a powerful community for learning as well as an engine for transformation of STEM education in the United States.

The Campaign for America's Future

Another task for NISET, and an essential element in the implementation of bold transformation, is the development of a popular consensus that an educational system, designed in the 19th and 20th centuries, can no longer serve the Nation without major changes. Thus, NISET can be called upon to appeal to the opinion leaders of the nation, the business community, scientists, engineers, educators, teachers, lawyers, clergy, media, leaders of higher education, politicians, and ordinary citizens to help explain the stakes. Additionally, NISET can be used to enlist support for changes such as those being advanced by our Commission and others and through state and local councils. We must sell the idea that our children deserve to look ahead to a future of hope and prosperity. We must help citizens understand the anachronistic nature of most schooling today, in which "post-Internet" young people are dropped into technology- poor environments, where they do not have the type of instruction, level of rigor, or expectations needed to address the challenges they will inherit or to imagine and create the future. We need to help the American public understand that the innovation system that has oftentimes given us products of American ingenuity and creativity is at risk. Seeking wide public support will require engagement with professionals who have public outreach expertise, and will also require the collaboration of media leaders.

Conclusions

The ingredients of this action plan rest heavily upon the new national NISET, which we present as a mechanism to enable a continuous transformation of STEM education and ultimately, of all U.S. education. However, we must be aware that the success of NISET requires P-20 councils, the collaboration of the NGA, the recognition and enthusiasm of the U.S. Congress, and a strong base of public support.

Our single major recommendation, to create an entity to support and assist in the effort, is largely made with careful consideration of our past failures to implement reform. Each member of an orchestra has a responsibility to perform at his or her highest level to create the symphony. Orchestrating transformation does not mean that each will play the same notes – it does mean that we will agree to the same music. Let us work together to sustain a strong and vibrant country with a robust and adapting economy for the 21st century in a world transformed by science and technology.

A Tale of Two Futures

If we were able to look into the future, we would be able to see the work of this Commission in the light of history. This is not possible. However, by building on current circumstances and conditions, we can imagine possible futures and the outcomes of our actions (or inactions). With this imagining comes some understanding of the possible effects of the choices that we make today. Two scenarios are presented below.

Scenario 1: Embracing the Challenge

The year 2007 was a turning point in U.S. history. Just as the launching of Sputnik 50 years earlier led to critical investments and the creation of many important agencies and initiatives to address the challenge to American security posed by the then Soviet Union, the decision to charter NISET and empower it to work across the many diff erent levels of government, higher education and civil society (with governors, state, Federal and local education agencies, institutes of higher education, accrediting bodies, business, industry, etc.) led to massive transformation of STEM education. Growing concern about the level of U.S. competitiveness in a knowledge-based economy prompted this work.

Programs of in-service STEM education revitalized the STEM teaching corps that was in place at the time. Innovative education and induction initiatives attracted STEM students to teaching and retained qualified educators. Teacher education students participated in exciting, re-vamped, college-level STEM courses and left their programs with enthusiasm for these fields. These highly qualified teachers were deployed into schools across the country where enhanced facilities, a world class curriculum, and exciting technology combined to enhance the science experiences for young people and support a positive attitude and "science way of thinking" for all students. Students emerged from these schools and from informal learning opportunities with 21st century skills, a love of learning, and excitement about STEM as it helped them understand the world around them. Some became STEM professionals; some became innovators, business and political leaders. All were personally enriched and empowered to move with confi dence into the future as their lives were increasingly transformed by science and technology. They were more agile workers, better parents, and more informed and engaged citizens. The economy thrived, and the standard of living improved for all, even as the United States reached out to support the use of science and technology (S&T) to address global challenges.

Prior to 2007, there had been good schools, excellent teachers, opportunities for student research, and engagement with problem-based learning, but these were not widespread. All too often, a student's "zip code" was a primary determinant of access, with students from high wealth areas receiving challenging educational experiences, while those in poor, urban, and rural schools were provided with uninspired and uninspiring STEM experiences.

The wake-up call led to unprecedented cooperation, convergence of intent and action and to the creation of a 21st century education for all of America's youth.

Scenario 2: Ignoring the Challenge (or Foregoing the Opportunity)

The NSB Commission issued its report in 2007. Despite its findings and its single recommendation to create an "implementing mechanism" (NISET) to support transformation in STEM education, it was difficult to get political and public traction for collaborative action. States continued to set their own standards and their own pace for change. Standards were often lowered to prevent massive takeover of schools by the states as required under NCLB legislation. The "illusion of rigor" lulled students and their parents into thinking that their children had been adequately prepared for living and working in the knowledge-based economy of the 21st century. However, the lack of knowledge and skills was painfully apparent when they entered higher education or the workforce. This inadequate preparation not only affected the students and their families directly, but in the aggregate, it affected overall U.S. competitiveness as the story of inadequate STEM education was found to have been repeated many times over. Despite the fact that past decisions had led to a weakened U.S. position in the global economy, policymakers "passed" on the challenge of assuming leadership, raising standards, and investing in creating a 21st century education for all children. Funding for education was not directed at transformation. Some students had received a wonderful, rich STEM education with well-prepared teachers and exciting STEM experiences. However, they were the exceptions. All too often family socio-economic and education levels were the main predictors of the quality of the STEM education experiences that students received. Th e talent of the increasingly diverse student population was left untapped. The STEM employment opportunities outside of education could not be ignored, especially for the most talented STEM educators who, in their frustration with the erosion of conditions in the schools, left to pursue more lucrative options in the workforce. Higher education bemoaned the quality of the STEM preparation of students who came to them, but did not perceive the relationship between the quality of their own teacher education initiatives and the students they would later receive.

Overall, there was a sense of pessimism about the directions that the country was headed. Citizens often voted in opposition to their own self-interest when it came to environmental, energy, and health concerns since they often did not understand what was at stake. Low wage jobs were the rule of the day, and children faced a lower standard of living than that of their parents.

The Bottom Line

Our people are our greatest asset, but failure to educate them could be a liability for us all. Our people, our children, our choice...will they be America's "ace in the hole" or our "Achilles' heel?" It is our move.

Action Plan

The United States can no longer afford to provide its young people with STEM education that is fragmented and uncoordinated across the various components of the formal education system. U.S. students must receive the skills and knowledge of science, technology, engineering, and mathematics within an educational structure that is aligned both horizontally and vertically. Additionally, this structure must be standards-based and nationally coordinated to ensure that all participants are adequately prepared to thrive in a technologically complex 21st century.

The grand challenge of this new century is raising the quality of education for all and narrowing the achievement gap in U.S. STEM education. The STEM education system must incorporate proven practices based on solid research on teaching and learning. The system must provide and enlarge capacity to undertake educational research for the ongoing development and study of innovative improvement practices. A balance must exist between acquiring content knowledge and developing analytical skills such as critical thinking, making connections between ideas, and building a capacity for life-long learning. Students need thoughtfully sequenced classes that focus on depth of understanding, not just coverage of topics. Coordination must be both horizontal among states and vertical across grade levels, from pre-K through graduate education. Undertaking this effort assumes an acceptance of high standards for all students and an acceptance of the value in coherent and coordinated standards, curricula, assessments, as well as professional development opportunities.

The Commission recognizes that a coherent P-20 national system requires:

- Horizontal coordination within and among states;
- Vertical alignment from pre-K through graduate education; and
- Fully integrated teachers in the system.

Addressing the issues posed in this action plan would be the responsibility of state P-20 councils, supported by the national coordinating entity, NISET, which would work closely with the National Governors Association, other state and local based education and STEM based groups, professional societies, teachers and higher education organizations among others. At the Federal level, we propose the National Science and Technology Council[3], Committee on Science, Subcommittee on Education and Workforce Development[4] provide the unified Federal voice that interacts with NISET.

Many different agencies and actors, at all levels, will need to work together to identify the contours of issues related to STEM education transformation in all its dimensions and to accept responsibility to work collectively toward meeting these challenges. We believe that the umbrella that NISET provides will allow an appropriate "implementing and learning community" to emerge.

The Commission was also charged with commenting on the role of the National Science Foundation in STEM education transformation. Statements about its unique role are provided below while other aspects of the NSF role are embedded, where appropriate, in the action plan below. It is clear that while NSF would have a role that would be integrated with other Federal actors, it also bears unique leadership responsibility by virtue of its mandate to see to the health of STEM education in the United States, and its strategic responsibility to focus on the integration of research and education. The comments to the Board about this role are made in recognition of this special context.

The Role of NSF

The National Science Foundation (NSF) has a unique responsibility to shape its own STEM education research and development strategy, in collaboration with the STEM education and research community, in ways that complement and support the larger implementation needs of this collaborative eff ort. This would mean, for example:

- Promoting innovation in education through support of research that responds to critical needs from the world of practice (such as new ideas that might emerge from school systems and P-20 councils) in addition to those that are initiated within the research programs of experts studying key issues related to STEM education;
- Supporting scientists and engineers who wish to pursue research and development on teaching and learning in education in their fields, perhaps in collaboration with education researchers with complementary and supporting interests and skills;
- Exploring research and development on issues related to scaling up promising practices or new organizational arrangements to support STEM education transformation;
- Finding ways to promote and scale up the successful educational research in order that all communities can benefit from the findings; and
- Building capacity for sustained research programs in STEM education, to ensure that innovative research methodologies, tools, and resources are developed to support deeper understanding of STEM educational issues.

Undertaking these additional roles in STEM education R&D will likely, over time, require new and additional investments from Congress.

The NSF portfolio has evolved over the years, and reflects the history of NSF's leadership in STEM education including basic research on learning; development of instructional materials, tools and resources; technology development; informal science education; pre-service teacher preparation; in-service teacher education; and large systemic initiatives aimed at improving mathematics and science education for all students. In particular, NSF has brought to the field the best knowledge and tools available for the professional development of all teachers. These products can be used by the U.S. Department of Education, other Federal agencies, and every state and district to support teachers and students in research-based programs so that every child has the opportunity to achieve to high standards.

The NSF's role is a continuum beginning with basic research on learning, research, and development in teacher education and teacher learning. NSF then seeks practical application of these research findings to help us better understand the role and impact of educational innovations and improvements. Finally, NSF implements new programs to evaluate how successfully they operate in a variety of contexts. The NSF's role includes not only the generation of knowledge and tools, but also support of activities that will build capacity and enhance the "improvement infrastructure" so that that infrastructure system eventually can provide on-going technical assistance to states and districts. Th e challenge for NSF is to create a better mechanism for integration and feedback across these roles. Research agendas must be informed by the needs from the field, in concert with the issues as understood by expert researchers. In turn, the results of research involve and feed back into the STEM education field to inform practice and into colleges and universities to inform the way that teachers are educated.

Outcome #1

Horizontal Coordination of STEM Education within and among States

Current Status

Currently, the U.S. STEM education system is far from coordinated. The system is fractured and disjointed within school districts and from state to state, both from the perspective of students and teachers. Content standards and the sequence in which content is taught vary by state. In our geographically mobile society, both students and teachers are likely to relocate during their academic or professional life. Students who move from one location to another may miss exposure to a critical fundamental concept in one school system and never have the opportunity to master that concept.[5] Teachers face barriers to their movement between states in the form of teacher certification standards set independently by each state and the inability to carry over pension funds.[6]

Actions Needed
   A. Development and adoption of national STEM content standards
   B. Linkage of student assessment with national STEM content standards
   C. Alignment of the preparation and credentialing of STEM teachers with national content standards

A. Development and Adoption of National STEM Content Standards [7]

States must adopt a common national definition of "adequate" STEM education for our nation's students that are benchmarked against international standards and that are based on available research.[8]

National STEM Content Standards Action #1: Define and Periodically Review Core National STEM Education Content Standards[9]

Lead Entities – The National Academies, Professional Disciplinary Societies, and Professional Teaching Organizations

The National Academies, professional disciplinary societies, and professional teaching organizations, will be assigned the task of defining and periodically reviewing core national STEM content standards.[10] These research-based standards would build on pre-existing broad standards[11] and should be clear, specifi c, defined, and articulated between each grade-level.[12]

National STEM Content Standards Action #2: Provide Financial Incentives for State Adoption[13]

Lead Entities – Congress and the Department of Education

Congress should appropriate to the Department of Education funds to provide financial incentives to states that act consistently with national content standards. Other incentives may also be appropriate.

National STEM Content Standards Action #3: Provide Input to Inform Curriculum Development within the Framework of National Content Standards[14]

Lead Entity – The National Science Foundation (NSF)
NSF will devise coordinated initiatives through its current programs to continue the development of research-based, innovative tools, materials, and resources to promote K-12 STEM learning.

National STEM Content Standards Action #4: Provide Input to Inform STEM Curriculum Pathways within the Framework of National Content Standards[15]
Lead Entities – State P-20 Councils
State P-20 councils will leverage the partnership among their members – state and local education agencies, institutions of higher education, local businesses and industry, local STEM-related employers, and others – to inform STEM curriculum pathways and critical workforce skill requirements within the parameters of the national STEM content standards. This allows STEM curriculum pathways to be responsive to local needs and to career technical education goals and eff orts.

B. Linkage of Student Assessment with National STEM Content Standards
Until recently, science has not been assessed under the No Child Left Behind Act (NCLB). As a result, science programs have been de-emphasized in many elementary schools as they focus on subjects, such as reading and mathematics, that are assessed under the legislation. Unless science is part of the evaluation, and counted as part of Adequate Yearly Progress (AYP), it will not receive the attention and resources required for every student to achieve basic science literacy and for highly motivated students to acquire the preparation needed for higher education in STEM fields. Because states do not currently share a common set of content standards upon which to base their assessments of student performance, their tests vary widely in the level of rigor and performance required. This allows for great variation in the quality of the education that students receive from state to state. Thus, comparisons and accomplishments are, at best, diffi cult to determine.

Student Assessment Action #1: Include Additional Measure of Science Learning for AYP[16]
Lead Entities – Congress and the Department of Education
Assessments of student performance under NCLB must be designed to reflect the knowledge, critical thinking skills, and problem-solving abilities required to meet real life challenges rather than the extent to which students have memorized the content required to pass the test. Science should be considered as part of AYP.[17]

Student Assessment Action #2: Develop National Content Standards for Assessment of Student Progress
Lead Entity – The National Assessment Governing Board (NA GB)[18]
The NAGB, in consultation with a wide range of experts, will be responsible for developing student assessments that derive from, and are aligned with, national content standards.[19]

Student Assessment Action #3: Provide Incentives to States Using National Content Standards for Assessment
Lead Entities – Congress and the Department of Education

Congress would appropriate funds to the Department of Education to provide incentives to states that voluntarily participate in standardized national testing that reflect national STEM content standards, problem-solving, and critical thinking skills. The National Assessment of Education Progress (NAEP) could act as a model for establishing these kinds of standards.[20]

Student Assessment Action #4: Participate Voluntarily in Standardized National Tests

Lead Entities –States

States should voluntarily participate in standardized national and international tests that reflect national STEM content standards.[21] Those states that participate would receive incentives.[22] States could collaborate in the development of tests, thus lowering the cost of test development.

C. Alignment of the Preparation and Credentialing of STEM Teachers with National Content Standards

STEM teachers should meet the requirements set by a national standard for STEM teacher quality. States would voluntarily align their credentialing of STEM teachers to meet national criteria. The value of this is two-fold. Such policies would ensure that teachers are prepared to teach the content specified in the national standards and facilitate teacher mobility within and among states.

Teacher Preparation Action #1: Create and Endorse National STEM Teacher Certifi cation Standards

Lead Entity – National Institute for STEM Education Transformation (NISET)

NISET will coordinate with the teaching, policy, employment, and content communities to create and endorse national STEM teacher certification standards. NISET will organize all relevant groups in deriving a consensus as to how this would be implemented. These standards will facilitate the ability of teachers qualified in one state to move to another and continue a STEM teaching career and will clarify requirements for bringing STEM professionals from other occupations into the classroom.[23]

Teacher Preparation Action #2: Create and Endorse National STEM Teacher Certifi cation Standards

Lead Entity – The National Science Foundation (NSF)

NSF would support research that can provide a foundation for determining and assessing teacher knowledge needed for effective STEM teaching at various stages of the career. They will also provide funding to develop and study examples of promising new models of fostering STEM teaching preparation and to create a mechanism whereby these new models can be replicated and brought to scale by other institutions.

Teacher Preparation Action #3: Provide Financial Incentives for National STEM Teacher Certifi cation Standards

Lead Entities – Congress and the Department of Education

Congress will appropriate funds to the Department of Education to provide financial incentives to those states or districts that recognize national certification, as outlined in the above actions, and employ certified, qualified, and effective teachers of STEM.

Teacher Preparation Action #4: Provide Teacher Education Based on National STEM Content Standards[24]
Lead Entities – Institutions of Higher Education (IHEs)
IHEs will provide teacher education based on national STEM content standards. They must promote interactions both externally with other accredited institutions (particularly between community colleges and four-year colleges) and internally between the college of education and the colleges of arts and sciences, engineering, and technology, as appropriate, to prepare future STEM teachers. These interactions should promote high quality teacher education focused on both content and the knowledge and skills associated with effective teaching. A key to this is the reworking of introductory courses to model pedagogy that motivates student interest in STEM fields. IHEs will utilize national STEM content standards and national STEM teacher qualification standards as guidance in developing their undergraduate curricula for STEM teacher education.

Teacher Preparation Action #5: Develop Policies Encouraging Institutions of Higher Education to Provide Teacher Education Based on National STEM Content Standards[25]
Lead Entities – Higher Education Accreditation Bodies and Disciplinary Societies
Both regional and specialized accreditation bodies and disciplinary societies must develop policies that require institutions of higher education to provide high quality teacher education that develops teacher competence and confidence in providing standards-based instruction.

Outcome #2

Vertical Alignment of STEM Education from Pre-K through Graduate Education

Current Status
Due to the lack of alignment among STEM standards, curricula, student assessments, and professional development of teachers, core concepts are not always taught and understood at the elementary and middle school levels, limiting academic success at the high school level. Furthermore, high schools often offer curricula that are uninspiring, poorly aligned, outdated, lacking in rigor, and wrought with low expectations. Most high school curricula do not show pathways to the workforce or communicate the exciting nature of science and engineering. High school graduates often enter college unprepared for first-year coursework[26] or arrive at the workplace without the skills employers require.[27] Additionally, career technical education programs, which are independent of the traditional high school to college pathway, may hinder students from successfully matriculating into further degree programs. In addition, educators may leave teacher education programs lacking in content knowledge that correlates with the disciplines they will be asked to teach in the classroom. Teacher education programs

may also fail to provide future teachers with a strong understanding of how students learn best and how knowledge connects to the real world.

Actions Needed
- A. Coordination between components of the STEM education system within states
- B. Alignment of student learning across grade levels in pre-K-12
- C. Alignment of post-high school student learning
- D. Inclusion of informal science education institutions and other stakeholders in the understanding of STEM

A. Coordination between Components of the STEM Education System within States

Each state will either establish or continue to support a P-20 council to engage multiple stakeholders in improving STEM education in their state at the pre-K through graduate school levels.[28] The merit of P-20 councils has been outlined in several previous reports,[29] and a number of states already have established P-20 councils. These P-20 councils will work with, and communicate through, NISET and the NGA.

Coordination within States Action #1: Create and Empower State P-20 Councils[30]
Lead Entity – State Governors

Every state will create or continue to support a non-partisan and independent P-20 council to be led and empowered by the governor of that state. Each P-20 council will represent the combined input of the governor, legislature, state education agency, higher education system, local school boards, teacher associations, business and industry, chamber of commerce, private foundations, economic development initiatives, informal science education institutions, civic groups, and other professional organizations. P-20 councils will review the STEM education system in their respective states, and each will develop a strategy for vertically aligning this system. Additionally, the councils will develop a vision and set of measurable goals and timelines for implementation of STEM education reform and alignment. NISET will provide technical assistance and support to enable coordination among all the state P-20 councils.

B. Alignment of Student Learning across Grade Levels in pre-K-12

Although national science and technology standards do exist, they span grade levels and are not grade specifi c.[31] In contrast, mathematics has recently developed "focal points" for each grade, and since their release in 2006, they are under consideration by many states.[32] Each state builds their curricula based on these existing standards, but do not horizontally coordinate timelines with other states. This makes it difficult for publishers who have to ensure their materials match state standards in a number of states. As a consequence, textbooks are often excessively long and cover too much material at too little depth. Courses, like their textbooks, end up being a mile wide and an inch deep.

Alignment of Student Learning Action #1: Develop Curricular Content Standards, Benchmarks, and Assessments for Each Grade Level[33]
Lead Entity – State and Local Education Agencies (SEAs and LEAs) with P-20 Councils

Using the national content standards developed in Outcome #1 and in collaboration with state P-20 councils, SEAs and LEAs will develop a common set of curricular content standards and benchmarks defining what students must master at each grade level in order to advance to the next grade level. Content standards and benchmarks will be in place through 1 2th grade, emphasize a few core concepts in a discipline, and demonstrate how these ideas are cumulatively developed.[34]

Alignment of Student Learning Action #2: Align pre-K-12 STEM Benchmarks with Higher Education Requirements[35]

Lead Entities – Institutions of Higher Education (IHEs) with P-20 Councils

IHEs, including two- and four-year colleges and technical schools, will work with P-20 councils to align STEM learning, which will provide pathways for success in college and the workforce. As a result, the learning gap between what high school graduates should know, and what they do know, will narrow.[36]

Alignment of Student Learning Action #3: Engage Administrators in Professional Development that Encourages and Supports Alignment[37]

Lead Entities – Local Education Agencies (LEAs)

Local school leadership is imperative for aligning STEM curricula and providing the support and infrastructure necessary for its successful delivery in the classroom. School leaders at all levels must be engaged, including school board members, school superintendents, curriculum directors, principals, assistant principals, and department chairs. In particular, LEAs must provide professional development for principals on ways to identify, reward, support, and implement effective STEM teaching and learning.

Alignment of Student Learning Action #4: Provide STEM Learning Opportunities for Changing Student Demographics

Lead Entities - States

States will provide challenging STEM learning opportunities that ensure access, participation, and benefit for all students. States will create these learning opportunities to address the changing demographics and complexities of providing quality education for the current and future student population, which present different needs and require more robust programs. This may mean supplementing formal education for these students with appropriate informal STEM education settings or after-school programs.

Alignment of Student Learning Action #5: Provide Challenging STEM Educational Opportunities to Gifted Students

Lead Entities – States

States will provide challenging STEM educational opportunities to their most gifted and talented students by establishing STEM academies, schools within schools, or other special programs for this population of future innovators. Students with strong interest and aptitude in STEM subjects must be nurtured and provided connections to research opportunities.[38]

Alignment of Student Learning Action #6: Collaboration between Local Business and Industry and School Systems on STEM Workforce Skill Requirements[39]

Lead Entities - Local Education Agencies (LEAs) and P-20 Councils

LEAs will ensure that their students are equipped with the requirements and skill sets for STEM-related jobs and will collaborate with STEM-related businesses and industry through state P-20 councils and other mechanisms in order to gain the required technical expertise.[40] This cross-communication will promote student interest in STEM fields and the career technical education programs that are called for.

Alignment of Student Learning Action #7: Inform School Guidance Counselors and Teachers of Potential STEM Career Fields and Skill Requirements[40]
Lead Entities – P-20 Councils
P-20 councils must work with all stakeholders to provide middle school, high school, and college guidance counselors and teachers the tools and information necessary to inform students about STEM career opportunities and the occupational and foundational skills required for those jobs. In an era when nearly all jobs require some technical literacy, this information flow is essential to prepare all students for productive lives after high school graduation.[42]

Alignment of Student Learning Action #8: Strengthen Elementary School STEM Programs
Lead Entity – Local Education Agencies (LEAs)
As learning in elementary grades provides the foundation for future student interest and success in STEM fi elds and captures children's natural curiosity about the world around them, LEAs must support science, engineering, and technology curricula and opportunities for learning in addition to instruction in mathematics. The time allotted for this learning should be equivalent to that of other subjects.

C. Alignment of Post-High School Student Learning

Alignment of Post-High School Student Learning Action #1: Reduce Transfer Barriers among Institutions of Higher Education
Lead Entities –Institutions of Higher Education (IHEs) and P-20 Councils
IHEs within each state will strengthen articulation agreements among themselves in order for students to transfer STEM coursework more easily (and without losing credit) between institutions.[43] P-20 councils will work with higher education systems to improve and strengthen articulation agreements to ensure that courses taken at accredited institutions transfer and that students are given credit toward degrees for completing equivalent courses.[44]

Alignment of Post-High School Student Learning Action #2: Recognize Coursework at Community Colleges as Part of Teacher Preparation
Lead Entities – Institutions of Higher Education (IHEs)
IHEs, in collaboration with state P-20 councils, will develop articulation agreements that recognize associate degrees in teacher education at community colleges and allow the credits to transfer into schools or colleges of education at universities.[45]

Alignment of Post-High School Student Learning Action #3: Establish Expectations for STEM Curriculum at the 13-20 Education Levels

Lead Entities – Institutions of Higher Education, P-20 Councils, Professional Societies, and Higher Education Organizations

P-20 councils, professional societies, and higher education organizations will work with higher education systems to establish basic STEM literacy expectations for all college graduates.[46] College graduates must understand science as a way of thinking and knowing. Curricula must acknowledge that different student populations exist within colleges and universities, including the general student population, students majoring in STEM fields, and those preparing to be pre- K-12 teachers; however, all students need to have a basic understanding of how the world works within and across the inter-related STEM disciplines.

Alignment of Post-High School Student Learning Action #4: Develop Mechanism for Professional Development of Teachers Outside University Graduate Structures

Lead Entities – P-20 Councils and Local Education Agencies (LEAs)

P-20 councils need to endorse and facilitate a mechanism whereby credit for professional development in STEM content areas can be awarded outside university graduate structures by LEAs. This should include mechanisms that allow teachers on salary schedules credit for taking in-service or professional development courses at community colleges.[47]

D. Inclusion of Informal Science Education Institutions and Other Stakeholders in the Understanding of STEM

Informal science education institutions play a valuable role in increasing interest in and excitement about STEM fields. These institutions and other stakeholders need to be engaged and work cooperatively with the formal school environment to promote an understanding of STEM fi elds.[48]

Informal Science Education Action #1: Align Formal and Informal Science Education Institutions through Collaboration[49]

Lead Entities –Local Education Agencies (LEAs), Informal Science Education Institutions, and the National Science Foundation (NSF)

Through collaboration with LEAs and NSF, informal science education institutions will provide unique complementary experiences that enhance and reinforce formal school learning goals. Through direct activities with students, professional development opportunities for teachers, and online learning resources, these institutions provide invaluable supplements to support teaching and learning.[50]

Informal Science Education Action Item #2: Develop Programs to Provide Research Experiences for High School Students

Lead Entity – The National Science Foundation (NSF)

NSF will initiate a research and development program to build and study models to provide STEM research experiences for high school students.

Informal Science Education Action Item #3: Identify and Create a Database of Existing, Effective Informal Science Education Programs[51]

Lead Entity – National Institute for STEM Education Transformation (NISET) and the National Science Foundation (NSF)

NISET and NSF will identify museums, media, traveling laboratories, libraries, online resources, and interactive experiences that demonstrate evidence of effectiveness in STEM education of students, families, educators, and the public at large. NSF will support the compilation of a database of exemplary programs to use in developing additional programs. NISET will review and disseminate this database, thus including the work of these informal settings as part of the resources for the formal system.

Informal Science Education Action Item #4: Develop and Support Programs that Increase the Public Engagement with Science
Lead Entity – National Science Foundation (NSF)
NSF will continue to support research that helps the field understand the most effective models and approaches for learning in informal settings. NSF will also continue to support research on programs that foster the public understanding of STEM through the media and provide access to informal STEM institutions for underrepresented groups and those who are geographically isolated from informal science education institutions.

Informal Science Education Action Item #5: Provide Students with Real-World STEM Experiences
Lead Entities – Business and Industry
Business and industry should develop and provide mentoring, shadowing, and internship opportunities for students in grades 7-12.[52] In addition, co-ops and internships have proven to be effective in retaining STEM majors in STEM fields in colleges and universities.

Outcome #3

Attract, Prepare, Retain, and Support STEM Teachers and Educators

Current Status

The strengthening of the STEM teaching profession requires a coordinated national effort to attract, prepare, and retain qualified and committed candidates to the teaching profession. The effectiveness of the STEM education system rests on the quality of the investment in and support of the nation's STEM teachers and educators. STEM educators in the United States must be viewed as a national resource that must be given thorough preparation prior to entering the classroom, adequate mentoring during the critical first few years in the classroom, opportunities for continual growth and enrichment of skills and knowledge, and proper support in order to be maximally effective STEM educators. Exemplary models of continued professional training and certification from other fields include medicine, architecture, and engineering. STEM educators require this level of professional development and training to reinstate American students at the forefront of global STEM education.

Actions Needed

A. Recruitment and retention of qualified and committed candidates into STEM teaching careers

B. Implementation of continuous, standards-based, data-driven, and relevant STEM teacher professional development
C. Support of teachers to ensure effective teaching

A. Recruitment and Retention of Qualified and Committed Candidates into STEM Teaching Careers

A quarter million qualified K-12 mathematics and science teachers will be needed over the next decade.[53] Unfortunately, 48 percent of our nation's middle schools and 61 percent of our high schools have already reported difficulty in hiring qualified candidates for mathematics and science teaching positions.[54] This widening gulf requires immediate action, beginning with the recommendations listed below.

STEM Teacher Recruitment and Retention Action #1: Provide Tuition Assistance for Promising STEM Teachers[55]

Lead Entities – Congress and the States

Congress will appropriate increased funds to the states in order to provide tuition and/or financial assistance to college students majoring in STEM content areas who commit to becoming K-12 teachers.[56] Some states are already doing this with their own funds, and the Commission is supportive of this. With the rising cost of education in the United States, a student's ability to subsidize tuition costs may be a strong recruitment incentive.

STEM Teacher Recruitment and Retention Action #2: Subsidize Loan Forgiveness for STEM Teachers[57]

Lead Entity – The Department of Education

The Department of Education will provide loan forgiveness to students majoring in STEM content areas that are tied to service in teaching. This kind of program will attract graduating students who are considering employment opportunities and beginning the process of student loan repayment.

STEM Teacher Recruitment and Retention Action #3: Expand Funding for STEM Teacher Education[58]

Lead Entity – National Science Foundation (NSF)

NSF will expand efforts such as its Robert Noyce Scholarship program[59] that provides financial support to college students for post-graduation STEM teaching in public schools.[60]

STEM Teacher Recruitment and Retention Action #4: Provide Additional Income to STEM Teachers

Lead Entity – The Federal Government

Although teacher compensation is set by local school boards, the Federal Government must step to the plate and assist local education agencies in supplementing STEM teacher salaries. Although all teachers are valuable resources for the nation, market forces offer career opportunities with substantially higher salaries to professionals with STEM training than these professionals would receive in teaching careers.[61] The National Science Board has previously stated that, "To attract and retain precollege science and mathematics teachers, resources must be provided to compensate teachers of mathematics, science, and technology comparably to similarly trained S&E professionals in other economic sectors."[62]

STEM Teacher Recruitment and Retention Action #5: Advocate Competitive Teacher Salaries[63]

Lead Entities – State P-20 Councils

State P-20 councils would assist state and local education agencies in actively pursuing ways to increase STEM teacher incomes to competitive levels.[64] Various mechanisms to achieve this include developing partnerships with local business and industry, government research laboratories, and/or institutions of higher education in order to help teachers augment incomes through summer employment.

STEM Teacher Recruitment and Retention Action #6: Establish Pension Portability for Teachers

Lead Entity – National Governors Association (NGA)

The NGA is encouraged to work with states to coordinate a system that allows teacher pensions to be portable among states. Teacher mobility across states is greatly diminished by the teacher pension system.

STEM Teacher Recruitment and Retention Action #7: Institute STEM-Specific Teacher Induction Programs

Lead Entities – The Department of Education and the National Science Foundation (NSF)

The Department of Education and NSF will provide sustained funding for the development and implementation of subject matter teacher induction programs to support teachers during their first 2 years of teaching. Th ese induction programs foster the professional community necessary for sustaining new teachers through mentoring, content specifi c professional development, and peer community development.

B. Implementation of Continuous, Standards-based, Data-driven and Relevant STEM Teacher Professional Development

The Federal Government, P-20 councils, states, LEAs, principals, local businesses, industry and other stakeholders should create professional development opportunities that deepen teachers' content knowledge, inquiry experiences, pedagogical skills, and understanding of instructional materials and their use in the classroom. Retaining high quality STEM teachers depends on facilitating access to opportunities for professional development and intellectual growth throughout their careers. Professional development must be sustained throughout teaching careers and support a professional learning community environment. It must incorporate available and emerging technologies, such as podcasting and e-mentoring, that can effectively deliver ongoing training in an asynchronous manner. Professional development must also provide teachers with access to STEM experts and updates on research findings. Providing teachers with a broad spectrum of professional development tools is critical to meeting the needs of the nation's STEM educators. Teachers should be prepared to teach to the standards, the curriculum for which they are responsible, and the student population in their classroom. They must be enabled to continually improve their practice.

Professional Development of Teachers Action #1: Fund Sustained Professional Development Programs
Lead Entity – The Department of Education and the National Science Foundation (NSF)
The Department of Education and NSF will provide funding for sustained professional development for teachers. NSF will provide funding for research, development, and implementation of focused teacher professional development models designed to enhance teachers' knowledge in ways that support students' STEM learning. NSF will also support the research and implementation needed to prepare these model approaches for going to scale. The Department of Education will provide funding for sustained professional development for teachers.

Professional Development of Teachers Action #2: Ensure STEM Teacher Access to Inquiry Based Pedagogy[64]
Lead Entity – National Science Foundation (NSF)
NSF needs to continue to develop, disseminate, and support research-based models, tools, and strategies to support development of content knowledge and content-specific teaching skills. Authentic experiences in science are needed for STEM teachers.

Professional Development of Teachers Action #3: Embed Professional Development during the School Day and Year[66]
Lead Entities – Local Education Agencies (LEAs) and School Principals
LEAs and school principals will support the development of professional learning communities and shared lesson planning time for teachers to improve teaching skills, the ability to evaluate student learning, and content knowledge in rapidly changing STEM fi elds.[67] Time for these activities would be included as part of the standard school year and school day.

Professional Development of Teachers Action #4: Support New Teachers through Appropriate Teaching Assignments and Mentoring
Lead Entities – Local Education Agencies (LEAs) and School Administrators
LEAs and school administrators have the responsibility to place new STEM educators into settings where they are most likely to succeed. State and local education agencies must implement policies to support mentoring of new teachers and eliminate the practice of assigning early career STEM teachers to the most challenging teaching situations. Likewise, administrators are encouraged to assign the most highly qualified and effective teachers to the most challenging students and environments. Additionally, school administrators must ensure that STEM teachers are not asked to teach non- STEM related classes.

Professional Development of Teachers Action #5: Provide Appropriate STEM Instructional Leadership and Infrastructure Support
Lead Entities – Local Education Agencies (LEAs)

LEAs will provide appropriate STEM instructional leadership and infrastructure support at all levels from the superintendent, curriculum director, principals, and assistant principals to the department chairs.

Professional Development of Teachers Action #6: Institute Mentoring Programs for Entering STEM Education Faculty at Institutions of Higher Education[68]

Lead Entities – Institutions of Higher Education (IHEs)

Colleges and universities should provide faculty development programs, including mentoring, for entering faculty who teach STEM courses. IHEs would reward faculty mentors for their involvement in the early career development of their colleagues as teachers. Pre-K-12 teachers who receive their education in colleges would benefit from having STEM content courses taught in such a way that their engagement with the subject matter is maximized and effective teaching strategies are modeled.

Professional Development of Teachers Action #7: Develop Programs to Link STEM Teachers with STEM Professionals

Lead Entity – National Science Foundation (NSF)

NSF must take the lead in developing programs that link classroom teachers with researchers in STEM fields and in STEM pedagogy and in studying these models to understand better the specific kinds of contributions such programs make to teacher effectiveness.

Professional Development of Teachers Action #8: Utilize Informal Science Education Institutions in Teacher Professional Development[69]

Lead Entities – Informal Science Education (ISE) Institutions

ISE institutions play a valuable role in continuing teacher professional development by broadening content knowledge, improving pedagogical skills, and providing real world, relevant experiences for the enhancement of teachers' content knowledge.

Professional Development of Teachers Action #9: Provide Professional Expertise to STEM Teachers[70]

Lead Entities – Professional Organizations

Professional STEM teaching organizations - such as the National Science Teachers Association (NSTA), National Council of Teachers of Mathematics (NCTM), National Association of Biology Teachers (NABT), and the International Technology Education Association (ITEA) - and disciplinary societies must provide continuing teacher professional development by using technology to supply "just in time" learning experiences. Organizations could use new technologies, such as e-mentoring, podcasts, etc., to reach teachers in all types of schools.

Professional Development of Teachers Action #10: Develop New Forms of Teacher Professional Development

Lead Entities – Institutions of Higher Education, Informal Science Education Institutions, Educational Research Organizations, the National Science Foundation, and Local Education Agencies

The entities named above will work cooperatively to research and develop new, innovative forms of teacher pre-service and in-service professional development based on science learning research to prepare teachers for real-world educational settings.

C. Support of Teachers to Ensure Effective Teaching

Teachers must be supported with the technology, teaching resources, mentoring, and planning time needed for effective teaching. Providing these resources to teachers is critical not only to their effectiveness, but also to their retention in the profession.

Teacher Support Action #1: Communicate Best Practices

Lead Entities – State and Local Education Agencies (SEAs and LEAs)

SEAs and LEAs will receive information from current research on the infrastructure required for quality STEM learning and best practices in STEM education. NISET could play a key role in the dissemination of this knowledge. National, state, and local associations would communicate these findings to Boards of Education, superintendents, principals, supervisors, and vice-principals through annual meetings of these groups.

Teacher Support Action #2: Provide Adequate Facilities and Infrastructure for STEM Learning

Lead Entities – State and Local Education Agencies (SEAs and LEAs)

SEAs and LEAs must provide adequate facilities and infrastructure (computers, laboratory equipment, and supplies) for STEM learning. This includes appropriate teacher planning time to implement curricula, teacher professional development, class and classroom size, safety equipment and training, and current technology. Students come to school technologically savvy, and operating STEM education classes without technology would guarantee failure.

Teacher Support Action #3: Provide Professional Development Opportunities to School Administrators

Lead Entities – National and State STEM Education Professional Organizations and Disciplinary Societies

National and state STEM education professional organizations and disciplinary societies must provide professional development opportunities for school boards, superintendents, and other administrators to identify, support, and encourage quality STEM education instruction. Annual meetings of these groups would provide an effective mechanism for providing professional development opportunities.

Teacher Support Action #4: Provide Professional Development Support Opportunities to Professional Support Providers

Lead Entities – State and Local Education Agencies (SEAs and LEAs), the Department of Education, the National Science Foundation (NSF), Informal Science Education Institutions, and Educational Research Organizations

The entities above would cooperatively create ongoing professional development opportunities and a learning community for the staff who are responsible for professional development in SEAs and LEAs.

Teacher Support Action #5: Provide Special Training in the Teaching of STEM Courses

Lead Entities – Institutions of Higher Education

Training of teachers rarely includes the very special requirements of how to teach science. Teachers should know that science comes in two parts: a content part and a process part. The blending of these is of overriding importance towards the STEM education objective. The training of STEM teachers must include an understanding of what is science, what is engineering, what is mathematics, and how they interact. The training of STEM teachers must include the sense that the world we live in is permeated by the science, mathematics, and engineering that converts concepts into the artifacts of our civilization and that create the sense of pleasure, joy, excitement, and empowerment, which drives the scientists as humans.

Unfinished Business

This Commission focused on many issues relevant to the transformation of STEM education and recommended specific mechanisms and actions to support this transformation. However, there are additional important educational issues that state and local councils will need to address. Outlined below are some of the most pressing of these issues. We especially look to the new national coordinating entity, NISET, to continue the transformations suggested here.

Special Populations

The Commission identified the need to address the major challenges subsumed under the goal of providing quality education to *all students*: raising the floor of expectations, access to quality programs, and removing the ceiling that limits the potential for growth and achievement for students with the greatest interests and aptitude for STEM. Addressing the needs of students with disabilities, English language learners, students from low socio-economic backgrounds, as well as students who have completed high school but who are not prepared for college or the workforce, is a challenge the entire community must acknowledge and accept. These unique student populations often come from impoverished families and attend racially or ethnically segregated and substandard schools. They need to be provided with opportunities and resources for success, including opportunities for STEM education and careers. Making use of the entire talent pool is a priority issue for STEM education since demographics will require major contributions to the workforce from those groups who have been "left behind." We are obligated to provide a level of education that will permit every young person to reach her/his potential.

It is also in our best interest to nurture our most talented students. Major revolutions of the 21st century - globalization and technology - require that we foster a culture of innovation and the support the next generation of innovators who will help shape our future. NISET would be expected to play a role in the organization of a national program for gifted education.

We can and must address both the skills gap and the performance gap. We cannot pit equity and access against competitiveness and innovation. The Nation can and must advance both.

Early Childhood Education (ECE)

A strong movement has emerged among the states for support of universal early childhood education. Fueled by changing family dynamics and research on brain development, states are responding to demands for such programs in support of promoting school readiness and hopes of greater success in K-12 education. As this movement grows with strong Federal support, more state investment, and positive outcomes for children, NISET and NGA would be expected to create new action plans that more prominently include STEM education as a component of ECE.

Learning about Learning

As we learn more about pedagogy, opportunities will emerge to inform the work of the teacher in the classroom and the faculty member in the laboratory and lecture hall. Especially important is the need to consider how best to support and assess conceptual understanding of STEM concepts, how the formal and informal systems for learning work together over a lifetime, and how to close the so-called "achievement gap."

Time for Schooling

It has been established that only about fifty per cent of the school day in American schools is devoted to learning. We have a shorter school day and school year than most industrialized nations. The long summer holiday has a negative affect on the continuity that is required in learning, especially for our most disadvantaged children, supporting loss of ground in their learning. Our present school calendar was set by a farming nation, and many educators believe it is time to change. Alternatives to this calendar have been adopted in many places that may act as test laboratories as districts consider other arrangements that can provide more time for learning. Here, too, the NISET mechanism with state collaboration would provide a forum to develop consensus on the issue of "time to learn."

This issue calls for thoughtful consideration of the use of non-school hours for students, such as the development and availability of quality informal programs that complement formal learning.

Time for Teachers

While the action plan addresses issues of continuous professional development of teachers, it does not address the need to create the time and circumstances for teachers to communicate with one another (i.e., mathematics and science teachers, chemistry and physics teachers, science and technology teachers and larger groups that include language, the arts and social sciences) to shore up the deep interconnections among the disciplines that underlie education. Time is also needed to support the interaction with local community college and university faculty, business, and political leaders as well as with parents and the larger community.

Curricula Matters

Research-based curricula are needed to support the standards that emerge. Many areas of study are not currently offered in most schools, such as those that focus on the nature of technology and engineering, applications of mathematics and science to these areas, or issues related to societal impact of science and technology. Local education agencies are unlikely to accept the notion of a single national curriculum. This Commission is not advocating a single national curriculum. We are advocates for national standards and believe that it may be possible to offer several high quality choices. National support is needed to create these standards. In all cases, there is the need to reduce the number and increase the depth of topics covered and to create seamless transitions, i.e., topics in middle school following smoothly from primary school and preparing students for study in high school and beyond.

Technology in Education

Technology has permeated much of our lives, but it oftentimes stops at the schoolhouse door. Technology has an important role to play in the transformation of STEM education at all levels, but the investments must be made to experiment, innovate and disseminate. Many of our students are growing up in a technology-rich environment that is radically different from the experiences of their teachers and those responsible for governance of schools. All citizens will need the technology to confront the world of the 21st century. Students are emerging from our 20th century classrooms knowing how to go online, explore Web territories unknown to their teachers and to those who educate teachers. Th ey call it Web 2.0. Students are learning from blogs and wikis and podcasts. They connect to knowledge content but also to people, ideas, and conversations. A major task for STEM education transformation is to design the 21st century classroom and 21st century learning experiences, and to prepare teachers for the altered culture of Internet-era students. On the whole, there is a need to focus much more on understanding the students: their interests and skills, their motivations and aspirations. This would allow us to build on the strengths that students bring to support their further learning and development.

The greatest promise of technology is its ability to create new environments for learning. Students explore virtual worlds through guided inquiry and experimentation. Computers are increasingly used to enhance hands-on experimentation by using real-time data acquisition and analysis with probes and probe-ware. Technology supports new forms of student collaboration within the classroom and across the world. These collaborations can enrich the curriculum, link to informal learners, stimulate thought, and prepare students for the kinds of collaborations that are integral to science, business, and government.

Appropriate technology not only delivers new, collaborative learning materials, it can provide guidance and embedded assessments that yield fine detail about student effort and progress at home, at school, and in informal settings. Data from learners' actions can be used by educators to alter the learning experience and use the ideas of Universal Design for Learning to better match the interests and needs of students. Finally, data from learners create unprecedented research opportunities that allow us to track large numbers of learners and understand details of their ideas and learning patterns. Research based on such data could help in the design of new generations of materials and curricula.

Technology can revolutionize teacher professional development. A mix of online courses, video case studies, discussions, and technological resources teachers can use with their students can create experiences for pre-service and in-service teachers that can increase their students' performance.

There are many technological innovations waiting to be explored that could improve STEM education, but there has been insufficient funding to develop them. As computers become less expensive, more portable, and more easily networked, the technology is far outpacing the ability of education to exploit its promise. It is not necessary to wait for the next generation of technology, however. There is already an adequate base of research and design experience to generate significant educational gains through more extensive use of today's technology. Current technologies need to be fully exploited in a new round of curriculum materials for STEM education. These materials can teach the current curriculum better because of technology. Advances in technology also make it possible to strengthen the curriculum with new content that can be taught earlier.

Higher Education

Post-secondary education in the United States includes many components from technical schools and community colleges to research universities: public, private, proprietary, single sex and minority-serving, liberal arts and technical institutes. The variety is staggering. All contribute in different ways to support the advancement and dissemination of knowledge and the development of skills necessary for citizenship, economic growth, and prosperity. Increasing numbers of our citizens take advantage of these places for learning. The knowledge-based economy that emerged over the 20th century will mean that, for an increasing number of future workers, 21st century employment will require some level of education beyond high school. The form and depth of that education will be critical to providing them with the level of knowledge and skills they will need to continue to learn for a lifetime.

A notable failure of higher education is the very low level of science and mathematics required of those who undertake study outside of STEM fields. A troubling example is the state of science and mathematics knowledge of primary school teachers. A lack of confidence is translated into an unwillingness and/or inability to teach these subjects. Under-prepared teachers may approach mathematics and science lessons with a palpable insecurity that their students can sense.

The traditional science requirement of a semester of "Rocks for Jocks" or "Physics for Poets" will no longer serve to produce the kind of responsible citizenship that the Nation needs. It is also fair to complain that most colleges continue to graduate teachers who are woefully unprepared or under-prepared to teach mathematics and science.

A 21st century college graduate should be capable of citizenship in our democratic society by active participation in decisions made on the national level as well as in the family and the community. We need standards of what such a graduate should know – a national consensus on the range, the rigor, and the duration of a 21st century science requirement. National input to such standards could be formulated by the National Academies and AAAS, perhaps organized by NISET. Whereas these would clearly not be prescriptive, the national attention to a discussion of the "STEM knowledge requirements of citizenship" can have a huge influence on the colleges and universities of the nation. It is quite clear that students need content knowledge related to the physical, biological, social, behavioral, economic, and earth sciences, as well as knowledge of technology and "process" – how did we find out what we know? how do we answer questions in the future? and how do we manage to survive, prosper and enjoy? In the age of the Internet and 24/7 information, students must have tools for discernment; we must give them the tools they need to make critical judgments of information, from Wikipedia, blogs, Britannica, Fox News, or ~e *New York Times*.

Another problem within institutions of higher education is the hole in the STEM pipeline that opens up after the first year of college. Even high school graduates who have demonstrated interest in and dedication to science through having invested heavily in AP mathematics and science courses and science fairs and clubs leave STEM majors. Such an exodus, often after their experience with poorly taught introductory courses in physics or chemistry in their freshman year, represents a disastrous loss of STEM talent and failure to maintain the flame that led these students initially to declare as STEM majors upon completing high school.

Dramatic counterexamples are emerging, however, from many liberal arts institutions, from a number of minority- serving institutions, women's colleges and community colleges, as well as from universities where powerful research results are emerging on the teaching of science from leaders such as Lillian McDermott, Eric Mazur, Carl Wieman, and others.

Sidebar Suggestions

A Science Way of Thinking

A frequently debated issue in STEM education is "How much science should non-science students know?" An easy response is: they should have acquired a "science way of thinking."

This seemingly exotic concept of "A Science Way of Thinking" was stressed in the 1930's by famed U.S. educator, John Dewey. Dewey urged scientists to convey the science way of thinking to all phases of education as a "SUPREME INTELLECTUAL OBLIGATION." Although this includes critical thinking, curiosity, skepticism, and verification by observation and measurement, its deeper meaning has to do with the sense of wonder and awe that emerges from the student's gradual realization that the natural world is orderly and comprehensible. The overarching laws of science enable predictions: sunrise, weather, and the hour and day of the return of Halley's Comet in 2061. Th e appreciation and respect implied here are tragically missing from our science classrooms.

The body of knowledge generally termed "scientifi c stuff" is the content of science, what we know about how the world works. There is also the process of science, the observation and measurements of phenomena, the slow conversion of phenomena to knowledge via the process of testing and rational thinking.

The fitting together of pieces of knowledge into a coherent framework is the art of science. This process evolves so that larger and larger elements in the domain are included. This knowledge, a "theory," tentative until disproved by fact or, by surviving extensive and repeated tests, is accepted as a law. Unfortunately, scientists still call it a theory.

Essential to the process of science is the storytelling. Who did what and why and how do we come to know? Science is a humane and accessible indulgence, carried out by humans called scientists. What they say they are doing, in addition to their personal and cultural perspectives, is the process of science.

But the teacher brews the wonder, colors the learning, and resonates with the students so that they exclaim, "Yes! This is the way it works." The chart of the periodic table glows with meaning. DNA, a once secret code, is now a user's manual for human genetics. Gravitation guides planets, comets, and falling apples. Superconductivity, so neatly demonstrated in classrooms labs, is a key to technologies that bring comfort and wealth: magnets for MRI, filters for city water systems, and rings for giant atom smashers. "How else, class, can we use this invention?" The tragedy is the rarity of this epiphany. Yet the "Science Way of Thinking" encapsulates the goal of science education for non-science students and scientists alike!

Employment, citizenship, parenthood, leisure will all be profoundly influenced by 21st century developments, making Dewey's quest for education, built on a science way of thinking, ever more crucial.

STEM Education Reform in a "Liberal Arts" World

A recent poll conducted by the American Council of Education underscored the weakness of the public's grasp of why education in the sciences and mathematics is crucial for non-science students.[71] This raises the issue of the age- old conflict between the role of science and that of the other liberal arts subjects. Yes, the public will accept a 3-year science requirement in high schools – but just barely. Yes, some (but not too much) science should be taught in college to non-science majors. Most colleges can still get away with a one semester "Rocks for Jocks" requirement to educate its graduates.

We need to look at STEM as an arrowhead of educational reform at all levels, but most especially in high schools and colleges. Th e 21st century STEM workforce must be communicators, must have a grasp of history and geography (must *easily* be able to find India on a map!), must be critical thinkers, and must understand in general terms how our government works. The vast influence of globalization as described in Tom Friedman's book, *The World is Flat,* stresses the importance of a liberal arts education that includes STEM fields.

The U.S. tradition of general education to grade level 14 is completely appropriate for the new century. This means that all students - high school graduates, students in higher education through grade 14 - must have a reasonable grasp of how science and technology work. Why? We live in a world where it is difficult to think of any employment that is not tinged by some scientific or technological issue or any area of life unaffected by them.

Law and science continuously intersect: patents, liability, international agreements, and Katrina and its lawsuits are a few issues. Healthcare and diagnostics are totally entwined with medical science. Understanding the dynamics of global climate change emerges from software that must take into account ocean solubility, atmospheric chemistry, reflectivity of ice and snow, solar radiation, and many other factors. National defense involves nuclear science, properties of toxic gases, communications technology, and radar and missile technology. Software is the third greatest employer in industry and includes the World Wide Web, Internet, laptops, and main frames. This merges into the chip industry and the micro miniaturization of electronics. To be ignorant of, for example, atoms, molecules, electrons, and energy, is to try to live in a country with no knowledge of the language spoken and no interest in learning it.

Some day all graduates of good colleges will have taken 2 years of laboratory science. However, the long-term success of STEM education reform will depend on a public grasp of, and support for, a grounding in STEM education for all students.

Television Interstitials

When asked to draw a picture of a scientist, most young people create an image of an older, eccentric-looking man. However, opportunities abound to show a very different picture – young men and young women who are bright, articulate, and driven by a love of science and technology, starring in a science fair near you! We must use the vision that these students provide to offer a different image of science, a different image of scientists, and an expanded image of teens. Our schools are blessed with young scientists – the students who star in science fairs – who are articulate and driven by a love of science and technology. Science fairs offer a vision of the excitement, drama, competition, and enthusiasm about science that are so seldom seen or imagined by the public. We need to offer the public a fresh view of the nature of science, how it works, and how deeply it enriches our culture. TV networks can make available creative interstitials: ninety seconds here, two minutes there, for these young ambassadors of science to talk about their projects. These spots could appear three or four times a day, three or four days a week. Science fairs can easily supply these short videos, filmed during the events. Many hundreds of such gems can be made available. The kids would be thrilled, the networks would be fulfilling their legal and moral commitments, and the public would be charmed and be made aware of the nature of science, how it works, and how deeply it enriches our culture.

End Notes

[1] The House Committee on Appropriations report, which accompanied the FY2006 Science, State, Justice, Commerce and Related Agencies Appropriations Bill, included report language endorsing the establishment of the STEM Commission. The report states, "The Committee understands that the Board has taken steps to establish a commission to make recommendations for NSF and Federal Government action to achieve measurable improvements in the Nation's science education at all levels. The Committee strongly endorses this eff ort." This chapter language was adopted in the final conference report for the Bill. Conference Committee, *Conference Report; Making Appropriations for Science, the Departments of State, Justice, and Commerce, and Related Agencies for the Fiscal Year Ending September 30, 2006, and for Other Purposes*, 109th Cong., 1st sess., 2005, H. Rep. 272, 184.

[2] The National Defense Education Act (NDEA) was passed in 1958 to aid science education in the U.S. in response to the launch of Sputnik by the Soviet Union. The NDEA was instituted primarily to stimulate the advancement of education in the elementary and secondary levels in science, mathematics, and modern foreign languages; but it has also provided aid in other areas, including technical education, and English as a second language. Of even greater significance, however, the act opened the way for future legislation that redefined many of the relationships between the Federal government and the education community. More information can be found at: *http://www.dod.mil/ddre/text/ t_ndea.html*

[3] The National Science and Technology Council (NSTC) was established by Executive Order in 1993. Th is Cabinet- level Council is the principal means within the executive branch to coordinate science and technology policy across the diverse entities that make up the Federal research and development enterprise. A primary objective of the NSTC is the establishment of clear national goals for Federal science and technology investments in a broad array of areas. Th e Council prepares research and development strategies that are coordinated across Federal agencies to form investment packages aimed at accomplishing multiple national goals. The work of the NSTC is organized under four primary committees; Science, Technology, Environment and Natural Resources and Homeland and National Security. More information can be found at *http://www.ostp.gov/nstc/index.html.*

[4] The Subcommittee on Education and Workforce Development is part of the NSTC Committee on Science.

[5] Also recommended in National Science Board, *Preparing Our Children: Math and Science Education in the National Interest* (Arlington, VA: 1999).

[6] This problem is discussed at length in a series of strategy briefs developed by State Higher Education Executive Officers (SHEEO) developed under the project *Enhancing the Teaching Profession: The Importance of Mobility to Recruitment and Retention* which was supported under a grant by the Ford Foundation. The three reports produced under this project are *Improving Pension Portability for K-12 Teachers,* Sandra S. Ruppert, (Denver, CO: Educational Systems Research, February, 2001) *http://www.sheeo.org/qualit y/mobility/pension.PDF; Teacher Recruitment, Staffi ng Classrooms with Quality Teachers,* Eric Hirsch, (Denver, CO: National Conference of State Legislators, February, 2001). *http://www.sheeo. org/quality/mobility/recruitment.PDF;* and *Solving Teacher Shortages Through License Reciprocity,* Bridget Curran, Camille Abrahams, and Theresa Clarke, (Denver, CO: National Governors Association Center for Best Practices. February, 2001). *http://www.sheeo.org/quality/mobility/reciprocity*

[7] An element of this recommendation is included in a portion of H.R. 325, the *SPEAK Act,* which requires the Secretary of Education to create the American Standards Incentive Fund to award grants to states that adopt

math and science standards and then align those standards with their teacher certification and professional development standards. Library of Congress, "Thomas; Legislation in Current Congress," http://thomas.loc.gov/cgi-bin/query (accessed March 15, 2007). A model for voluntary education content standards is defined and explained in Finn, Jr., C.E., Julian, L., Petrilli, M.J. *To Dream the Impossible Dream: Four Approaches to National Standards and Tests for America's Schools*, Thomas B. Fordham Foundation, p.22-27 (August, 2006).

[8] Th e Third International Mathematics and Science Study (TIMSS) observed that mathematics and science curricula in U.S. high schools lack coherence, depth, and continuity and cover too many topics in a superficial way. Standards must emphasize depth of understanding over exhaustive coverage of content. National Center for Education Statistics, "Th ird International Mathematics and Science Study," *Institute of Education Sciences* (Washington, DC: U.S. Department of Education, 2003), http://nces.ed.gov/timss/index.asp (accessed March 15, 2007).

[9] Also recommended in American Association for the Advancement of Science, *A System of Solutions: Every School, Every Student* (Washington, DC: American Association for the Advancement of Science, 2005), Carnegie Commission on Science, Technology, and Government, *In the National Interest: The Federal Government in the Reform of K-12 Math and Science Education* (New York: 1991).

[10] A current piece of legislation, H.R. 325 (and its Senate companion bill, S. 224), the *SPEAK Act*, assigns this responsibility to the National Assessment Governing Board. These bills task the Board with creating or adopting voluntary math and science education content standards for grades K-12 (the standards should reflect knowledge needed to enter college or the workforce). Additionally, the bills require the Secretary of Education to establish the American Standards Incentive fund to award competitive four-year grants to states which agree to adopt such standards as the core of their own math and science standards and align these standards with their teacher certification and professional development requirements. Library of Congress, "Thomas; Legislation in Current Congress," http://thomas.loc.gov/cgi-bin/ query/C?c110:./temp/~c110agnnE4 (accessed March 15, 2007).

[11] These grade-specific standards could build upon pre-existing standards such as: National Council of Teachers of Mathematics, *Principles and Standards for School Mathematics* (Reston, VA: NCTM, 2000); International Technology Education Association, *Standards for Technological Literacy* (Reston, VA: ITEA, 2000); American Association for the Advancement of Science, *Benchmarks for Science Literacy* (Oxford Unity Press, 1993); National Research Council, *National Science Education Standards* (Washington, DCL National Academy Press, 1996); and Douglas Gorham, Pam Newberry, and Theodore Bickart, "Engineering accreditation and Standards for Technological Literacy," *Journal of Engineering Education* 92 (2003).

[12] The Third International Mathematics and Science Study (TIMSS) observed that mathematics and science curricula in U.S. high schools lack coherence, depth, and continuity and cover too many topics in a superficial way. Standards must emphasize depth of understanding over exhaustive coverage of content. National Center for Education Statistics, "Th ird International Mathematics and Science Study," *Institute of Education Sciences* (Washington, DC: U.S. Department of Education, 2003), http://nces.ed.gov/timss/index.asp (accessed March 15, 2007).

[13] Also recommended in Carnegie Commission on Science, Technology, and Government, *In the National Interest: the Federal Government in the Reform of K-12 Math and Science Education* (New York: 1991).

[14] Also recommended in Carnegie Commission on Science, Technology, and Government, *In the National Interest: the Federal Government in the Reform of K-12 Math and Science Education* (New York: 1991).

[15] Also recommended in Carnegie Commission on Science, Technology, and Government, *In the National Interest: the Federal Government in the Reform of K-12 Math and Science Education* (New York: 1991), and The National Science Board, *Preparing Our Children: Math and Science Education in the National Interest*. (Arlington, VA: National Science Foundation, 1999.)

[16] Also recommended in the National Science Board Commission on Precollege Education in Mathematics, Science and Technology, *Educating Americans for the 21st Century: A Plan of Action for Improving Mathematics, Science and Technology Education for All American Elementary and Secondary Students So That Their Achievement is the Best in the World by 1995* (Arlington, VA: National Science Foundation, 1983); The National Science Board, *America's Pressing Challenge - Building a Stronger Foundation: A Companion to Science and Engineering Indicators*, NSB-06-02 (Washington DC: Government Printing Office, 2006); and the Domestic Policy Council of the Office of Science and Technology Policy. *America's Competitiveness Initiative; Leading the World in Innovation* (Washington DC: Government Printing Offi ce, 2006).

[17] Using such metrics as an added measure of AYP is reflected in H.R. 35, the *Science Accountability Act of 2007*. Th is act would amend the Elementary and Secondary Education Act of 1965 to require the use of science assessments in the calculation of adequate yearly progress. Library of Congress, "Thomas; Legislation in Current Congress," http://thomas.loc.gov/cgi-bin/query (accessed March 15, 2007).

[18] The National Assessment Governing Board (NAGB), appointed by the Secretary of Education but independent of the Department, sets policy for the National Assessment Education Program (NAEP) and is responsible for developing the framework and test specifications that serve as the blueprint for the assessments. The NAGB is a bipartisan group whose members include governors, state legislators, local and state school officials,

educators, business representatives, and members of the general public. Congress created the 26-member Governing Board in 1988.

[19] A current piece of legislation, H.R. 325 (and its Senate companion bill, S. 224), the *SPEAK Act*, assigns this responsibility to the National Assessment Governing Board. These bills task the Board with creating or adopting voluntary math and science education content standards for grades K-12 (the standards should reflect knowledge needed to enter college or the workforce). Additionally, the bills require the Secretary of Education to establish the American Standards Incentive fund to award competitive four-year grants to states which agree to adopt such standards as the core of their own math and science standards and align these standards with their teacher certification and professional development requirements. Library of Congress, "Thomas; Legislation in Current Congress," *http://thomas.loc.gov/cgibin/query* (accessed March 15, 2007).

[20] An element of this recommendation is included in a portion of H.R. 325, the *SPEAK Act*, which requires the Secretary of Education to create the American Standards Incentive Fund to award grants to states that adopt math and science standards and then align those standards with their teacher certification and professional development standards. Library of Congress, "Thomas; Legislation in Current Congress," *http://thomas.loc.gov/cgi-bin/query ~c110eyIIwF*: (accessed March 15, 2007). NAEP is the only nationally representative and continuing assessment of what America's students know and can do in various subject areas. Since 1969, assessments have been conducted periodically in reading, mathematics, science, writing, U.S. history, civics, geography and the arts. National NAEP reports information for the nation and specific geographic regions of the country. It includes students drawn from both public and nonpublic schools and reports results for student achievement at grades 4, 8, and 12. More information can be found by going to: *http://nces.ed.gov/nationsreportcard*

[21] Also recommended in the National Governors Association and Council on Competitiveness, *Innovation America: A Partnership* (Washington, DC: National Governors Association, February 24, 2007). Page 9. *http://www.nga.org/Files/ pdf/0702INNOVATIONPARTNERSHIP.PDF*

[22] An element of this recommendation is included in a portion of H.R. 325, the *SPEAK Act*. Library of Congress, "Thomas; Legislation in Current Congress," *http://thomas.loc.gov/cgi-bin/query* (accessed March 15, 2007).

[23] Interstate Agreement (2005-2010) by the National Association of State Directors of Teacher Education and Certification (NASDTEC). This agreement has 41 state participants as well as the District of Columbia. Its purpose is to establish a process under which a person prepared or certified in one Member state may obtain a certificate from another Member state. *http://www.nasdtec.org/docs/NIC_2005-2010.doc;* and Problem discussed in a paper presented at the STEM Institute for Alternative Certification of Teachers meeting, Online Science Methods for Lateral Entry Science Teachers, William R. Veal, Dorothy Mebane and Keri Randolph (Arlington, VA: Science, Technology Engineering and Math Education Institute for Alternative Certification of Teachers, May 5-7, 2006). *http://www.stemtec.org/act/PAPERS/ William Veal.doc*.

[24] Also recommended in National Science Board Commission on Precollege Education in Mathematics, Science and Technology, *Educating Americans for the 21st Century: A Plan of Action for Improving Mathematics, Science and Technology Education for All American Elementary and Secondary Students So That Their Achievement is the Best in the World by 1995* (Arlington, VA: National Science Foundation, 1983); National Science Board, *Preparing Our Children: Math and Science Education in the National Interest* (Arlington, VA: National Science Foundation, 1999); Building Engineering and Science Talent, *A Bridge for All: Higher Education Design Principles to Broaden Participation in Science, Technology, Engineering and Mathematics* (Washington, DC: BEST, 2004); and Business-Higher Education Forum, *A Commitment to America's Future: Responding to the Crisis in Mathematics and Science Education* (Washington, DC: Business-Higher Education Forum, January 2005).

[25] Also recommended in National Science Board, *Preparing Our Children: Math and Science Education in the National Interest* (Arlington, VA: National Science Foundation, 1999).

[26] "One-third of our high school graduates are not prepared to enter postsecondary education or the workforce." Council of Chief State School Officers, *Mathematics and Science Education Task Force, Report and Recommendations* (June 2006 through October 2006), p. 1.

[27] Also recommended in National Commission on Mathematics and Science Teaching for the 21st Century, *Before It's Too Late: A Report to the Nation* (Washington, DC: 2000).

[28] Examples of these regional organizations are mentioned in the "P-16 Collaboration in the States" by the Education Commission of the States (ECS). Updated June 2006. Denver, CO. *http://www.ecs.org/clearinghouse/69/26/6926.pdf*

[29] Also recommended and discussed in the National Governors Association and Council on Competitiveness, *Innovation America: A Partnership*. (Washington, DC: National Governors Association, February 24, 2007).

[30] Also recommended in National Science Board Commission on Precollege Education in Mathematics, Science and Technology, *Educating Americans for the 21st Century: A Plan of Action for Improving Mathematics, Science and Technology Education for All American Elementary and Secondary Students So ~at Their Achievement is the Best in the World by 1995* (Arlington, VA: National Science Foundation, 1983); The National Science Board, America's Pressing Challenge - Building a Stronger Foundation: *A Companion to Science and Engineering Indicators*, NSB-06-02 (Washington DC: Government Printing Office, 2006); the Domestic

Policy Council of the Office of Science and Technology Policy. *America's Competitiveness Initiative; Leading the World in Innovation* (Washington DC: Government Printing Office, 2006.); National Science Board, *Preparing Our Children: Math and Science Education in the National Interest* (Arlington, VA: National Science Foundation, 1999); American Association for the Advancement of Science, *A System of Solutions: Every School, Every Student* (Washington, DC: American Association for the Advancement of Science, 2005); Business- Higher Education Forum, *A Commitment to America's Future: Responding to the Crisis in Mathematics and Science Education* (Washington, DC: Business-Higher Education Forum, January 2005); and National Governors Association and Council on Competitiveness, *Innovation America: A Partnership* (Washington, DC: National Governors Association, February 24, 2007) page 5,7,8.

[31] These grade-specific standards could build upon pre-existing standards such as; International Technology Education Association, *Standards for Technological Literacy* (Reston, VA: ITEA, 2000); American Association for the Advancement of Science, *Benchmarks for Science Literacy* (Oxford Unity Press, 1993); and National Research Council, *National Science Education Standards* (Washington, DCL National Academy Press, 1996).

[32] National Council of Teachers of Mathematics, *Principles and Standards for School Mathematics* (Reston, VA: NCTM, 2000).

[33] Also recommended in National Science Board, *Preparing Our Children: Math and Science Education in the National Interest* (Arlington, VA: National Science Foundation, 1999) and Business-Higher Education Forum, *A Commitment to America's Future: Responding to the Crisis in Mathematics and Science Education* (Washington, DC: Business-Higher Education Forum, January 2005).

[34] These grade-specific standards could build upon pre-existing standards such as: National Council of Teachers of Mathematics, *Principles and Standards for School Mathematics* (Reston, VA: NCTM, 2000).

[35] Also recommended in Business-Higher Education Forum, *A Commitment to America's Future: Responding to the Crisis in Mathematics and Science Education* (Washington, DC: 2005).

[36] According to the Alliance for Excellent Education, the nation is losing $3.7 billion a year due to insufficient preparation for college and the workforce. Students are not learning the basic skills to move forward on these two trajectories. ~ at figure includes $1.4 billion which is spent on remedial education for recent high school graduates. ~ e additional costs account for the public resources that support remedial coursework at two-year institutions, the cost of tuition, and the cost of lost time and wages. Alliance for Excellent Education, *Inadequate High Schools and Community Colleges Remediation* (Washington DC: 2006). http://www.nam.org/s_nam/sec.asp?CID=86&DID=84 (accessed 3 May 2007).

[37] Also recommended in National Commission on Mathematics and Science Teaching for the 21st Century, *Before It's Too Late: A Report to the Nation* (Washington, DC: U.S. Department of Education, 2000).

[38] Currently special schools exist in a numbers of states. Examples include the Illinois Mathematics and Science Academy in Illinois (http://www.imsa.edu/), North Carolina School of Science and Math in North Carolina (http://www.ncssm.edu/), and the Bronx High School of Science, (http://www.bxscience.edu/about.jsp).

[39] National Science Board Commission on Precollege Education in Mathematics, Science and Technology, *Educating Americans for the 21st Century: A Plan of Action for Improving Mathematics, Science and Technology Education for All American Elementary and Secondary Students So That Their Achievement is the Best in the World by 199*5 (Arlington, VA: National Science Foundation, 1983).

[40] An example of such a relationship between the STEM education community and industry is illustrated in a provision proposed in H.R. 37, the *National Science Education Tax Incentive for Business Act of 2007*. This bill amends the Internal Revenue Code to allow a general business tax credit for contributions of property or services to elementary and secondary schools and for teacher training to promote instruction in STEM fields. Library of Congress, "Thomas; Legislation in Current Congress," http://thomas.loc.gov/cgi-bin/query (accessed March 15, 2007).

[41] Also recommended in National Science Board, "America's Pressing Challenge – Building a Stronger Foundation," *Companion to Science and Engineering Indicators 2006* (Arlington, VA: National Science Foundation, 2006).

[42] The U.S. Department of Labor projects that new jobs requiring science, engineering and technical training will increase by 51% between 1998 and 2008; a rate of growth that is roughly four times higher than average job growth nationally. Opstal, Debra van and Michael E. Porter. *U.S. Competitiveness 2001: Strengths, Vulnerabilities, and Long-Term Priorities.* (Washington DC: Council on Competitiveness, January 2001). http://www.compete.org/pdf/competitiveness2001.pdf

[43] Also recommended in *Getting it Done: Ten Steps to a State Action Agenda, A Guidebook of Promising State and Local Practices*, National Governors Association Center for Best Practices, (Washington, DC: National Governors Association, March, 2005). Pages 19-21. http://www.nga.org/portal/site/nga/menuitem.9123e83a1f6786440ddcbeeb501010a0/?vgnextoid=0517a32889da2010VgnVCM1000001a01010 aRCRD Currently, Florida (http://scns.fl doe.org/scns/ public/pb_index.jsp), Texas (http://www.tccns.org/ccn/phil.htm), Georgia (http://www.usg.edu/academics/handbook/ section2/2. 04/2.04. 05.phtml), California (http://www.curriculum Colorado (http://www.cccs.edu/cccns/Home.html) and Oregon (http://oregonstate.edu/ap/curriculum/common.html) each employ a common course numbering system.

[44] For an example, look at the Ohio Articulation and Transfer Policy, http://regents.ohio.gov/transfer/policy/index.php. Th is policy was created to improve transfer student mobility and includes provisions to maximize the award and application of credit for prior learning and equitable treatment for transfer students. Ohio State University has completed three transfer agreements with three northeast Ohio community colleges and with the Columbus State Community College.

[45] According to the American Association of Community Colleges, 20 percent of teachers began their post-secondary schooling at community colleges, and 4 out of 10 teachers completed math and science courses at community colleges. American Association of Community Colleges, *Teaching by Choice; Community College Science and Mathematics Preparation of K-12 Education* (American Association of Community Colleges: Washington, DC, 2004).

[46] Examples include the Accreditation Board for Engineering and Technology, http://www.abet.org/ and the National Association of State Universities and Land Grant Colleges (NALSUGC), http://www.nasulgc.org/

[47] Currently in some cases teachers are not given credit for professional development for STEM content courses at community colleges due to their low course numbers.

[48] National Science Teachers Association Position Statement of Informal Science Education. NSTA recognizes and encourages the development of sustained links between the informal institutions and schools. http://www.nsta.org/about/positions/informal.aspx

[49] Also recommended in National Science Board Commission on Precollege Education in Mathematics, Science and Technology, *Educating Americans for the 21st Century: A Plan of Action for Improving Mathematics, Science and Technology Education for All American Elementary and Secondary Students So That Their Achievement is the Best in the World by 199*5 (Arlington, VA: National Science Foundation, 1983).

[50] Currently, by the time children reach the age of 18, they spend almost four times the amount of time in informal or unstructured activity compared to time spent in school, so the opportunities of informal science activities in a child's total learning must not be missed. National Science Foundation, *Investing in America's Future: Strategic Plan FY2006- 2011* (Arlington, VA: National Science Foundation, 2006).

[51] Also recommended in National Science Board Commission on Precollege Education in Mathematics, Science and Technology, *Educating Americans for the 21st Century: A Plan of Action for Improving Mathematics, Science and Technology Education for All American Elementary and Secondary Students So That Their Achievement is the Best in the World by 199*5 (Arlington, VA: National Science Foundation, 1983); The National Science Board, *America's Pressing Challenge - Building a Stronger Foundation: A Companion to Science and Engineering Indicators*, NSB-06-02 (Washington DC: Government Printing Office, 2006); and National Science Board, *Preparing Our Children: Math and Science Education in the National Interest* (Arlington, VA: National Science Foundation, 1999).

[52] National Governors Association and Council on Competitiveness, *Innovation America: A Partnership*, (Washington, DC: National Governors Association, February 24, 2007). p.7

[53] U.S. Commission on National Security/21st Century, *Road Map for National Security: Imperative for Change*, Phase III Report, p. 39 (February 15, 2001).

[54] Council of Great City Schools, *The Urban Teacher Challenge: Teacher Demand in the Great City Schools* (Washington, DC: Council of Great City Schools. 2000). Page 9-11.

[55] Also recommended in National Commission on Excellence in Education, *A Nation at Risk: The Imperative for Educational Reform* (Washington, DC: U.S. Department of Education, 1983); National Commission on Mathematics and Science Teaching for the 21st Century, *Before It's Too Late: A Report to the Nation* (Washington, DC: U.S. Department of Education, 2000); and Building Engineering and Science Talent, *A Bridge for All: Higher Education Design Principles to Broaden Participation in Science, Technology, Engineering and Mathematics* (Washington, DC: BEST, 2004).

[56] Also found in National Academy of Engineering, and Institute of Medicine of the National Academies, *Rising Above the Gathering Storm: Energizing and Employing America for a Brighter Economic Future* (Washington, DC: National Academy of Sciences, 2005).

[57] Also recommended in National Commission on Excellence in Education, *A Nation at Risk: The Imperative for Educational Reform* (Washington, DC: U.S. Department of Education, 1983); National Commission on Mathematics and Science Teaching for the 21st Century, *Before It's Too Late: A Report to the Nation* (Washington, DC: U.S. Department of Education, 2000); The National Science Board, *America's Pressing Challenge - Building a Stronger Foundation: A Companion to Science and Engineering Indicators*, NSB-06-02 (Washington DC: Government Printing Office, 2006); Building Engineering and Science Talent, *A Bridge for All: Higher Education Design Principles to Broaden Participation in Science, Technology, Engineering and Mathematics* (Washington, DC: BEST, 2004) and National Governors Association and Council on Competitiveness, *Innovation America: A Partnership* (Washington, DC: National Governors Association, February 24, 2007). Page 6.

[58] Also recommended in National Commission on Excellence in Education, *A Nation at Risk: The Imperative for Educational Reform* (Washington, DC: U.S. Department of Education, 1983); National Science Board, *America's Pressing Challenge - Building a Stronger Foundation: A Companion to Science and Engineering Indicators*, NSB.-06-02 (Washington DC: Government Printing Office, 2006); and National Commission on

Mathematics and Science Teaching for the 21st Century, *Before It's Too Late: A Report to the Nation* (Washington, DC: U.S. Department of Education, 2000).

[59] The Robert Noyce Scholarship Program seeks to increase the number of teachers with a strong content knowledge in mathematics. This National Science Foundation program provides scholarship funds for talented undergraduate mathematics majors to become teachers in high need school districts. Likewise, stipends are available for professionals (who already have a bachelor's degree) seeking to become mathematics teachers committed to teaching in a high needs school. Scholarship and stipend recipients agree to teach two years in a high need school district for every year of scholarship funds received.

[60] This idea is reflected in a current piece of legislation, H.R. 362, the "10,000 Teachers, 10 Million Minds Science and Math Scholarship Act." Library of Congress, "Thomas; Legislation in Current Congress," *http://thomas.loc.gov/cgi-bin/query C?c110:./temp/~c110XaKNA8* (accessed March 15, 2007).

[61] National Education Association: "The average starting salary for a mathematics teacher is $12,769, based on 198 1- 82 figures. This compares with $22,368 for an engineer and $16,980 for accounting graduates."; "In 1997, teachers earned an average of $35,048 -- 71% of the average earnings of a worker with a baccalaureate degree. Nationally, the average starting salary for teachers in 1997 was $25,735. Persons earning baccalaureate degrees in mathematics and science can make twice that salary in private industry." *Before It's Too Late*, National Commission on Mathematics and Science Teaching for the 21st Century U.S. Department of Education, 2000; and "Four out of ten mathematics and science teachers leave the profession because of job dissatisfaction; about 57% of these site salaries as the deciding factor. By contrast, 29% leave because of student discipline problems, and 21% leave because of poor student motivation." National Commission on Mathematics and Science Teaching for the 21st Century 10 March 2000.

[62] ~e National Science Board, *America's Pressing Challenge - Building a Stronger Foundation: A Companion to Science and Engineering Indicators*, NSB-06-02 (Washington DC: Government Printing Offi ce, 2006).

[63] Also recommended in National Commission on Excellence in Education, *A Nation at Risk: The Imperative for Educational Reform* (Washington, DC: U.S. Department of Education, 1983); The National Science Board Commission on Precollege Education in Mathematics, Science and Technology, *Educating Americans for the 21st Century: A Plan of Action for Improving Mathematics, Science and Technology Education for All American Elementary and Secondary Students So That Their Achievement is the Best in the World by 1995* (Arlington, VA: National Science Foundation, 1983); National Science Board, "America's Pressing Challenge – Building a Stronger Foundation," *Companion to Science and Engineering Indicators 2006* (Arlington, VA: National Science Foundation, 2006); and National Commission on Mathematics and Science Teaching for the 21st Century, *Before It's Too Late: A Report to the Nation* (Washington, DC: U.S. Department of Education, 2000).

[64] Also recommended in Business-Higher Education Forum, *A Commitment to America's Future: Responding to the Crisis in Mathematics and Science Education* (Washington, DC: Business-Higher Education Forum, January 2005); Hart- Rudman Commission, *Road Map for National Security: Imperative for Change (Phase III)* (Washington, DC: 2001); ~ e Research and Policy Committee of the Committee for Economic Development, *Learning for the Future: Changing the Culture of Math and Science Education to Ensure a Competitive Workforce* (Washington, DC: 2003); and Executive Office of the President/President's Council on Advisors on Science and Technology, *Sustaining the Nation's Innovation Ecosystem: Maintaining the Strength of Our Science and Engineering Capabilities* (Washington, DC: 2004).

[65] Also recommended in National Science Board, "America's Pressing Challenge – Building a Stronger Foundation," *Companion to Science and Engineering Indicators 2006* (Arlington, VA: National Science Foundation, 2006).

[66] Also recommended in American Association for the Advancement of Science, *A System of Solutions: Every School, Every Student* (Washington, DC: American Association for the Advancement of Science, 2005).

[67] This idea is reflected in a piece of legislation from the 109th Congress, S. 3710, "Teacher Center Act of 2006." ~ is bill would provide grants to local education agencies for the establishment, operation and support of new and existing teacher centers in order to provide high-quality professional development and training. Library of Congress, "~ omas; Legislation in Current Congress," *http://thomas.loc.gov/cgi-bin/query* (accessed 15 March 2007).

[68] Also recommended in National Commission on Mathematics and Science Teaching for the 21st Century, *Before It's Too Late: A Report to the Nation* (Washington, DC: U.S. Department of Education, 2000).

[69] Also recommended in National Science Board, "America's Pressing Challenge – Building a Stronger Foundation," *Companion to Science and Engineering Indicators 2006* (Arlington, VA: National Science Foundation, 2006)

[70] Also recommended in National Commission on Mathematics and Science Teaching for the 21st Century, *Before It's Too Late: A Report to the Nation* (Washington, DC: U.S. Department of Education, 2000).

[71] *Math and Science Education and United States Competitiveness: Does the Public Care?* "Less than one-third of the public (31 percent) believe that math and science classes offered to students not majoring in those fields are "very relevant" to life after graduation. In addition, only a slight majority of the public (54 percent) believe that all students should have to take more math and science courses."

http://www.acenet.edu/AM/Template.cfm?Section=Search&TEMPLATE=/ CM/ContentDisplay.cfm&CONTENTID=19215 For the Executive Summary of Survey (graphs, methodology) go to: *http://www.solutionsforourfuture.org/site/DocServer/Global_Competitiveness_Executive_Summary.pdf?docID=641* and for the Summary of Survey results: *http://www.cte.mnscu.edu/researchcorner/Future%20Work/MATH%20AND%20SCIENCE%20EDUCATION%20AND%20UNITED%20STATES%20COMPETITIVENESS.pdf*

GLOSSARY

10-14 Pathways	Boundary-spanning curricular or institutional structures that enhance students' transition and access to colleges from secondary education.
Accreditation	Recognition by an agency or an association that an institution, program of study, individual, or service meets its criteria for accreditation
Articulation Agreement	Policy that allows a student to apply credits earned in specific programs at one institution toward advanced standing, equal transfer, or direct entry into specific programs at another institution
Assessment	Mechanisms to measure the learning and performance of students. Types of assessment include achievement tests, performance tasks, and developmental screening tests. Under No Child Left Behind, tests are aligned with academic standards
Benchmarks	A description of the level of student knowledge expected at specific grades, ages, or developmental levels.
Certification	Issuance of a formal document that certifies or declares that an educator possesses a set of skills, knowledge, and abilities, usually granted after completion of education, training, or experience in the related areas
Curriculum	The subjects and courses required to fulfill an educational program
Horizontal Coordination	Coherence among and within the fifty states to negotiate and integrate education policies into an overall strategy
Informal Science Education	The learning of science experienced outside of (ISE) the classroom
Informal Science Education (ISE) Institutions	Venues where the informal learning of science occurs including museums, national parks, and science fairs
Infrastructure	Basic framework, foundation, and resources of a system, organization, or activity that supports STEM education
Inquiry experiences	Process in which students investigate, work-through, and solve problems
In-service education	Continuing education for teachers following completion of

	pre-service training and employment. Also referred to as staff or professional development
Institutions of Higher Education	Accredited community colleges, four-year colleges, and universities
Instructional leadership	Administrators and educators who shift the emphasis of school activity more directly onto instructional improvements that lead to enhanced student learning and performance
Local Education Agencies	A public board of education or other authority within a state that maintains administrative control of public schools in a city, county, township, school district, or other political subdivision of a state
National Board Certification	A national teacher certification created in 1987 after the release of the Carnegie Forum on Education and the Economy's Task Force on Teaching as a Profession's, *A Nation Prepared: Teachers for the 21st Century*. These certifications are offered by the National Board for Professional Teaching Standards (NBPTS) and off er teachers the chance to voluntarily become nationally certified by demonstrating and maintaining high and rigorous standards in the Five Core Propositions developed by the NBPTS.
P-20 Council(s)	Body of education stakeholders including state and local policy makers, teachers, administrators, and parents designed to improve education and to address issues in its educational system
Pedagogy	The art and method of teaching
Pre-service preparation	Professional development and training of teachers prior to employment, usually while studying in institutions of higher education
Professional Development	Skills required to help teachers and administrators build knowledge and skills through continuing education programs such as conferences, classes and workshops
Research-based models tools, and strategies	Models, tools, and strategies based on empirical evidence that educators and administrators may use to teach more effectively
Standards	Standards denote points of reference against which individuals are compared or evaluated. Standards usually take two forms in curriculum: content standards that describe expected student knowledge in various subject areas and performance standards that specify expected learning levels and assess the degree to which content standards have been met
State Education Agencies	Agencies primarily responsible for the state supervision of public elementary and secondary schools
STEM	Science, Technology, Engineering and Mathematics
Vertical Alignment	Alignment of student learning between grade-levels (pre-K through graduate education)

Meeting Participants

The Commission on 21st Century Education in Science, Technology, Engineering, and Mathematics would like to thank the following experts who addressed the Commission at one or more of our Meetings.

Mr. Norman Augustine
Retired Chairman and CEO, Lockheed Martin Corporation, and Chair, Committee on Prospering in the Global Economy of the 21st Century

Dr. Arden L. Bement, Jr.
Director, National Science Foundation

Mr. Arne Duncan
Chief Executive Officer, Chicago Public Schools

Dr. William C. Harris
President and CEO, Science Foundation Arizona

Mr. Bill Kurtis
President, Kurtis Productions, Inc.

Mr. Michael Lach
Director of Mathematics and Science, Chicago Public Schools
The Honorable Daniel Lipinski United States House of Representatives

Dr. Cora Marrett
Incoming Assistant Director, Directorate for Education and Human Resources, National Science Foundation

Dr. Stephanie Pace Marshall
President, Illinois Mathematics and Science Academy

Mr. David R. Mosena
President and Chief Executive Officer, Museum for Science and Industry, Chicago
The Honorable Janet Napolitano *Governor of Arizona*

Mr. Robert J. Shea
Counselor to the Deputy Director for Management, Office of Management and Budget

Dr. Donald E. Thompson
Acting Assistant Director, Directorate for Education and Human Resources, National Science Foundation

Dr. Iris Weiss
President, Horizon Research

Working Group Members

The Commission on 21st Century Education in Science, Technology, Engineering, and Mathematics would like to thank the following working group members who donated their time and expertise to assist the Commission in identifying STEM education related issues and potential action items.

Dr. Linda Atkinson
Associate Director, K20 Center, University of Oklahoma

Mr. Steve Cousins
Superintendent, Reeths-Puff er School District, Michigan

Dr. John Falk
Professor, Oregon State University, and President, Institute for Learning Innovation

Dr. Suzanne Mitchell
Teacher Quality Enhancement Project Director, Arkansas Department of Higher Education

Ms. Jeanne Narum
Director, Project Kaleidoscope

Dr. Mary John O'Hair
Vice-Provost for School and Community Partnerships, University of Oklahoma

Ms. Gwen Pollock
Director of Professional Development, National Science Teachers Association, and Principal Educational Consultant, Illinois State Board of Education

Dr. William Schmidt
Professor, Michigan State University, and U.S. Research Coordinator for the Third International Mathematics and Science Study (TIMSS)

Dr. Robert Semper
Executive Associate Director, The Exploratorium

Dr. Jon Strauss
Member, National Science Board, and President Emeritus, Harvey Mudd College

Dr. Jerry Valadez
K-12 Science Coordinator, Fresno Unifi ed School District

Dr. Iris Weiss
President, Horizon Research

Dr. Gerald Wheeler
Executive Director, National Science Teachers Association

Mr. James Woodland
Director, Science Education, Nebraska Department of Education

APPENDIX G. PUBLIC COMMENTS ON DRAFT NATIONAL ACTION PLAN

In August 2007 the Board solicited and received public comments on a draft of the national action plan. The final action plan incorporates the public's comments as appropriate. Comments, both critical and supportive, were received from the states, organizations, and individuals listed below. Titles and affiliations are listed as provided by the commenter.

States and Organizations

American Association of Physics Teachers – Toufic M. Hakim, Ph.D., Executive Officer
American Geological Institute – P. Patrick Leahy, Ph.D., Executive Director, and Gail M. Ashley, Ph.D., President
American Institute of Biological Sciences – Douglas J. Futuyma, Ph.D., President
American Institute of Physics – H. Frederick Dylla, Ph.D., Executive Director and CEO
American Meteorological Society – Keith L. Seitter, Ph.D., C.C.M., Executive Director
American Society of Mechanical Engineers Center for Public Awareness – Vince Wilczynski, Ph.D., Vice President
Association for Computing Machinery – Robert Schnabel, Ph.D., Chair, Education Policy Committee
Association of Science-Technology Centers – Bonnie VanDorn, Executive Director
Botanical Society of America – William M. Dahl, Executive Director
Commonwealth of Virginia – The Honorable Thomas R. Morris, Secretary of Education
Council of Graduate Schools – Debra W. Stewart, President
Greater Philadelphia Regional Compact for Science, Technology, Engineering and Mathematics (STEM) Education – Steering Group of the Member Organizations: Delaware Valley Industrial Resource Center, Math Science Partnership of Greater Philadelphia, Select Greater Philadelphia, Philadelphia Education Fund, WHYY
International Technology Education Association – Kendall N. Starkweather, Ph.D., Executive Director and CEO
National Center for Technological Literacy (NCTL), Museum of Science, Boston – Dr. Ioannis Miaoulis, Center Director and President of the Museum of Science; Dr. Yvonne Spicer, V.P. for Advocacy & Educational Partnerships; Dr. Cary Sneider, V.P. for Educator Programs; Dr. Christine Cunningham, V.P. for Research; Mr. Richard Blumenthal, V.P. for Publishing; Ms. Patti Curtis, Managing Director, Washington Office of the NCTL

National Council of Teachers of Mathematics – Jim Rubillo, Executive Director National High Magnetic Field Laboratory – Gregory S. Boebinger, Director National School Boards Association – Anne L. Bryant, Executive Director National Science Digital Library – Kaye Howe, Director

National Science Teachers Association – Dr. Gerald Wheeler, Executive Director **Sigma Xi** – James W. Porter, President

Society of Manufacturing Engineers Education Foundation – Glen H. Pearson, President, and Bart Aslin, Director

State of Hawai'i – The Honorable Linda Lingle, Governor of Hawai'i

State of Maryland – Dr. Nancy S. Grasmick, State Superintendent of Schools

State of West Virginia –The Honorable Joe Manchin III, Governor of West Virginia **State of Wisconsin** – The Honorable Jim Doyle, Governor of Wisconsin

Tennessee Department of Education – Linda Jordan, Science K-12 Coordinator

Individuals

William Abikoff, Professor of Mathematics, University of Connecticut **Diane W. Adams, M.A.**, Star Tannery, Virginia

Dr. Ayodele Aina, Chair, Mathematics and Computer Sciences, Cheyney University of Pennsylvania

Robert Akeson

Martin Apple, Ph.D., President, Council of Scientific Society Presidents

Diola Bagayoko, Ph.D., Southern University System Distinguished Professor of Physics, Adjunct Professor of Science and Mathematics Education, Director, LS-LAMP and the Timbuktu Academy

Darlyne Bailey, Ph.D., Dean & Assistant to the President, Campbell Leadership Chair in Education and Human Development, College of Education and Human Development, University of Minnesota

Art Bardige, President, Enablearning

Christopher F. Bauer, Professor and Chair, Department of Chemistry, University of New Hampshire

Robert J. Beichner, Ph.D., Co-Director, NCSU STEM Education Initiative, Alumni Distinguished Professor of Physics, North Carolina State University

Daniel B. Berch, Ph.D.

Anita Bernhardt, Science & Technology Specialist and Regional Representative, Maine Department of Education

Pierre Bierre, Founder and CEO, BuildExact Corp

Karen J.L. Burg, Ph.D., Hunter Endowed Chair and Professor of Bioengineering, Interim Vice Provost for Research & Innovation, Clemson University

Crista Carlile, Science Curriculum Coordinator, Des Moines Public Schools **Jay Cole**, Education Policy Advisor to West Virginia Governor Joe Manchin III **Terry Daugherty**, Batchelor Middle School, Bloomington, Indiana

M. Daniel DeCillis, Ph.D., Senior Research Associate and Director of Web Operations, California Council on Science and Technology

Diana Dummit, Co-PI, Institute for Chemistry Literacy through Computational Science, National Center for Supercomputing Applications, University of Illinois at Urbana-Champaign

Thom Dunning, Director, National Center for Supercomputing Applications, and PI, Institute for Chemistry Literacy through Computational Science, National Center for Supercomputing Applications, University of Illinois at Urbana-Champaign

Francis Eberle, Ph.D., Executive Director, Maine Mathematics and Science Alliance

Tami R. Ellison, how2SCIENCE

Patricia L. Eng, P.E., Derwood, Maryland

Gualterio Nunez Estrada, Sarasota, Florida

Noreen Ewick, Middle School Teacher, Holyoke, Massachusetts

r. Evelina Félicité-Maurice, NASA Heliophysics Projects Division, Education and Public Outreach Program Planning Manager

Dr. Teresa Franklin, Associate Professor, Instructional Technology Educational Studies Department, College of Education, Ohio University

Bill Gibbard, Science Coordinator, Allentown School District

Howard Gobstein, Vice President, Research and Science Policy, National Association of State Universities and Land Grant Colleges (NASULGC)

Al Gomez, Engineering Instructor, CTE Coordinator, Sun Prairie Area School District, Wisconsin

Daniel L. Goroff, Co-Director, Scientific and Engineering Workforce Project based at the National Bureau of Economic Research

Charles R. Granger, Ph.D., Professor of Biology and Education Curators' Distinguished Teaching Professor, Departments of Biology and Education, University of Missouri-St. Louis

Raymond R. Grosshans, Ph.D., Program Coordinator, Center for Advanced Energy Studies, Idaho National Laboratory

Jong-on Hahm, Ph.D., Research Professor, George Washington University

Carol Hakobian, Fifth Grade Teacher, Serrania Avenue School, Woodland Hills, California **Trisha Herminghaus**, Anchorage, Alaska

Andrea Hickson, Middle School Teacher, Holyoke, Massachusetts

Pao-sheng Hsu

Dale Ingram, Education and Outreach Coordinator, LIGO Hanford Observatory, Richland, Washington

Eric Jakobsson, Director of Research to Learning, Institute for Chemistry Literacy through Computational Science, National Center for Supercomputing Applications, University of Illinois at Urbana-Champaign

Larry Johnson

Cathy Kessel

Andrew C. Klein, Ph.D., P.E., Director, Educational Partnerships, Idaho National Laboratory **Professor Lawrence Klein**, Massachusetts

William Knight, Physical Scientist, NOAA/NWS

Eve Lewis, Sing Science, LLC

Edward S. Lowry, Bedford, Massachusetts

Denise Mann

Mike Mansour, Retired Middle School Science Teacher, Lake Orion, Michigan

J.V. Martinez, Ph.D., Senior Advisor for Scientific Institutional Outreach, Department of Energy

Kari McCarron, Senior Legislative Assistant, Massachusetts Institute of Technology Washington Offi ce Della McCaughan, Mississippi

F. Joseph Merlino, Principal Investigator and Project Director, Math Science Partnership of Greater Philadelphia

Bernadette Monahan, M.A., Star Tannery, Virginia

John Mosto, Member, Massachusetts Department of Education Math/Science Advisory Council **Mary Obringer**, Science Teacher

Deborah A. Pace, Ph.D., Professor and Coordinator of Administration, Department of Mathematics and Statistics, Stephen F. Austin State University

Robert Baird Paterson

Walter Paul, Ph.D., Belle Mead, New Jersey

Carl Pennypacker, University of California at Berkeley and Co-Leader, Hands-On Universe

Dr. Wes Perusek, Director, Ohio Space Grant Consortium (NASA) Invention Innovation Centers Project

Ralph Peterson, Science Teacher, North Gem High School, Bancroft, Idaho

Evelyn A. Puaa, Mathematics Educator, Mathematics Teacher Educator, Doctoral Student, Hawai'i **Johann Rafelski**, Professor of Physics, University of Arizona

Samuel M. Rankin, III, Ph.D., Associate Executive Director, American Mathematical Society **Bob Raynolds, Ph.D.**, Research Associate, Denver Museum of Nature & Science

Catherine Reed, Director, Bachelor's Plus Early Pathway, California State University, East Bay

Elsie M. Colon Rodriguez, Director, Turabo Alliance for Better Schools, Exploring my Universe!, GEAR UP

Laurie F. Ruberg, Ph.D., Associate Director, Center for Educational Technologies, Wheeling Jesuit University

Mark Sanders, Professor & Program Leader, Technology Education, Affi liate Faculty Member, Engineering Education, Virginia Tech

Barb Sauer, Winneconne High School, Wisconsin **Patricia Seawell**, Gene Connection:Chem Connection

Cecily Cannan Selby, Co-Chair, NSB 1983 Commission: "Educating Americans for the Twenty- First Century"

Diane Spect, South Carolina

Daniel L. Stabile, Ph.D., Bishop O'Connell High School, Arlington, Virginia **Deiadra D. Swartz**, Concerned Writer/Professor/Lawyer & Mom, Parker, Colorado

Dr. Herbert D. ~ier, Academic Administrator Emeritus, University of California, Berkeley; Co-Director, Education and Public Outreach, UC Berkeley BIOMARS Institute; and Founding Director, SEPUP

Claudia Toback, CMT Educational Consulting

Joe Tuggle, Graduate Student, BaBar Collaboration, Stanford Linear Accelerator Center

Todd Ullah, Ed.D., Director of Secondary Science Programs, Los Angeles Unified School District

Dr. Gordon E. Uno, Chair and David Ross Boyd Professor of Botany, Department of Botany and Microbiology, University of Oklahoma

Alice P. Wakefield, Early Childhood Teacher Educator, Old Dominion University
Darryl N. Williams, Ph.D., Executive Director, iPRAXIS, Inc.
Edee Wiziecki, Co-PI, Institute for Chemistry Literacy through Computational Science, National Center for Supercomputing Applications, University of Illinois at Urbana-Champaign
David E. Wojick, Ph.D., Star Tannery, Virginia
Joanne Zosel, High School Mathematics and Science Teacher

Obtaining the Board Action Plan

The action plan is available electronically at: Impilivww.nsigovInsbldocuments/20071 stern action.pdf

Paper copies of the action plan can be ordered by submitting a Web-based order form at: hup://www.nsfgoapublicationsiorderpubisp or contacting NSF Publications at 703-292-7827.

Other options for obtaining the documents: TTY: 800-281-8749; FIRS: 800-877-8339.

For special orders or additional information, contact the National Science Board Office: NSBOffice@nsfgov or 703-292-7000.

CHAPTER SOURCES

The following chapters have been previously published:

Chapter 1 – This is an edited, excerpted and augmented edition of a National Center for Education Statistics publication, Report Code NCES 2009-161, dated July 2009.

Chapter 2 – This is an edited, excerpted and augmented edition of a United States Congressional Research Service publication, Report Order Code RL33434, dated March 21, 2008.

Chapter 3 – This is an edited, excerpted and augmented edition of a National Science Foundation publication, Report Code NSB-07-122, dated November 19, 2007.

Chapter 4 – This is an edited, excerpted and augmented edition of a National Science Foundation publication, Report Code NSB-07-114, dated October 30, 2007.

INDEX

"

"competitiveness", 53, 129
"query", 181

2

20th century, 175, 176
21st century, 103, 104, 111, 127, 131, 148, 152, 155, 156, 173, 175, 176, 178

A

academic performance, 32
academic success, 109, 162
access, 61, 90, 119, 124, 129, 130, 132, 152, 155, 164, 167, 169, 173, 185
accountability, 132
accounting, 20, 184
accreditation, 85, 162, 180, 185
achievement test, 185
administrators, 47, 48, 120, 130, 170, 172, 186
ADP, 132
adults, 131
advancement, 129, 176, 179
Africa, 34
African Americans, 62, 70
age, 3, 7, 14, 20, 35, 176, 178, 183
agricultural sciences, 2, 3, 4, 5, 6, 7, 8, 9, 10, 11, 12, 13, 14, 15, 18, 19, 20, 25
Alaska, 8, 18, 191
ambassadors, 179
America COMPETES Act, 51
American Competitiveness Initiative, 30, 31, 53
appointments, 43, 46
aptitude, 164, 173
architecture, 167

Armenia, 35
articulation, 126, 133, 165
Asia, 41, 134
aspiration, 109
assessment, vii, 29, 31, 33, 53, 83, 84, 114, 130, 132, 159, 181, 185
Austria, 36, 108
authorities, 147
authority, 186
automata, 98
average earnings, 184
awareness, 88, 90, 115, 127

B

Bahrain, 35
banking, 86
barriers, 71, 73, 109, 114, 125, 159
base, 2, 22, 47, 69, 86, 107, 117, 119, 120, 127, 140, 154, 160, 176
base year, 22
basic research, 118, 158
behavioral sciences, 2
Belgium, 35, 36, 108
benchmarks, 107, 122, 132, 164
benefits, 89, 106
biotechnology, 62, 69
blame, 88, 89
blogs, 175, 176
blueprint, 129, 180
board members, 164
Brazil, 41, 42
bridges, 120
broadcast media, 121, 140
Broadcasting, 140
Bulgaria, 35
Bureau of Labor Statistics, 128

bureaucracy, 153
Bush, President, 63
Business Roundtable, 53, 55, 136, 140
businesses, 160, 165, 169

C

Cabinet, 130, 179
calculus, 7, 19
caliber, 76, 96
campaigns, 86, 90
candidates, 109, 124, 167, 168
career development, 171
career prospects, 62, 70
categorization, 21
cation, 114, 125, 126, 161
causal relationship, 3
CBS, 140
CCR, 97, 98
Census, 128
central planning, 115
certificate, 5, 9, 10, 12, 13, 16, 17, 18
certification, 26, 37, 49, 50, 52, 85, 90, 106, 125, 126, 128, 159, 161, 162, 167, 180, 181, 186
challenges, 54, 60, 64, 66, 74, 79, 82, 84, 89, 91, 96, 97, 104, 106, 108, 118, 122, 151, 153, 154, 155, 157, 160, 173
Chamber of Commerce, 138, 140
chemicals, 99
Chicago, 187
childhood, 174
children, 103, 111, 128, 129, 149, 154, 156, 165, 174, 183
Chile, 35
China, 41, 42, 69, 84, 134
cities, 50
citizens, 39, 46, 48, 50, 60, 73, 94, 103, 127, 149, 154, 175, 176
citizenship, 132, 176, 178
City, 47, 93, 139, 150, 183
class, 3, 85, 109, 111, 112, 148, 155, 172, 177
classes, 5, 20, 81, 82, 83, 85, 87, 107, 112, 157, 170, 172, 184, 186
classification, 54
classroom, 48, 71, 109, 113, 115, 119, 121, 124, 126, 128, 140, 161, 162, 164, 167, 169, 171, 172, 174, 175, 185
classroom teacher, 48, 113, 140, 171
classroom teachers, 48, 171
climate change, 178
cognitive impairment, 98
coherence, 104, 111, 112, 115, 116, 117, 121, 124, 131, 180

collaboration, 47, 48, 63, 66, 71, 120, 121, 126, 149, 153, 154, 157, 158, 164, 165, 166, 174, 175
collaborative approaches, 70
College Station, 101
college students, 11, 43, 54, 65, 87, 120, 125, 168
colleges, 5, 62, 63, 70, 71, 73, 74, 83, 85, 92, 97, 113, 126, 148, 151, 152, 158, 162, 164, 165, 166, 167, 171, 176, 177, 178, 183, 185, 186
commerce, 70, 163
common sense, 70
communication, 61, 69, 70, 71, 89, 110, 111, 112, 121, 165
communication skills, 61, 70
communities, 30, 31, 66, 103, 105, 117, 147, 158, 161, 170
community, 39, 49, 51, 62, 63, 64, 65, 74, 81, 83, 86, 87, 88, 95, 104, 109, 113, 117, 118, 119, 121, 148, 151, 152, 153, 154, 157, 162, 165, 166, 169, 172, 173, 174, 176, 177, 179, 182, 183, 186
compensation, 109, 125, 152, 168
competition, 66, 88, 179
competitive advantage, 69
competitive grant program, 50
competitiveness, 29, 31, 53, 54, 106, 121, 129, 130, 138, 147, 151, 155, 156, 173
compilation, 167
complement, 59, 72, 114, 152, 153, 157, 174
compulsory education, 35
computational grid, 98
computer, 2, 3, 4, 5, 6, 7, 9, 10, 11, 12, 13, 14, 15, 18, 19, 20, 25, 30, 39, 46, 51, 83, 86, 98, 119, 128
computer science, 30, 39, 51, 86
computer systems, 128
conference, 127, 179
Conference Report, 127, 179
Congress, viii, 30, 31, 51, 53, 57, 63, 73, 94, 96, 102, 103, 105, 106, 110, 111, 112, 113, 129, 130, 131, 132, 138, 139, 142, 144, 148, 151, 152, 154, 158, 159, 160, 161, 162, 168, 180, 181, 182, 184
consensus, 72, 90, 108, 122, 154, 161, 174, 176
conservation, 27
cooperation, 58, 90, 149, 155
cooperative agreements, 48
coordination, 29, 31, 44, 51, 105, 109, 110, 111, 112, 114, 115, 121, 129, 153, 154, 157, 163
Corporation for Public Broadcasting, 140
cost, 46, 50, 61, 69, 82, 99, 141, 161, 168, 182
course work, 49
covering, 73, 128
CPB, 140
creativity, 86, 154
critical thinking, 107, 112, 122, 157, 160, 161, 177
culture, 47, 70, 80, 85, 86, 173, 175, 179

curation, 119
currency, 148
curricula, 47, 49, 50, 71, 80, 84, 110, 118, 119, 121, 122, 126, 131, 148, 157, 162, 163, 164, 165, 172, 174, 175, 180
curriculum, 44, 48, 63, 64, 71, 72, 73, 79, 80, 82, 83, 84, 87, 89, 90, 108, 122, 155, 160, 164, 169, 171, 175, 176, 182, 186
curriculum development, 44
Cyprus, 34
Czech Republic, 36, 108

D

data collection, 3, 22, 23, 68, 74
data set, 119
database, 65, 88, 90, 115, 167
datasets, 24
decentralization, 29
deficiencies, 51, 114
democracy, 127
Denmark, 36, 108
Department of Agriculture, 129
Department of Defense, 54, 87, 110, 129, 151
Department of Energy, 51, 128, 192
Department of Health and Human Services, 44
Department of Transportation, 77
depth, 72, 109, 112, 126, 128, 131, 157, 163, 175, 176, 180
deviation, 53
digital content, 119
directors, 164
dissatisfaction, 62, 133, 184
distribution, 10, 11, 12, 37, 41, 59, 119
District of Columbia, 181
diversity, 46, 61, 63, 71, 153
DNA, 177
Domestic Policy Council, 53, 132, 136, 180, 182
draft, 97, 103, 150, 189
drawing, 105

E

Eastern Europe, 41
economic development, 151, 163
economic growth, 61, 85, 176
economics, 2
economy, 31, 60, 65, 79, 89, 91, 94, 96, 104, 106, 155
education reform, 69, 72, 90, 92, 97, 127, 163, 178
educational attainment, 30, 41, 54
educational career, 148
educational experience, 63, 83, 84, 89, 91, 92, 96, 129, 155

educational opportunities, 65, 84, 164
educational policy, 51
educational practices, 112, 114, 118, 120, 122
educational programs, 89
educational quality, 43
educational research, 118, 119, 148, 157, 158
educational settings, 172
educational system, 31, 51, 130, 154, 186
educators, 49, 68, 98, 106, 109, 113, 114, 118, 124, 130, 154, 155, 156, 162, 167, 169, 170, 174, 175, 181, 186
Egypt, 34
electrons, 178
Elementary and Secondary Education Act, 132, 180
elementary school, 43, 52, 160
employers, 59, 68, 69, 72, 89, 95, 96, 109, 160, 162
employment, 66, 68, 95, 148, 156, 161, 168, 169, 176, 178, 185, 186
employment opportunities, 148, 156, 168
empowerment, 173
energy, 62, 69, 104, 156, 178
enrollment, 2, 3, 4, 5, 6, 7, 13, 19, 20, 24, 26, 41, 125
environment, 58, 61, 62, 63, 69, 70, 81, 83, 85, 166, 169, 175
environmental factors, 61
Environmental Protection Agency, 42
EPA, 42
equipment, 86, 124, 141, 172
equity, 173
erosion, 156
Estonia, 34
ethics, 65, 88
ethnic groups, 7, 154
ethnicity, 26, 48
EU, 48, 130
Europe, 41, 69
evidence, 31, 45, 167, 186
executive branch, 130, 151, 179
Executive Office of the President, 129, 130, 184
Executive Order, 130, 179
experiences, 63, 64, 65, 71, 72, 81, 83, 84, 88, 90, 91, 119, 120, 124, 125, 155, 156, 166, 167, 169, 170, 171, 175, 185
expertise, 46, 104, 105, 119, 126, 154, 165, 188
exploitation, 148
exposure, 62, 72, 81, 83, 109, 159

F

facilitators, 85
faculty development, 43, 171
families, 7, 20, 22, 82, 156, 167, 173
Federal funds, 129

Federal Government, 63, 109, 112, 115, 127, 130, 135, 139, 147, 152, 168, 169, 179, 180
federal programs, 43
financial, 42, 43, 44, 63, 90, 120, 125, 128, 159, 162, 168
financial incentives, 159, 162
financial support, 43, 90, 120, 168
Finland, 36, 108
flame, 177
flexibility, 109, 122
fluid, 99
food, 62, 69
force, vii, 1, 23, 37, 54, 94, 120
Ford, 101, 140, 144, 179
foreign language, 51, 129, 179
foreign nationals, 73
formal education, 156, 164
formation, 131
formula, 48
foundations, 74, 110, 113, 119, 163
France, 36, 41, 54, 108
funding, 45, 48, 64, 85, 111, 113, 115, 116, 118, 129, 130, 131, 132, 161, 169, 170, 175
funds, 29, 42, 44, 45, 52, 129, 130, 159, 161, 162, 168, 184

G

GAO, 21, 29, 30, 42, 44, 45, 53, 54, 129
GEAR, 192
General Accounting Office, 128
general education, 178
Georgia, 57, 58, 59, 71, 76, 77, 78, 79, 88, 91, 92, 93, 96, 101, 146, 182
global climate change, 178
global economy, vii, 1, 127, 156
global education, 65, 84
global scale, 60, 94
global warming, 86
globalization, 103, 106, 173, 178
governments, 106, 111, 115, 116
governor, 113, 135, 163
GPA, 7, 19, 26
grades, 32, 33, 37, 72, 81, 131, 165, 167, 180, 181, 185
graduate education, 95, 129, 130, 134, 157, 186
graduate program, 73
graduate students, 43, 46, 48
grant programs, 52
grants, 46, 47, 48, 50, 52, 53, 55, 73, 80, 115, 179, 180, 181, 184
growth, 30, 43, 54, 61, 85, 98, 124, 129, 167, 169, 173, 176, 182

guidance, 48, 59, 61, 65, 66, 80, 88, 90, 104, 114, 117, 162, 165, 175
guidance counselors, 61, 65, 80, 88, 90, 165
guidelines, 44, 105, 111, 114, 116, 121, 122, 123, 125, 126, 131

H

Hawaii, 99
health, 36, 45, 61, 62, 69, 85, 156, 157
Health and Human Services, 44
health education, 36
heat transfer, 98
HHS, 44, 45
high school, 3, 4, 7, 8, 9, 17, 19, 22, 23, 26, 37, 43, 47, 50, 62, 64, 82, 87, 88, 90, 105, 109, 114, 120, 124, 128, 129, 131, 132, 162, 163, 164, 165, 166, 168, 173, 175, 176, 178, 180, 181, 182
high school diploma, 9, 17, 26, 109
higher education, 48, 53, 66, 105, 106, 109, 113, 115, 117, 120, 123, 124, 126, 130, 131, 152, 154, 155, 156, 157, 160, 162, 163, 165, 166, 169, 176, 178, 186
hiring, 52, 132, 168
Hispanics, 62, 70
historically black colleges and universities, 62, 85
history, 39, 58, 59, 73, 151, 155, 158, 178, 181
homeland security, 62, 70
Hong Kong, 34, 36
House, 127, 133, 139, 142, 144, 179, 187
House of Representatives, 187
housing, 62, 69, 73
human, 61, 116, 120, 177
human capital, 116, 120
Hungary, 34, 36, 108
Hunter, 190

I

Iceland, 36, 108
identification, 119
identity, 62, 72
image, 65, 72, 74, 80, 86, 99, 178
images, 70
imagination, 71, 86
improvements, viii, 61, 80, 102, 106, 107, 109, 110, 111, 127, 131, 147, 158, 179, 186
income, 7, 8, 20, 26, 82, 125
India, 41, 69, 178
individuals, 31, 45, 46, 48, 54, 61, 131, 186, 189
Indonesia, 34, 36
induction, 155, 169
industry, 40, 60, 65, 68, 70, 72, 73, 74, 79, 82, 84, 85, 87, 89, 95, 96, 97, 106, 110, 113, 115, 120,

148, 149, 151, 155, 160, 163, 165, 167, 169, 178, 182, 184
information technology, 62, 69
Information Technology, 54
infrastructure, 42, 43, 47, 112, 151, 158, 164, 171, 172
ingredients, 154
injury, iv
insecurity, 176
Institute of Education Sciences, 21, 131, 136, 138, 180
institutions, 3, 5, 6, 18, 20, 22, 23, 37, 43, 44, 45, 46, 48, 50, 53, 54, 59, 63, 66, 81, 85, 89, 95, 109, 117, 120, 121, 126, 130, 160, 161, 162, 163, 165, 166, 167, 169, 171, 176, 177, 182, 183, 186
instructional materials, 116, 118, 120, 130, 158, 169
integration, 51, 69, 157, 158
integrity, 153
intellect, 103
international affairs, 130
international standards, 131, 159
Internet, 140, 154, 175, 176, 178
internship, 47, 84, 90, 91, 96, 167
interpersonal skills, 62
investment, vii, 1, 79, 86, 130, 148, 167, 174, 179
investment bank, 86
investments, 64, 71, 79, 81, 119, 130, 155, 158, 175, 179
Iowa, 48, 77, 93, 102
Iran, 34
Ireland, 36, 108
isolation, 82
Israel, 34, 41
issues, viii, 29, 48, 54, 57, 58, 59, 60, 64, 68, 69, 70, 79, 82, 83, 89, 91, 92, 94, 95, 96, 97, 102, 103, 104, 111, 118, 121, 130, 147, 148, 154, 157, 158, 173, 174, 178, 186, 188
Italy, 34, 35, 108

J

Japan, 34, 35, 41, 42, 108
job dissatisfaction, 133, 184
Jordan, 34, 190
jumping, 128

K

Kentucky, 132, 146
kill, 148
kindergarten, 105, 130, 132, 134
knowledge-based economy, 106, 107, 109, 155, 156, 176
Korea, 34, 35, 41, 108

L

labor force, 23, 54, 94
labor market, 74
labor markets, 74
lack of confidence, 176
languages, 38, 51, 129, 179
Laplace transform, 73
Latvia, 34, 36
laws, 73, 147, 149, 177
laws and regulations, 147, 149
lawyers, 154
lead, 54, 66, 80, 81, 105, 118, 119, 151, 171, 186
leadership, 47, 60, 61, 63, 64, 66, 69, 70, 71, 72, 73, 79, 80, 83, 84, 85, 89, 90, 94, 96, 97, 104, 110, 111, 114, 116, 124, 152, 156, 157, 158, 164, 171, 186
leadership development, 84
Leahy, 189
learners, 133, 154, 173, 175
learning culture, 47
learning environment, 121
learning skills, 70
Lebanon, 34
legislation, 31, 51, 111, 129, 131, 134, 154, 156, 160, 179, 180, 181, 184
legislative proposals, 30, 31, 49
leisure, 178
lesson plan, 119, 170
level of education, 19, 26, 173, 176
lifelong learning, 61, 72, 73, 74, 95
lifetime, 174, 176
light, 59, 60, 68, 87, 94, 155
literacy, vii, 29, 30, 35, 127, 147, 148, 160, 165, 166
Lithuania, 34
local community, 174
local government, 148
Lockheed Martin, 187
logistics, 62, 69, 95
love, 62, 85, 155, 178

M

Macedonia, 34
magnets, 177
Maine, 190, 191
majority, vii, 10, 13, 29, 30, 31, 45, 46, 70, 149, 184
Malaysia, 34
man, 102, 142, 144, 145, 178
management, 59, 61, 70, 71, 95, 114, 131, 133, 153
manufacturing, 69, 71, 99
marketing, 61, 71, 86
marketplace, 103

Maryland, 47, 190, 191
mass, 90
mass media, 90
materials, 58, 59, 98, 99, 116, 118, 120, 121, 130, 148, 158, 160, 163, 169, 175, 176
mathematical knowledge, 103
mathematics education, 53, 94, 127, 152
matter, iv, vii, 29, 30, 32, 131, 137, 169, 171
McKinley, William, 99
measurement, 177
measurements, 177
media, 66, 74, 90, 121, 140, 154, 167
median, 128
medical, 63, 86, 178
medical science, 178
medicine, 73, 80, 86, 167
membership, 112, 148, 149, 153
mentor, 48, 65, 98
mentoring, 44, 47, 63, 83, 84, 87, 88, 90, 109, 124, 167, 169, 170, 171, 172
messages, 65, 86, 88, 90
methodology, 54, 185
Mexico, 35, 41, 108, 145
minorities, 61, 63, 65, 66, 70, 72, 80, 81
minority students, 63, 70, 80, 86, 88, 120
mission, 52, 114, 116, 129, 152
missions, 153
Missouri, 102, 142, 144, 191
mixing, 99
modeling, 47
models, 63, 65, 69, 74, 80, 82, 83, 87, 114, 118, 122, 125, 148, 161, 166, 167, 170, 171, 186
modification, 154
modules, 71, 120
Moldova, 34
molecules, 178
monitoring, 152, 153
Montenegro, 36
Morocco, 34
motivation, 64, 81, 133, 184
MRI, 177
museums, 98, 148, 167, 185
music, 36, 154

N

nanotechnology, 62, 69
NAS, 31, 49, 50, 152
National Aeronautics and Space Administration, 42, 51, 65, 87, 110, 128, 151
National Association of Manufacturers, 140
National Center for Education Statistics, v, 1, 4, 5, 6, 9, 10, 11, 12, 14, 15, 18, 20, 21, 32, 35, 36, 38, 53, 54, 128, 129, 131, 133, 136, 138, 180, 195

National Defense Authorization Act, 51
National Institutes of Health, 29, 42, 129
national interests, 147
national parks, 185
national policy, viii, 57, 103
National Public Radio, 140
National Research Council, 66, 67, 131, 137, 180, 182
national security, 51, 60, 94, 103, 127, 148, 151
National Survey, 128
Native Americans, 62, 70
natural resources, 27
natural science, vii, 2, 4, 5, 6, 7, 9, 10, 11, 12, 13, 14, 15, 18, 19, 27, 29, 30
natural sciences, 2, 4, 5, 6, 7, 9, 10, 11, 12, 13, 14, 15, 18, 19, 27
Netherlands, 34, 35, 108
New Zealand, 34, 35, 108
next generation, 62, 69, 106, 107, 127, 130, 173, 176
No Child Left Behind, 53, 105, 122, 134, 135, 154, 160, 185
Nobel Prize, 86
Norway, 34, 35, 41, 108
NPR, 140

O

Office of Management and Budget, 44
officials, 106, 113, 130, 153, 180
OH, 150
Oklahoma, 101, 143, 188, 192
online learning, 166
operations, 113, 141
opportunities, 20, 43, 45, 48, 49, 50, 58, 62, 65, 66, 68, 69, 72, 84, 87, 92, 103, 109, 115, 120, 124, 133, 148, 153, 155, 156, 157, 164, 165, 166, 167, 168, 169, 172, 173, 174, 175, 178, 183
Opportunities, 51, 52, 86, 133, 164, 172
oral presentations, 48
organize, 161
outreach, 44, 45, 51, 65, 72, 91, 121, 126, 149, 154
outreach programs, 51
outsourcing, 63, 69, 74, 81, 86, 90
oversight, viii, 57, 95, 103, 153

P

Pacific, 7, 8, 9, 16, 18, 20
pairing, 83
parallel, 59, 94
parenthood, 178
parents, 7, 19, 61, 65, 80, 86, 87, 90, 130, 148, 149, 155, 156, 174, 186

Index

participants, 48, 58, 60, 64, 68, 69, 72, 78, 81, 82, 83, 85, 86, 89, 90, 95, 104, 127, 156, 181
pathways, 63, 160, 162, 164
pedagogy, 125, 126, 148, 162, 171, 174
percentile, 6, 18
performance, 30, 32, 47, 49, 52, 66, 81, 82, 83, 105, 120, 122, 125, 132, 148, 151, 160, 173, 175, 185, 186
personal choice, 103
pessimism, 156
pharmaceutical, 99
Philadelphia, 189, 192
Philippines, 34
physical sciences, 2, 3, 4, 5, 6, 7, 9, 10, 11, 12, 13, 14, 15, 18, 19, 20, 24, 38, 39
physics, 82, 128, 174, 177
PISA, 30, 35, 54, 107, 108, 128
Poland, 35, 108
policy, vii, viii, 1, 30, 31, 49, 51, 53, 57, 58, 66, 73, 94, 102, 103, 106, 109, 110, 111, 129, 130, 133, 134, 151, 152, 161, 179, 180, 183, 186
policy issues, viii, 57, 103
policy makers, 106, 130, 186
policymakers, 105, 112, 116, 118, 119, 156
political leaders, 155, 174
population, 3, 4, 22, 41, 50, 54, 62, 69, 70, 119, 127, 156, 164, 166, 170
portfolio, 85, 118, 121, 158
Portugal, 35, 108
poverty, 52, 86
precedent, 151
preparation, 19, 20, 37, 49, 59, 61, 62, 63, 79, 83, 86, 89, 105, 109, 120, 124, 126, 151, 156, 158, 159, 160, 161, 167, 182, 186
primary school, 175, 176
principles, 98, 148
private foundation, 74
private schools, 22, 129
probability, 22, 23
probe, 175
problem solving, 71
problem-based learning, 74, 155
problem-solving, 49, 112, 160, 161
problem-solving skills, 112
professional development, 44, 47, 49, 53, 98, 109, 114, 116, 118, 120, 121, 122, 125, 157, 158, 162, 164, 166, 167, 168, 169, 170, 171, 172, 174, 175, 180, 181, 183, 184, 185
professional growth, 124
professionals, 30, 52, 109, 120, 125, 126, 130, 133, 154, 155, 161, 168, 184
profit, 6, 18
programming, 27, 83, 121

progress reports, 149
project, 45, 47, 48, 58, 59, 63, 71, 72, 86, 87, 98, 103, 104, 179
proliferation, 86
promote innovation, 118
prosperity, 107, 154, 176
prosthesis, 98
prosthetic device, 98
psychology, 2
public education, 111, 115, 129, 151
public interest, 148
public policy, 152
public resources, 182
public schools, 128, 129, 168, 186
public sector, 60, 62, 70, 95, 96
public service, 72
public support, 154
publishing, 59
Puerto Rico, 22

Q

quality of life, 61, 85, 127
query, 180, 181, 182, 184
questionnaire, 22

R

race, 110, 151
radar, 178
radiation, 178
reading, 53, 160, 181
reciprocity, 134, 179
recognition, 44, 58, 104, 105, 154, 157
recommendations, iv, vii, viii, 1, 31, 49, 51, 57, 58, 59, 64, 68, 94, 96, 97, 106, 107, 111, 112, 116, 121, 127, 147, 149, 151, 168, 179
recruiting, 49, 109
redistribution, 69
reflectivity, 178
reform, 59, 79, 80, 84, 90, 92, 95, 97, 106, 127, 132, 147, 148, 152, 154, 163, 178
Reform, 135, 139, 178, 180, 183, 184
reforms, 51, 69, 72, 80, 90
regulations, 149
relevance, 63, 71, 82, 86
remediation, 83
replication, 45
requirements, 62, 87, 114, 124, 125, 148, 160, 161, 165, 173, 176, 180, 181
research and development, 51, 130, 157, 158, 166, 179
researchers, 46, 98, 99, 119, 120, 140, 158, 171

resources, 27, 63, 65, 66, 83, 89, 98, 105, 109, 115, 116, 119, 120, 121, 124, 133, 140, 148, 158, 160, 166, 167, 168, 172, 173, 175, 182, 185
response, 22, 83, 103, 177, 179
responsiveness, 58
restructuring, 110
retention rate, 62, 70, 80, 89, 92, 96
Richland, 191
robotics, 88
Romania, 34
rural areas, 50
rural schools, 155
Russia, 41

S

sabotage, 138
safety, 172
Saudi Arabia, 34
scaling, 114, 122, 158
scholarship, 50, 65, 88, 90, 184
school improvement, 47
school learning, 166
schooling, 154, 183
science education, 47, 127, 131, 147, 148, 158, 163, 166, 167, 177, 179, 180, 181
scope, 45, 79, 91, 141
screening, 185
SEC, 94
second language, 129, 179
secondary education, 16, 17, 18, 176, 185
secondary school students, vii, 29, 51
secondary schools, 51, 52, 120, 182, 186
secondary students, 31, 42, 138
secondary teachers, 126
security, 51, 60, 62, 70, 94, 103, 106, 107, 127, 148, 151, 155
selectivity, 6
self-interest, 156
seminars, 48, 65, 89
Senate, 133, 139, 144, 180, 181
Serbia, 34, 36
services, iv, 61, 69, 83, 132, 149, 152, 182
sex, 176
shape, 107, 157, 173
shock, 110, 151
shortage, 109
signals, 74
simulations, 119
Singapore, 34
social environment, 63, 70, 81, 83
social perception, 79
social problems, 61, 86
social sciences, 65, 82, 83, 174

society, 60, 61, 106, 109, 147, 155, 159, 176
sociology, 2
software, 23, 119, 178
solubility, 178
South Africa, 34
South America, 41
South Dakota, 47
South Korea, 41, 108
Soviet Union, 129, 155, 179
Spain, 35, 41, 108
specialists, 128
specialization, 38
specifications, 129, 180
spending, 44, 45, 48, 52, 119, 129
Spring, 128
stability, 89
stakeholder groups, 103, 106, 113, 153
stakeholders, viii, 68, 71, 95, 102, 105, 106, 111, 112, 113, 114, 116, 124, 125, 126, 129, 130, 148, 163, 165, 166, 169, 186
standard deviation, 53
standard of living, 155, 156
Stanford, Leland, 138
state borders, 114
states, 32, 33, 35, 41, 44, 45, 46, 52, 55, 105, 108, 109, 111, 112, 113, 114, 115, 119, 121, 122, 124, 125, 127, 128, 129, 130, 131, 132, 153, 156, 157, 158, 159, 160, 161, 162, 163, 168, 169, 174, 179, 180, 181, 182, 185, 189
statistics, 27, 37, 38, 128, 131, 132, 133, 137
statutes, 149
Stokes, Louis, 104, 120, 131, 150
storytelling, 177
structural changes, 112
structure, 23, 99, 106, 152, 153, 156
student achievement, 37, 47, 109, 131, 181
student motivation, 133, 184
student populations, 22, 166, 173
student teacher, 47
supervision, 149, 186
supervisors, 172
support staff, 80
survey, 2, 3, 22, 23, 37, 42, 49, 54, 55
Sweden, 34, 35, 108
Switzerland, 35, 108
synthesis, 118

T

takeover, 156
talent, 69, 70, 73, 82, 89, 156, 173, 177
target, 22, 42, 43, 90
target population, 22, 43
target populations, 43

teacher preparation, 120, 126, 158
teacher training, 182
teaching effectiveness, 125
teaching evaluation, 73
teaching strategies, 118, 171
teams, 48, 61, 63, 71, 83, 84, 86
technical assistance, 116, 158, 163
techniques, 98, 99
technologies, 2, 6, 9, 10, 12, 13, 15, 25, 27, 62, 119, 176, 177
teens, 179
TEM, vii, viii, 20, 29, 30, 60, 81, 102, 103, 104, 123, 124, 130, 147, 167, 178
terrorism, 62, 69
tertiary education, 41, 54
test scores, 131
testing, 32, 47, 161, 177
textbooks, 108, 124, 128, 163
Thailand, 36
threats, 103
time frame, 45
Title I, 22, 53
Title IV, 22
Title V, 51, 52
torus, 99
tourism, 74
toxic gases, 178
training, 45, 46, 55, 61, 63, 70, 71, 81, 85, 109, 124, 130, 148, 167, 168, 169, 172, 173, 182, 184, 185, 186
training programs, 81
traits, 89
transformation, 103, 107, 111, 151, 152, 153, 154, 155, 156, 157, 158, 173, 175
transformations, 173
transportation, 62, 69, 129
tuition, 50, 63, 82, 125, 168, 182

U

U.S. Department of Labor, 182
U.S. history, 155, 181
undergraduate education, 45, 134
UNESCO, 54
unions, 110, 153
United Kingdom, 34, 36, 41
United Nations, 54
universities, 6, 18, 52, 62, 63, 64, 65, 68, 70, 71, 73, 79, 81, 83, 85, 89, 90, 91, 92, 95, 96, 97, 126, 148, 151, 158, 165, 166, 167, 171, 176, 177, 186

urban, 154, 155
urban schools, 154
Uruguay, 36
USA, 50, 76, 77
USDA, 129

V

validation, 45
variables, 21, 23, 24, 26
vehicles, 74
vein, 74
venue, 87
Vermeer, 143
Vice President, 77, 78, 101, 102, 143, 145, 189, 191
video, 119, 127, 175, 179
videos, 179
vision, 98, 148, 153, 163, 178
visualization, 98
voters, 103
voting, 112

W

wages, 182
war, 42, 127, 175
Washington, 20, 21, 44, 53, 54, 66, 67, 75, 76, 77, 102, 104, 127, 128, 129, 130, 131, 132, 133, 134, 135, 136, 137, 138, 139, 142, 143, 146, 149, 180, 181, 182, 183, 184, 189, 191, 192
Washington, George, 191
water, 61, 62, 69, 86, 177
weakness, 60, 94, 178
Wisconsin, 93, 190, 191, 192
workers, 51, 54, 60, 94, 155, 176
workforce, 39, 46, 51, 52, 57, 58, 59, 60, 63, 64, 66, 68, 70, 72, 94, 95, 96, 103, 104, 105, 106, 111, 120, 124, 126, 127, 128, 130, 131, 147, 148, 156, 160, 162, 164, 173, 178, 180, 181, 182
working conditions, 109
working groups, 149
workload, 82, 85
workplace, 109, 132, 162
World Bank, 41, 54
World Wide Web, 178

Y

yield, 110, 175
young people, 74, 132, 154, 155, 156, 178
young women, 178